Audition in Childhood

Audition in Childhood: Methods of Study

Edited by
DANIEL S. BEASLEY, PhD
Memphis State University
Memphis, Tennessee

College–Hill Press, Inc.
San Diego, California

College-Hill Press, Inc.
4284 41st Street
San Diego, California 92105

Library of Congress Cataloging in Publication Data
Main entry under title:

Audition in childhood: Methods of study.

     1. Auditory perception in children. 2. Communication disorders in children. 3. Developmental psychology. I. Beasley, Daniel S. [DNLM: 1. Communication—In infancy and childhood. 2. Auditory perception—In infancy and childhood. 3. Child development—Physiology. 4. Child development disorders—Physiology. WV 272 A9116]
BF723.A77A93   1984   155.4'13   83-26272

ISBN 0-933014-12-0

Printed in the United States of America.

This volume is dedicated
to the fond memory of
Thomas H. Shriner, Jr.

1938 - 1980

TABLE OF CONTENTS

CONTRIBUTORS

JUDITH B. AMSTER, PhD
School of Education & Allied
   Professions
University of Miami
Coral Gables, Florida 33124

WALTER W. AMSTER, PhD
Chief, Audiology & Speech
   Pathology Service
Veterans Administration
   Medical Center
Miami, Florida 33125

KATHRYN A. BEAUCHAINE, MA
Boys Town National Institute for
   Communication Disorders in
   Children
Omaha, Nebraska

STEVEN P. BORNSTEIN, PhD
Ithaca College
Ithaca, New York

DAVID G. CYR, PhD
Boys Town National Institute for
   Communication Disorders in
   Children
Omaha, Nebraska

RAYMOND G. DANILOFF, PhD
University of Vermont
Burlington, Vermont

ALBERT R. DE CHICCHIS, PhD
Veterans Administration Hospital
Augusta, Georgia

DAUN C. DICKIE, PhD
Ingham Intermediate School District
Mason, Michigan

THEODORE J. GLATTKE, PhD
University of Arizona
Tucson, Arizona

G. ROBERT HOPPER, PhD
Audiology & Speech Pathology
   Service
Veterans Administration
   Medical Center
Miami, Florida 33125

ROBERT W. KEITH, PhD
University of Cincinnati
   Medical Center
Cincinnati, Ohio

KAREN M. KRYGIER, MA
Memphis State University
Memphis, Tennessee

FRANK E. MUSIEK, PhD
Dartmouth-Hitchcock
   Medical Center
Hanover, New Hampshire

DANIEL J. ORCHIK, PhD
The Shea Clinic &
   Deafness Foundation
Memphis, Tennessee

CHERYL A. RUNGE, MS
Stanford University
   Medical Center
Stanford, California

HELEN K. SMITH, PhD
School of Education
   & Allied Professions
University of Miami
Coral Gables, Florida 33124

GISELA WILSON, PhD
Department of Neurophysiology
   Neuroscience Program
University of Wisconsin
Madison, Wisconsin

Consulting Editor:
RAYMOND G. DANILOFF
University of Vermont
Burlington, Vermont

PREFACE

This is the third book in a three-volume series dedicated to the memory of Thomas H. Shriner, Jr. The series was conceived shortly after Tom's untimely death December 22, 1980 and includes a book of readings on language by two of Tom's former students, Tanya Gallagher and Carol Prutting, a book of readings in the speech sciences by his personal colleague and lifelong friend, Ray Daniloff, and the present volume on audition. Each of these volumes in its own way represents Tom Shriner's dedication to better understanding of normal and nonnormal human communication and to the process of generating and studying ideas. Language as a total system unique to human behavior was Tom's major focus, yet he understood better than many that understanding "language" required a knowledge of the arts and sciences and their inherent relationships and an appreciation of the philosophical and sociological consequences of that knowledge. This dedication to learning and thinking was evidenced in Tom's writings and his teaching activities, particularly when he was exercising his rare talent of drawing relationships between the seemingly unrelated and his ability to so elegantly bring these relationships to bear upon the phenomenon of human communication. Tom Shriner was a genuine scholar.

The authors who have so graciously contributed to this work either knew Tom personally or knew of and respected his work and his love of learning. The reader may very well have some difficulty detecting a general theme to the readings in this volume, other than the general relationship to audition and tenuous emphasis upon children. The variety of topics and the controversial nature of several of the presentations here are intended to reflect Tom's view of human communication as a complex phenomenon, the study of which should never be closed to fresh viewpoints. And therein lies the major theme of this memorial to Tom Shriner, namely his total dedication to researching the relationships among the various ideas and thoughts of those interested in study of human communication.

Tom Shriner strongly eschewed labels and neat categories, choosing instead to find order in the study of diversity. Thus, he knew so well that the auditory system did not stand alone from the production of language, and indeed, at one time or another, Tom studied and researched, formally or informally, each of the topics presented in this volume. His own research into the study of auditory processing and perception in children set a scientific trend that has lasted for 15 years. His understanding of the need for knowledge of the neurophysiological underpinnings in language development dates at least from his days as a research professor at the Children's Research Center at the University of Illinois. Because of his breadth of knowledge, Tom knew that research involving the total auditory mechanism was required if we were to understand audition and the various roles it plays in human communication. And Tom particularly enjoyed seeing his students assume a confident position, supported by science and philosophy, when attempting to resolve issues of a controversial and emotional nature. In his own words, "read, read, read, and assume nothing."

Tom Shrinér had little tolerance for those who looked for "cookbooks" or chose to follow blindly the pronouncements of a popular voice. He actively sought not answers, but simply better questions. It was not out of character for Tom to take a seemingly absurd position, argue the position, and at that moment when complete frustration on the part of the student was about to be broached, to simply smile and with a quick glance and a sharp twinkle in his eye, say "Umhm, maybe you're right." And to those of us who knew and studied with Tom, we knew we had just been given another lesson in learning to think.

There is little that can be added to what has already been so eloquently said by Ray Daniloff, Tanya Gallagher, and Carol Prutting in the prefaces of the previous two volumes and Jim Curtis in the foreword. As the first student to have worked with Tom after his days at Iowa, I came to appreciate the man who was Tom Shriner: the philosopher and scientist, the intellectual streetfighter, the scholar, the Everyman, the selfless giver, the non-taker. To those who knew him, Tom was an enigma, as complex as the subject he loved, a man who suffered as his own harshest critic, but could show untold warmth and consolation to others if they erred simply because they had tried.

There is a sadness that will remain with those of us to whom he gave so much and with whom he shared his warmth and kindness and caring. But there is a gentle, quiet pride and joy in knowing that there was a moment in our lives when he shared with us his essence as a human being, with the understanding that we also must share these qualities with our students, our colleagues, our friends, and anyone of lesser opportunity. For this, Tom, we thank you, and to this end this book is dedicated.

ACKNOWLEDGMENT

The editor expresses his appreciation to Renée Friemoth-Lee, Mike McDaniel, and particularly to his wife, Stephanie, for their assistance in editing the chapters in this book. Appreciation also is extended to Marie Walters and Shirley Rias for their unmatched skills on a word processor.

Daniel S. Beasley

FOREWORD

*T*homas H. Shriner, Jr. was born on February 12, 1938 in Fallowfield Township, Pennsylvania. On December 22, 1980, less than two months prior to his 43rd birthday, death cut short his career as a productive scholar and researcher and inspiring teacher.

Tom Shriner's academic history includes a Bachelor of Science in Education degree with a major in Speech and Hearing awarded by State College, California, Pennsylvania in 1962, a Master of Arts degree in Speech Pathology and Audiology in 1964 and a Ph.D. degree in Speech Pathology and Audiology in 1965, both awarded by the University of Iowa, and two post-doctoral fellowships — one at the University of Iowa for the year 1965-1966, and one at the Massachusetts Institute of Technology for the year 1969-1970. He served in the United States Marine Corps during the years 1957-1959.

Following his post-doctoral year at the University of Iowa Dr. Shriner was appointed Research Assistant Professor in the Children's Research Center, Department of Speech, University of Illinois. He held this position and rank until 1969. In 1970 he returned to Illinois from his post-doctoral year at MIT with the rank of Associate Professor in the Department of Speech. At Illinois he taught courses in Development of Spoken Language and Psychology of Speech and seminars in Language Development, Language Measurements, Auditory Cognition, and Language Research. Following the 1970-1971 academic year he left the University of Illinois to accept a position as Associate Professor and Director of the Infant Language Laboratory, Mailman Center for Child Development, University of Miami School of Medicine. In addition to his research activities as laboratory director, he taught courses in Linguistics: Science and Application and Special Studies in Speech in the Department of Speech and Hearing Sciences, University of Miami.

Although Dr. Shriner had doubtless acquired an interest in language behavior during his undergraduate studies with Dr. Ray Bontrager at California State College, his interest in the area of language development in infants and children apparently began while he was a graduate student at the University of Iowa. His doctoral dissertation, directed by Dr. Dorothy Sherman, was a report of research on the measurement of language development. His post-doctoral studies at both Iowa and MIT were devoted to continued development of his special research interest in language development, including its relationship to auditory perception.

It is probably significant that this interest in children's language had its early beginnings while he was a graduate student in a department that supported a substantial clinical program concerned with speech, language and hearing disorders, as well as extensive programs of research into the fundamental processes of speech, language and hearing and the disorders of speech, language and hearing. This context not only encouraged and fostered the development of his specialized interest in children's language, it did so as part of a broad program of studies in human communication processes and disorders. In this context Dr. Shriner had the opportunity to take courses and seminars which provided a broad background concerning both normal and abnormal speech and hearing processes, to engage in research and to interact directly, on a day-to-day basis, with fellow graduate students and with faculty who were involved both with research into these processes and with the clinical management of persons with disorders of speech, language and hearing. One of Dr. Shriner's earliest published papers was not a report of research on language, but was a collaboration with Dr. Kenneth L. Moll that reported research on an aspect of motor activity during speech production. He also served as a graduate assistant to Dr. Wendell Johnson, who was not only a pioneering researcher in the area of stuttering, but had broad interests and wrote extensively in the area of personal and social effects of language behavior. It is not too much to suggest that this broad exposure to many varied aspects of human communication provided Dr. Shriner with a particularly broad and rich context in which to develop his interests in language development and may have contributed to both the breadth of his scholarship and thinking with respect to more specifically linguistic and auditory processes and to his pragmatic approach to the analysis and understanding of issues in language behavior.

One of the most frequent comments concerning Tom Shriner's work both as a scholar and teacher, from both former students and colleagues, concerned the breadth of his interests in the total communication process and his insistence that language processes could only be understood in a context which considered human communication as a total process. These comments indicate that this was a distinguishing characteristic that set him apart from many of his contemporaries who approach the study of language more narrowly. One of his former students, now a faculty member at a large state university, commented that he was one of the very early linguistic pragmatists, certainly the first such thinker with whom this person had come into contact. The breadth of his research and scholarly interests is clearly evident in the titles of his publications and convention papers, and it is appropriately reflected in the broad scope of the contributions to these memorial volumes.

Tom Shriner's record as a productive scholar is well documented by the pages of his publication in scientific journals and by published convention proceedings that reflect his contributions. In the all too brief time allowed to him he authored, or co-authored, more than twenty research articles and nearly as many convention papers. The quality of his work has been recognized, and its influence extended, by the reprinting of no less than five of these research articles in book collection form. He was an invited contributor to the Revised Handbook of Speech Pathology (1971). He served as an associate editor of the Journal of Speech and Hearing Research from 1969 to 1972, as a guest editor of the American Speech and Hearing Association Monograph Series, and as guest editor of the Bulletin of the Division for Children with Communication Disorders of the Council for Exceptional Children. He was invited to be a visiting professor at the University of Minnesota during the summer of 1969, and he was called on frequently as a lecturer and contributor to workshops in speech, hearing and language. All this and more in a brief post-doctoral career that spanned less than a decade and a half.

Finally, but perhaps most importantly, Tom Shriner was a superb teacher. He must have been, for during his brief tenure at the University of Illinois an amazing number of talented graduate students chose Dr. Shriner as the person with whom they wanted to work most closely. The record shows that during the short period of four years one Senior Honors thesis, two Master's theses and four doctoral dissertations were completed under Dr. Shriner's direction. In addition his influence was felt by the numerous students who enrolled in his courses and seminars, or who participated in many informal discussion groups.

Because my close personal contact with Tom Shriner came at an earlier time, while he was a graduate student at the University of Iowa, what follows is primarily based on comments of his former students. It is clear from their statements that his influence was profound. They express the highest respect for him as a scholar and thinker and deep affection for him as a person. They unanimously report that he was completely unselfish with his time, that he gave of himself unstintingly, that he was always available for counsel and discussion of problems. His relationships with students were never authoritarian. He seemed to them more like a fellow student sharing in their quest for knowledge than a mentor directing that quest. They never felt subordinate or dominated. And yet he was able to stimulate them with new ideas, challenge them to new ways of thinking, and to help them in the difficult process of learning to expose ideas and thinking to critical analysis and testing. Moreover, it is very evident from these former students' reports that he had the gift of making this challenge enjoyable, exciting, and exhilarating. According to one former student, an important key to Dr. Shriner's teaching was his emphasis on the importance of learning how to ask questions, not just any questions, but the critical ones that would go to the core of an idea and test the validity of that idea or of a line of reasoning. Quite obviously he taught far more by example than by precept, and the example his students saw was that of a scholar, a disciplined, inquiring mind, tirelessly searching for new understanding, and having fun in the searching.

That he was a highly successful teacher cannot be doubted. Not only was he respected by both students and colleagues, but the successes enjoyed by his former students bears testimony to his teaching effectiveness. All four of the persons who completed Ph.D. degrees under his tutelage have gone on to achieve success as faculty members at major universities. Tom would have been justifiably proud of their accomplishments, but too humble to claim the share of credit that his students more than gladly accord him.

These three memorial volumes are eloquent testimony to the high regard in which Thomas H. Shriner was held by his students and colleagues and to the influence which he had on their thinking and development. The fact that some of the contributions in these volumes are the work of students bears witness to the fact that this influence continues to be felt. Although he is no longer with us, Tom Shriner's example of dedication to his students and to his field of scholarship continues, and will continue, as it is repeated daily in the work of his former students and colleagues and their students.

James F. Curtis

1
DICHOTIC LISTENING IN CHILDREN

Robert W. Keith
The University of Cincinnati Medical Center

T he use of dichotic listening tests in the evaluation of children with possible learning disabilities is on the increase in audiology clinics. Unfortunately, however, there is no standard protocol for clinical administration and interpretation of these tests. The purpose of the present chapter is to review the subject in light of increased interest in the relationship between dichotic test results and language, learning, and reading problems. The emphasis is on administration of these tests to children, with special attention given to methods of test administration, scoring, and interpretation of results. In the concluding remarks, a method of clinical application and interpretation of dichotic listening tests is recommended that may result in more effective use of these studies in clinical practice.

HISTORY

Dichotic listening tests involve the simultaneous presentation of different acoustic stimuli to the two ears. Commonly used stimuli include digits, consonant–vowel (CV) nonsense syllables incorporating the six stop consonants [p, t, k, b, d, g] paired with the vowel /a/, words, sentences, and other combinations of acoustic stimuli. Testing is usually done under headphones although dichotic studies have been done using sound field speakers. The listener is required to repeat or write what is heard, according to a prescribed set of instructions.

The first studies on dichotic listening that have been extensively cited were by Kimura (1961, 1963, 1967), who presented three different groups of digits (1, 2, and 3 pairs) to 120 right-handed girls and boys between the ages of 4 and 9. Kimura's results showed that digits presented to the right ear were recalled better than those presented to the left ear, even for the youngest children tested. The finding of a "right ear advantage" was interpreted as indicating a language specialization for left cerebral hemisphere, to which the right ear has relatively direct anatomic connections.

A summary of research subsequent to that of Kimura was published by Berlin and McNeil (1976) who analyzed and codified 300 studies. Dichotic listening tests have become the simplest and most widely used technique for studying dominance, and the current clinical application of this technique cannot be separated from studies of hemispheric function. There is reason to be concerned about the apparent simplicity of the dichotic listening technique, however, and clinical data must be interpreted with extreme care—a point that will be reemphasized frequently.

To a great extent, studies in dichotic listening deal with two questions posed by Studdert-Kennedy (1975):

1. What is the mechanism for perceptual asymmetries: anatomic or attentional?
2. What is the nature and extent of the right and left hemisphere's particular functions?

METHODS OF STUDYING HEMISPHERIC SPECIALIZATION

Witelson (1977), Knox and Roeser (1980), and Kinsbourne (1979) have reviewed several techniques for identifying the language area of the brain. They include studies of patient populations with abnormal brain function and normal populations of subjects. In patient populations, the devastating effect of left hemispheric damage on language skills of adults has been known since Broca's work of the mid 1800s and extensively studied. In addition, persons with agenesis of the corpus callosum or patients with midline cerebral commissuratomy also have been studied for information about the specialized functions of each half of the cortex (Musiek, Wilson, & Pinheiro, 1979; Musiek, Wilson, & Reeves, 1981; Springer & Gazzaniga, 1975).

In 1960, Wada and Rasmussen reported that injection of sodium amytol into the carotid artery induced a temporary loss of function in the ipsilateral cerebral hemisphere, a technique which has been used to study right and left hemispheric function for both language and music. Kinsbourne (1979) described a unilateral electroconvulsive shock (ECS) method that generates a transitory cognitive impairment which may be used to study hemispheric function. Obviously, these methods have limited application and are selectively used on patients for whom the technique is medically appropriate.

In normal populations, hemifield tachistoscopic viewing is a method of studying hemispheric function in the visual system. Brief visual presentation of linguistic or nonlinguistic stimuli are presented to the right or left visual field. Since the visual image to the right of the fovea in both eyes goes to the right hemisphere, and to the left of the fovea to the left hemisphere, scores similar to those in dichotic listening can be derived showing visual field superiority for words, letters, and other stimuli. Other methods of note include the observation of lateral orienting effects in which subjects who adopt a particular mental set are said to turn their eyes in the direction opposite the active cerebral hemisphere. Vocal–manual interference techniques utilize simultaneous activities (e.g., speaking and finger tapping) to determine the disrupting effects of the verbal task or the hand movement. Event-related electrophysiological potentials (Donchon & McCarthy, 1979; Molfese, 1978; Mononen & Seitz, 1977; Seitz, 1976) have been used in the last decade to study right and left hemispheric function. More recently, changes in the amount of blood flowing in areas of the human cortex have been studied with the aid of radioactive isotope techniques (Lassen, Ingvar, & Skinhoj, 1978), a technique based upon the contention that enhanced functional level in a tissue can be sustained only by increasing the rate at which oxygen is consumed.

RESULTS OF STUDIES OF HEMISPHERIC SPECIALIZATION

Table 1-1 is a summary, albeit simplistic, of the suggested functions of the right or left hemisphere. Although the motor production of speech is controlled from one hemisphere, there probably exists what Shankweiler and Studdert-Kennedy (1975) have called "a continuum of lateralization for speech perception." Moscovitch (1981) stated that, although there was little evidence to suggest that the right hemisphere contributes to normal performance on traditional linguistic tasks, there was growing evidence that it played an important role in processing paralinguistic aspects of language such as emotional tone, context, inference, and connotation. These are, according to Moscovitch, those aspects of language that may be included as part of pragmatics or the discourse function of language. Wada, Clarke, and Hamm (1975) noted that when the hemisphere dominant for speech is inactivated by carotid sodium amytol injection, patients are unable to comprehend spoken commands, but remain capable of automatic speech and melodic expression. Thus, the difference between speech and language production (a single hemispheric function) and speech and language perception (a dual hemispheric function) must be kept clear when employing measures of auditory perception.

Relationship Between Cerebral Dominance and Language

According to Heçaen and Sauguet (1971), at least 19 of 20 persons are left dominant for language. Among the 1 in 20 minority, 75 percent are right lateralized for language while 25 percent have language representation in both hemispheres. When handedness is considered, approximately 96% of normal right-handed and 70% of left-handed people have language functions represented in the left hemisphere (Rasmussen & Milner, 1975, cited in Knox & Roeser, 1980). The remaining 4% of the right-handed people displayed right hemisphere speech dominance, while equal percentages of left-handed people exhibited bilateral and right hemisphere speech representation. Knox and Roeser (1980) note that this research clearly dispels the belief that speech is represented in the hemisphere contralateral to the preferred hand.

There is anatomic evidence of structural differences between the hemispheres that may underlie cerebral dominance. Within the speech dominant hemisphere, Heschl's gyrus contains the primary auditory reception area, while the auditory association cortex occupies the floor of the Sylvian fissure behind the primary auditory area in the region known as the planum temporale. The auditory association cortex on the left also is known as Wernicke's area.

Of the brains studied by Geschwind (1979), the planum temporale was larger on the left in 65% and larger on the right in 11%, and approximately equal on the two sides in 24%. Wada et al. (1975) noted that the left planum temporale was larger than the right in approximately 90% of both adults and infants. On the average, the left planum was one-third larger than the right. For left-handed people there is a larger percentage of asymmetry in both adults (Geschwind, 1979) and infants (Wada et al., 1975). While the relationship between structure and function is not clearly known, anatomical data suggests that a larger left planum might indicate a greater degree of verbal ability, and a larger right planum might signify

TABLE 1-1

Clinical, experimental and anthropological data suggesting the differential functioning of the cerebral hemisphere.

Left Hemisphere	Right Hemisphere
Speech/Verbal	Spatial/Musical
Logical, Mathematical	Holistic
Linear, Detailed	Artistic, Symbolic
Sequential	Simultaneous
Controlled	Emotional
Intellectual	Intuitive, Creative
Dominant	Minor (quiet)
Worldly	Spiritual
Active	Receptive
Analytic	Synthetic, Gestalt
Reading, Writing, Naming	Facial Recognition
Sequential Ordering	Simultaneous Comprehension
Perception of Significant Order	Perception of Abstract Patterns
Complex Motor Sequences	Recognition of Complex Figures

a higher degree of musical potential (Galaburda, Le May, Kemper, & Geschwind, 1978). Whether distributions of talent have anatomic correlates needs further exploration, but it is important to note that there is in the anatomic data a continuum of distribution between size of right and left asymmetries.

Effect of Non-Left-Hemispheric Dominance on Speech and Language

For many years there has been speculation that children with specific learning problems, including reading and language disorders, may have atypical cerebral dominance, a hypothesis first advanced by Orton (1937). There is little direct evidence, however, on the relationship between brain asymmetry and language/learning/writing disorders. Geschwind (1979) described cytoarchitecture mapping showing that the left temporal planum of a highly verbal lawyer was approximately seven times as large on the left as the right, while the brain of a dyslexic patient showed little asymmetry in that region. Hier, Le May, Rosenberger, and Perlo (1978) studied 24 dyslexic patients using computerized brain tomography (CT) and found that 10 (42%) of the subjects had brains that were wider in the right parieto-occipital region than the left, and 8 (33%) had brains that were wider on the left; 6 (25%) had brains that were approximately symmetrical. Rosenberger and Hier (1980) obtained CT scans on 53 learning-disabled adults and young children with verbal intellectual deficits, defined as depressed scores on the "verbal" scales of standard intelligence tests. Twenty-two (42%) of the subjects showed reversal of the usual right–left asymmetry. When subjects with a history of delayed speech were omitted from the learning-disabled group, the difference in proportion of reversed asymmetry compared to their control group was no longer significant.

Results of dichotic listening tests with dyslexic children have shown conflicting results. One author reported finding neither ear advantage nor left ear superiority for digits and words (Thomson, 1976), and others have shown a normal right ear advantage in dyslexic readers, although absolute scores were reduced compared to normal readers (McKeever & VanDeventer, 1975; Newell & Rugel, 1981). A study of normal reading subjects demonstrated a mild positive correlation between left ear superiority on dichotic listening task and scores on a standardized reading test (Richardson & Firlej, 1979). Obviously the issue of reversed cerebral dominance in poor readers is far from resolved.

Knox and Roeser (1980) provided some enlightening data by separating their severely dyslexic subjects into two subgroups: "dysphonetic dyslexics" exhibiting phonetic processing difficulties and "dyseidetic dyslexics" who demonstrated normal phonetic processing skills but poor recall of the visual gestalt of a word. The results of their dichotic testing showed a significant right ear advantage for the control group and dyseidetic dyslexics, but none for the dysphonetic group. They suggested that dyslexia should not be viewed as a unitary disorder, but rather one comprising at least two distinct subgroups.

Results of dichotic listening studies of language-disordered children have generally failed to verify a theory of reversed cerebral dominance (Ayers, 1977; Curcio, Rosen, & MacKavey, 1976; Hynd, Obrzut, Weed, & Hynd, 1979; Obrzut, Hynd, Obrzut, & Pirozzolo, 1981; Springer & Eisenson, 1977; Witelson & Rabinovitch, 1972). Nevertheless, some findings indicate that dichotic listening tests differentiate normal from learning-disabled children when certain test procedures and interpretations are used. The findings of Hynd et al. (1979) and Obrzut et al. (1981) suggest the use of dichotic listening tasks with free recall and directed ear procedures. Under these conditions learning-disabled children tend to show the following:

1. Poorer overall performance with lower scores in the free recall conditions.
2. Right ear advantage (REA) in the directed-right condition.
3. Left ear advantage (LEA) in the directed-left condition.

In normal children, the right ear advantage does not increase significantly on directed-right listening when compared to free recall conditions, and a right ear advantage is maintained on directed-left listening. This interpretation of directed ear listening tasks also is supported by work of Curcio et al. (1976).

A fourth dichotic test finding observed by this author in some children with disorders of oral or written language is a marked left ear advantage for either free recall or both directed ear listening conditions. The key to interpretation of clinically meaningful LEA is based on normative data obtained from children showing that the REA is not great and that small shifts between REA and LEA on repeated testing for dichotic consonant–vowel (CV) stimuli is normal. Therefore, LEAs for CVs should exceed at least 1 standard deviation before being considered abnormal.

Effect of Developmental Changes with Age on Dichotic Listening Results

Gilbert and Climan (1974), reporting on dichotic listening results in 2–3-year-old children, found an 18% average REA (calculated by $R-L/R+L$) with 24 of

31 children demonstrating an REA. Of the remaining seven subjects, six demonstrated an LEA and one demonstrated an equal preference for both ears. There was no significant difference in the degree of REA for males and females. Using CV syllable stimuli, Berlin, Hughes, Lowe-Bell, & Berlin (1973) found similar results for children aged 5 to 13 years (see Table 1-2). A criterion difference of at least two items was required to classify an ear advantage. Their results showed developmental trends only when children were required to identify both numbers of a stimulus pair, a result they attributed to increased channel capacity with increasing age. They, too, found no difference between results obtained from boys and girls.

Obrzut et al. (1981) found no developmental effects of age on dichotic CV tests administered to 64 normal children ranging in age from 7 years, 6 months to 13 years, 2 months. Results of their listening conditions, including free recall and directed ear testing, shown in Table 1-3, indicated a normally persistent REA under all listening conditions, including directed-left.

The results of Berlin et al. were extended by Schulman-Galambos (1977) through college age with similar findings. The difference between right and left ear scores (for dichotic words) ranged from 8.9 to 22% for various ages, with a mean of 14.4%. Schulman-Galambos found that mean overall accuracy increased up to Grade 3, and then began to level off. Approximately 30% of all subjects showed no particular ear advantage while small LEAs were seen in less than 10% of all subjects tested. Thus, there appears to be no developmental trend on "simple" dichotic listening tasks, with maturational effects shown on tasks involving more complex listening strategies (Anooshian & McCulloch, 1979; Geffen & Sexton, 1978). Schulman-Galambos data were obtained using free recall instructions to listeners. Recent data obtained in our laboratory indicate that adults and children may perform differently under conditions of free recall and directed ear listening. Preliminary data indicate that adults switch ear advantage under directed ear conditions while children generally maintain a right ear advantage under all conditions. These data indicate that developmental changes may be demonstrated under certain listening conditions.

Reliability of Dichotic Listening Test Results and Stability of Predicting Ear Advantage

Recent literature has shown increased interest in reliability of dichotic test results. For most investigators, decisions regarding presence of ear advantage are based on small percentage differences between ears, frequently as low as 6%, with most normal studies showing a mean REA between 6 and 15%. The larger the initial REA or LEA the greater the probability that the same laterality will be found on retest, and both the direction and size of the average ear advantage will remain essentially invariant (Blumstein, Goodglass, & Tartter, 1975; Speaks & Niccum, 1977). When subjects have small differences between ears, there is a possibility that test results may show a change in ear advantage on retest. Trial-to-trial reversals are more likely to occur when initial ear advantage is equal to or less than the standard deviation, and may occur in 20–25% of the population (Blumstein et al., 1975; Speaks & Niccum, 1977). Children yield the same stability of results as adults

TABLE 1-2
Dichotic Results on Children 5-13 years of age (From Berlin et al., 1973)

			Number of Children	Approximate % of Correct Responses		
Age	REA	LEA	No Apparent Ear Advantage	Right	Left	Both
5	16	14	10	77	63	37
7	21		9	80	60	42
9	23		7	80	58	47
11	21		9	80	57	53
13	21	5	4	80	53	57

TABLE 1-3
Number of Correctly Reported Dichotic CV Syllables (Obrzut et al., 1981)

			Listening Conditions			
				Directed		
Subject Age	Free Recall		Left		Right	
	Left	Right	Left	Right	Left	Right
7.4–10.4						
$\overline{X}$	10.56	13.31	11.38	13.69	10.94	14.19
SD	1.86	2.39	3.16	3.00	2.41	1.91
10.4–13.2						
$\overline{X}$	11.06	13.81	10.88	13.19	11.06	13.88
SD	1.48	2.51	1.36	1.94	2.08	2.42

Note. A total score of 30 was possible for each ear.

and subjects reach their maximum performance at an early age for dichotic listening tests (Millay, Roeser, & Godfrey, 1977). When instructions require the subject to respond to both stimuli, the first ear reported will show better scores and higher reliability than the second ear reported (Curcio et al., 1976; Millay et al., 1977). Left-handed persons show greater test–retest variability on dichotic listening tasks than right-handed (Hines, Ferrell, Bowers, & Satz, 1980), and although there is high intersubject variability of absolute dichotic CV scores, there is low intrasubject variability on retest (Millay et al., 1977). Further, the method used in reporting the research or clinical data may affect the interpretation of score magnitude, although it should not affect interpretation of ear advantage. Thus, while there are varied opinions about the reliability of dichotic test scores and stability of ear advantage (Millay et al., 1977; Schulman-Galambos, 1977; Speaks & Niccum, 1977), dichotic tests, nevertheless, appear to be as reliable as other audiological tests of equal difficulty and can be used in a clinical setting if carefully interpreted.

OTHER FACTORS AFFECTING DICHOTIC TEST RESULTS

There are multiple factors affecting test results that must be considered by the scientist and clinician, including at least the following: acoustic features of the signal, phonetic and acoustic features of the stimuli, methods of scoring, and linguistic content of the signal.

Acoustic Features of the Signal

The intensity of the signals must be carefully calibrated to ensure presentation at intended levels to the two ears. Most investigators present the signals at equal sound pressure level (SPL) in normal hearing subjects. Cullen, Thompson, Hughes, Berlin, and Sampson (1974) have shown that the signals must be at least 50-dB SPL (approximately 30 dB above normal hearing thresholds) to assure maximum performance, and 70-dB SPL is commonly used. The calibration of dichotic CV materials can be checked on an oscilloscope where the rms voltage of the steady state vowel portion of the syllable should equal the peak-to-peak voltage of the 1000-Hz calibration tone.

There is little data available on effects of small differences in intensity between ears on dichotic results. Berlin et al. (1972) found intensity effects with differences as low as 10 dB between ears. Dobie and Simmons (1971) presented dichotic CV materials at equal intensities and with interaural intensity differences of 15, 25, and 35 dB. Their results showed response decrements in the test ear when the CV to the opposite ear was at 15 dB higher intensity, particularly for the left ear score. Until more data is available on this subject, it must be assumed that even small intensity differences between ears can affect dichotic CV data, making it imperative that accurate pretest threshold data be obtained and that audiometer calibration be carefully monitored.

There is a scant data available on effects of signal-to-noise ratio (S/N) of test materials. Berlin et al. (1973) have reviewed data indicating that a S/N of 30 dB or poorer, especially with channel asymmetry, may have significant effects on dichotic listening results.

It also is possible that small differences in temporal onset may affect dichotic CV test results, although there appears to be little data published on this point. While this chapter has dealt only with simultaneous presentation of signals, there is a substantial body of literature dealing with lead and lag effects of 30 msec or greater on dichotic test results. Current technology allows for the careful control of the signal onset, duration, and other acoustic parameters and should be considered when constructing such measures.

Phonetic and Acoustic Features of the Stimulus

Berlin and McNeil (1976) note that in all the dichotic CV listening experiments conducted in their laboratory (presumably on adult subjects), voiceless stop consonants were more intelligible than voiced consonants when syllables were aligned at their onset. They consider this finding in adults so robust that if voiceless consonants were presented systematically to the left ear and voiced consonants to the right, the results would show a left ear advantage. Curiously, this finding was reversed in the results obtained from young children (Berlin et al., 1973), but to date follow up research on that finding has not been published. Berlin and McNeil (1976) also commented that velar syllables were repeated correctly more often than alveolar syllables, which in turn were more accurately repeated than labial syllables.

Methods of Scoring

A number of scoring procedures are available for reporting results of dichotic listening tests. They include:

Right Ear Correct	(REC)	
Left Ear Correct	(LEC)	
Right–Left	(R–L)	REC – LEC
Total Items Correct	(TC)	REC + LEC
Double Correct	(DC)	Number of Correct Syllable Pairs
Neither Correct	(NC)	
Percent of Correct	(POC)	Right Ear Correct/Total Correct
Percent of Error	(POE)	Left Ear Errors/Total Errors

All the methods except for POC and POE can be reported as a raw score or percentage, although the latter is preferable to avoid errors of interpretation since the number of items presented can vary. When the examiner is interested in comparing individual or group results to a population norm, the absolute scores computed on the basis of REC or LEC, including TC, DC, NC, and R–L is required. However, Harshman and Krashen (1972) pointed out that raw counts of errors made by each ear are influenced by many factors including the difficulty of the stimulus set, the amount of guessing used by the subject, and the degree to which the subject can "profit" from guessing. For example, there is a significant negative correlation between R–L and accuracy of response. For "easy" stimuli, both ears will do well (if there is no underlying perceptual asymmetry), yielding a small percent difference between ears. For "difficult" material, especially semantically vague stimuli such as dichotic CV syllables, both ears will do poorly, again yielding a small percent difference between ears. Further, the POC suffers from the same correlation with accuracy, giving biases in the same direction as R–L; specifically as accuracy increases ear difference will seem to decrease.

Therefore, when the purpose of the investigation is to determine the degree of underlying asymmetry in the perceptual process, the POE method is preferred. Harshman and Krashen state that the POE will show the degree of underlying perceptual asymmetry regardless of ease of stimulus materials, amount of guessing by the subject, and subject age. Both the POC and POE show increasing degrees of REA left hemisphere lateralization as the ratio increases above 50%.

Linguistic Content of the Signal

One of the more profound effects on dichotic test material results from the linguistic content of the acoustic signal. The focus has been on results obtained using dichotic CV material which have minimal linguistic value. Certain dichotic listening tests are available that use both competing words (Staggered Spondaic Word Test (SSW), Katz, 1977) and sentences (Competing Sentence Test, Willeford, 1977), and these yield very different results from dichotic CV materials.

Porter and Berlin (1975) stated that CV materials are processed lower in the central nervous system than tasks that demand semantic–syntactic analysis. Thus, CV materials do not show a marked ear advantage because their light linguistic load does not fully engage the higher level mechanisms involved in language processing. Normally, these stimuli are processed nearly equally in the two hemispheres. As the linguistic load increases, the signal appears to be processed very differently and the language dominant hemisphere assumes its role. For younger children linguistically complex materials (words and sentences) may be processed primarily in the language dominant (usually left) hemisphere, yielding a strong REA, because of the relatively direct anatomic ear-to-left-hemisphere connections. The left ear score suffers because the complex neural message cannot be adequately transmitted from the right hemisphere through the auditory pathway in the corpus callosum to the language centers in the left hemisphere. As the central nervous system matures, the left ear scores improve until they equal the right ear, and laterality effects are no longer observed. This developmental trend is not seen with dichotic CV material because of their minimal linguistic–semantic cues with emphasis on the acoustic and phonetic competition.

The model suggested here is exemplified in Figure 1-1, where typical results of a normal 6-year-old child are shown for dichotic CV syllables, dichotic words from the competing portions of the SSW (Katz, 1977), and competing sentences from the Willeford (1977) battery. The dichotic CV results are similar to those found in Table 1-3. The SSW results show a strong REA with greater difference between ears than CV syllables and improved overall scores. The competing sentence test finds 100% correct response in the right ear and a 40% difference between right and left ears. Normative data on competing sentences show that the right ear score in 6-year-olds ranges from 90 to 100%, with the left ear normally ranging from 0 to 100% for words and sentences. The left ear scores in normal children continue to improve until the age of approximately 11 years, when they reach 100%, while dichotic CV syllables remain essentially unchanged from childhood through adulthood. Typical findings for a normal 11-year-old are shown in Figure 1-2.

For competing sentences, the finding of a strong REA in young children is so consistent that it is rare to find a child with less than 90–100% correct responses on the right. These findings may indicate that sentence materials, with their heavy linguistic load, may be the most appropriate stimuli for assessing hemispheric function in children. This view is especially appealing because of its similarity to results of anatomical studies which show asymmetries favoring the left brain and results of sodium amytol testing showing that persons who have language function

FIGURE 1-1

Typical results of dichotic listening test expected from a normal 6-year-old. Responses are reported for dichotic CV tests for undirected ear listening conditions. The competing conditions of the SSW and the Competing Sentence Test of the Willeford battery are obtained under directed ear listening conditions. There are no published data available for directed ear dichotic CV testing in 6-year-olds.

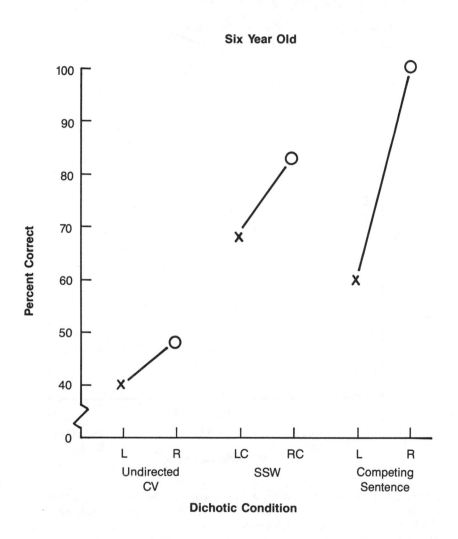

FIGURE 1-2
Typical results of dichotic listening tests expected from a normal 11-year-old. The tests reported are the same as shown in Figure 1-1.

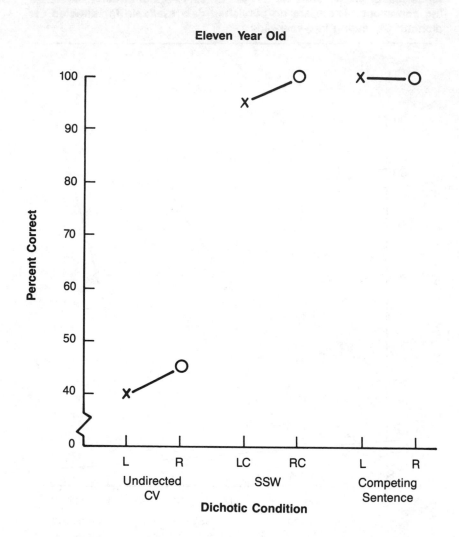

established in the right hemisphere are extremely rare (Blumstein et al., 1975). If dichotic sentence materials more accurately identify the dominant hemisphere in children, the value of dichotic CV testing lies not so much in establishing the dominant hemisphere for language, as in determining the way in which the listener processes more subtle, less linguistically distinct units of speech.

With this model, it is not surprising that small ear differences occur for dichotic CV tasks and that no ear advantage or small left ear advantages are frequently seen in normal subjects. Stronger REAs are expected if the syllables engage the language hemisphere. On the other hand, a marked discrepancy between ear advantage found with dichotic CV syllables and dichotic words or sentences, strong reversals in ear advantage on directed dichotic listening tasks (strong REA on directed right and strong LEA on directed left), or overall poor performance on dichotic listening tasks may be significant diagnostic signs of underlying neurological disorganization that is related to a wide range of specific learning disabilities including problems with auditory perception, language, and reading. In general, results need to show remarkable LEA or poor performance that is repeatable on retest and correlated with some other auditory or language (oral or written) finding before they can be considered clinically meaningful. Even then, poor performance on measures of functional asymmetry should be considered as potentially symptomatic rather than pathogenic, as suggested by Hynd, Obrzut, and Obrzut (1981) in discussing the relationship between dichotic listening results and cognitive function. The interpretation used here is closely related to the neuropsychological perspective on assessment and intervention of children with learning problems (Obrzut & Hynd, 1983).

CLINICAL PROCEDURES FOR ADMINISTERING DICHOTIC LISTENING TESTS

In spite of the amount of research on dichotic testing published to date, there appears to be no standardized method of instructing subjects, scoring responses, or reporting results. What follows are a number of suggestions for clinical testing that are based on a reading of the literature and the author's experience. These suggested procedures are open for revision when better techniques are demonstrated.

Pretest Considerations

Dichotic listening tapes of the highest quality should be used, with well-calibrated, noise-free, two-channel electronic equipment. Care must be taken to ensure that appropriate half-track or quarter-track tapes are ordered for the audiotape playback unit. To obtain maximum subject response, dichotic stimuli are presented at a minimum of 40-dB SL and preferably at 50-dB SL (approximately 70-dB SPL).

Prior to dichotic testing, normal and symmetrical hearing at the octave frequencies 500 through 4000 Hz, and 6000 Hz should be determined. There is little data available on the effects of hearing loss on dichotic test results, and any attempt at interpretation of results obtained on subjects with high-frequency hearing loss, asymmetrical, or even symmetrical, hearing loss (Ling, 1971) would be difficult to defend. The subject's ability to discriminate the stimuli is assessed under non-competing conditions to assure adequate recognition of and response to the signals. Finally, practice items are administered to familiarize the subject with the task and to ensure an understanding of the response requirements.

Listener Instructions and Scoring

For simultaneous dichotic presentation (0-msec lag), results are obtained under three listening conditions: free recall, directed-right, and directed-left. When instructing listeners, be sure that they know which is their right and left ear since many learning-disabled children and adults have problems in this regard. Only a single response for simultaneous (0-msec lag) testing is required. When dichotic CV tests with lead/lag items are used, a double response is required.

In order to avoid cross-modality confusion, the listener is asked to verbally repeat the stimulus. Children and adults who have problems with reading and writing may achieve a poorer score if they are required to respond using a check sheet or written responses. Some children with articulation and language disorders may not be able to repeat accurately the test words or syllables, and this limitation should be considered when testing. The oral response requires a high-fidelity talk-back system to avoid errors of discrimination on the part of the examiner.

When scoring, the examiner should circle the correct response and strike the missed syllable of the stimulus pair. If neither syllable is correct the examiner strikes both and notes the response that was given. When the listener perseverates on a single response for several items, he should be reinstructed. During directed ear listening, the examiner should remind the listener of his task if doubt exists about the ear to which he is attending.

When a double response is required, the examiner continues to score responses as noted above. If a double response is given and one is correct, credit should be given regardless of the order of the response. When a double response is given and both are correct, they should be scored double correct regardless of order.

The greatest problem in scoring dichotic CV results, whether in a free recall or directed ear test, is knowing to which ear the listener is attending, whether the listener is switching attention from ear to ear, or whether the signal opposite the directed ear intruded. While giving credit for all correct responses, regardless of order, may elevate the overall accuracy, it does not penalize the child who has problems in sequencing. Further, this scoring method will not affect computation of ear advantage. Examples of scoring are shown in Table 1-4.

Interpretation

To assess the results of dichotic CV tests, percentage scores from each ear are compared to normative results obtained from children of similar age and intelligence. The percentage of error (POE) score is used to determine degree of hemispheric asymmetry without regard to overall accuracy. Results of dichotic CV tests are considered abnormal if there is (a) poor overall performance shown by percent correct scores, (b) strong LEA on free recall, (c) a strong LEA on directed-left and strong REA on directed-right, (d) LEA on directed right.

Obviously these steps require adequate normative data that are not presently available. It is necessary for each clinic to establish its own set of norms for its specific audiotapes, equipment, and subject population. Even when normative data are made available it is necessary to verify them in individual clinics. In addition, there are no accepted guidelines for defining "good" performance or "strong" ear

TABLE 1-4
Examples of methods used in scoring dichotic CV test results.

	Simultaneous Single Response Directed-Right			120-Msec Lag Double Response		
	Right	*Left*		*Left*	*Right*	
	DA	(GA)	D	KA	BA	
	(KA)	PA	D	BA	(PA)	
	(PA)	TA		(GA)	(PA)	
	(DA)	TA	D	GA	BA	P
	(BA)	PA	D	GA	TA	P
	BA	(GA)		(DA)	BA	D
	DA	(BA)		(GA)	(DA)	
	(GA)	DA	D	KA	TA	P
K	TA	DA	?	BA	(DA)	
	(KA)	GA		(GA)	(KA)	
	6	3	Raw Score	4	5	
	60%	30%	% Correct	40%	50%	
	63%		POE = Left Errors	54%		
			Total Errors			

advantage. Until more is known, absolute performance that exceeds 2 standard deviations from the mean should be considered abnormal, with performance between 1 and 2 standard deviations considered borderline. An ear advantage is considered "strong" if it exceeds three times the normal difference obtained between ears. Tables 1-5 and 1-6 include examples of a central auditory and auditory language test battery administered to two boys with problems in reading. Note that the results in Table 1-6 show abnormal dichotic test results in a dysphonetic child similar to results reported by Knox and Roeser (1980).

Abnormal performance on dichotic CV tests may indicate abnormal hemispheric asymmetries or performance deficits due to delayed maturation of the auditory pathways that are symptomatic of neurological organization underlying a learning disability. The specific disability may be in multiple areas of language or academic performance. Only occasionally does an abnormal finding indicate the presence of a central lesion in children. However, when circumstances of history or other physical findings indicate such, the clinician should be alert to that possibility and make appropriate referrals for further neurological testing.

In addition, following the general principles of all diagnostic testing, dichotic CV results cannot be interpreted in isolation. A battery of central auditory and language measures is necessary to determine the wide range of abilities and

TABLE 1-5
Example of a central auditory test battery, including normal dichotic test results, obtained on an 11-year, 8-month-old boy with difficulties in reading. His hearing and auditory discrimination in quiet are normal.

WISC-R:
Verbal:	"Top of Average Range"
Performance:	"Bottom of Bright Average"

Achievement:
   6 to 31 percentile

Reading:
   +2 years behind grade level (11th percentile)

AUDITORY TESTS

Test	Result (R)	(L)		Interpretation
1000-Hz Low-Pass Filtered Speech	86%	80%		Normal
Word Discrimination (+6 dB S/N)	92%	84%		Normal
Dichotic CV Identification			*POE*	
Free Recall	43%	23%	58%	Normal REA
Directed Right	50%	26%	59%	
Directed Left	40%	20%	57%	
SSW (% of error)				
Noncompeting	5%	0		Normal
Competing	2%	16%		
Willeford Competing Sentence Test	100%	90%		

AUDITORY LANGUAGE

Test	Result	Interpretation
Token Test for Children	57	Normal = 54.7 ±4
Peabody Picture Vocabulary Test	108	97th percentile
Visual Auditory Digit Span Test	27	90th percentile
GFW Sound Symbol Test		
Sound Analysis	28	83rd percentile
Sound Blending	19	40th percentile
Border Test of Developmental Dyslexia		
Sight Reading Level	5th grade	Mild delay
Spelling		
Known	70%	Normal
Unknown	70%	

TABLE 1-6
Example of a central auditory test battery, including abnormal dichotic test results obtained on a 10-year, 8-month-old boy with a history of difficulties in reading, difficulty following auditory directions, auditory attention and memory. His hearing and auditory discrimination in quiet are normal.

WISC–R:

Verbal IQ = 80
Performance IQ = 100
Full Scale IQ = 88

PIAT:

Reading Comprehension = 9th percentile

AUDITORY TESTS

Test	Result (R)	(L)		Interpretation
Word Discrimination (+4 S/N)	84%	76%		Normal
Dichotic CV				POE
Free Recall	33%	46%	45%	
Directed Right	36%	30%	45%	
Directed Left	16%	50%	37%	Strong LEA
SSW				
Noncompeting	2%	0		Below CA
Competing	8%	38%		

AUDITORY LANGUAGE

		Interpretation
Peabody	73	16th percentile
Token Test for Children	55	Normal = 54.7 ± 5
Visual Auditory Digit Span	22	Average = 24 ± 2.7 (Poor written response)
Border Test of Developmental Dyslexia		
Sight Reading Level	6th grade	Normal
Spelling		
Known	70%	Spells by rote memory
Unknown	10%	Unable to spell phonetically; poor understanding of sound symbol relationships.

disabilities exhibited by the child. A test battery approach has been described elsewhere (Keith, 1977, 1981a, 1981b, 1981c) and is recommended reading for those interested in this subject.

In addition to dichotic CV tests, a diagnostic battery should include dichotic stimuli with greater linguistic content. For example, the SSW (Katz, 1977) and the Competing Sentence Test (Willeford, 1977), in this author's opinion, provide additional useful diagnostic information. While neither have been reviewed here in detail, both have been criticized for technical difficulties resulting from alignment criteria, signal-to-noise ratio, calibration, and overall tape quality. The SSW has recently been improved in this regard, and the Competing Sentence Test could also be improved, making it more acceptable for research and clinical application.

SUMMARY

Recent literature indicates growing evidence of probable underlying neurological bases of language and reading disorders in some children. These neurological constraints may be detectable using dichotic listening tests. Obviously, a great deal of additional information is required before dichotic tests can be applied, without reservation, to the clinical situation. Nevertheless, such measures may be useful in helping to better categorize subgroups within the learning-disabled population, thereby leading to more appropriate recommendations for remediation. Eventually they may be useful in predicting the time course of remediation and the long-term expectation for learning functional skills. Other clinical applications of these tests will undoubtedly result from future research and clinical experience. In the meantime, dichotic test results should be used but should be interpreted with care.

REFERENCES

Anooshian, L. & McCulloch, R. Developmental changes in dichotic listening with categorized word lists. *Developmental Psychology*, 1979, *15*, 280–287.

Ayers, A. J. Dichotic listening performance in learning-disabled children. *American Journal of Occupational Therapy*, 1977, *31*, 441–446.

Bakker, D., Van Der Vlugt, H., & Claushuts, M. The reliability of dichotic ear asymmetry in normal children. *Neuropsychologia*, 1978, *16*, 753–757.

Berlin, C., Hughes, L., Lowe-Bell, S. & Berlin, H. Dichotic right ear advantage in children 5 to 13. *Cortex*, 1973, *9*, 393–401.

Berlin, C., Lowe-Bell, S., Cullen, J., Thompson, C., & Stafford, M. Is speech special? Perhaps the temporal lobectomy can tell us. *Journal of the Acoustical Society of America*, 1972, *52*, 702–705.

Berlin, C. & McNeil, M. R. Dichotic listening. In N. Lass (Ed.) *Contemporary issues in experimental phonetics*. New York: Academic Press, 1976.

Blumstein, S., Goodglass, H. & Tartter, V. The reliability of ear advantage in dichotic listening. *Brain and Language*, 1975, *2*, 226–236.

Cullen, S., Thompson, C., Hughes, L., Berlin, C., & Samson, D. The effects of varied acoustic parameters on performance in dichotic speech perception tasks. *Brain and Language*, 1974, *1*, 307–322.

Curcio, F., Rosen, J., & Mackavey, W. Cerebral dominance: Its relation to age and reading. Final report, U. S. Department of Health, Education, and Welfare (National Institute of Education, Project 3-2046, Grant NE-G-00-2-0085), 1976.

Dobie, R., & Simmons, B. A dichotic threshold test: Normal and brain damaged subjects. *Journal of Speech and Hearing Research*, 1971, *14*, 71–81.

Donchon, E. & McCarthy, G. Event related brain potentials in the study of cognitive processes. In *The neurological bases of language disorders in children: Methods and directions for research* (NINCDS Monograph 22, NIH Publication 79-440). Washington, DC: U. S. Government Printing Office, 1979.

Galaburda, A., LeMay, M., Kemper, T., & Geschwind, N. Right-left asymmetries in the brain. *Science*, 1978, *199*, 852–856.

Geschwind, N. Anatomical foundations of language and dominance. In *The neurological bases of language disorders in children: Methods and directions for research* (NINCDS, Monograph 22, NIH Publication 79-440). Washington, DC: U. S. Government Printing Office, 1979.

Geschwind, N. & Levitsky, W. Left-right asymmetries in the temporal speech region. *Science*, 1968, *161*, 186–187.

Geffen, G., & Sexton, M. The development of auditory strategies of attention. *Developmental Psychology*, 1978, *4*, 11–17.

Gilbert, J. H. V., & Climan, I. *Dichotic studies in 2-3-year-olds: A preliminary report*. Paper presented at the Speech Communication Seminar, Stockholm, August, 1974.

Harshman, R., & Krashen, S. *An "unbiased" procedure for comparing degree of lateralization on dichotically presented stimuli*. Paper presented at 83rd annual meeting of the Acoustical Society of America, April, 1972.

Heçaen, H., & Sauguet, J. Cerebral dominance in left-handed subjects. *Cortex*, 1971, *7*, 19–48.

Hier, D., LeMay, M., Rosenberger, P., & Perlo, V. Developmental dyslexia. *Archives of Neurology*, 1978, *35*, 90–92.

Hines, D., Ferrell, E., Bowers, D., & Satz, P. Left-handers show greater test–retest variability in auditory and visual asymmetry. *Brain and Language*, 1980, *10*, 208–211.

Hynd, G., Obrzut, J., & Obrzut, A. Are lateral and perceptual asymmetries related to WISC–R and achievement test performance in normal and learning disabled children? *Journal of Consulting and Clinical Psychology*, 1981, *49*, 977–979.

Hynd, G., Obrzut, J., Weed, W., & Hynd, C. Development of cerebral dominance: Dichotic listening asymmetry in normal and learning-disabled children. *Journal of Experimental Child Psychology*, 1979, *28*, 445–454.

Katz, J. The Staggered Spondaic Word Test. In R. W. Keith (Ed.), *Central auditory dysfunction*. New York: Grune & Stratton, 1977.

Keith, R. W. (Ed.), *Central auditory dysfunction*. New York: Grune & Stratton, 1977.

Keith, R. W. Audiological and auditory-language tests of central auditory function. In R. W. Keith (Ed.), *Central auditory and language disorders in children*. San Diego: College-Hill Press, 1981a.

Keith, R. W. Tests of central auditory function. In R. Roeser & M. Downs (Eds.), *Auditory disorders in school children*. New York: Thieme Stratton, 1981b.

Keith, R. W. Central auditory test battery. In N. Lass et al. (Eds.), *Speech, language, and hearing*. Philadelphia: Saunders, 1981c.

Kimura, D. Cerebral dominance and the perception of verbal stimuli. *Canadian Journal of Psychology*, 1961, *15*, 166–171.

Kimura, D. Speech lateralization in young children as determined by an auditory test. *Journal of Comparative and Physiological Psychology*, 1963, *56*, 899–902.

Kimura, D. Functional asymmetry of the brain in dichotic listening. *Cortex*, 1967, *3*, 173–178.

Kinsbourne, M. Language lateralization and developmental disorders. In *The neurological bases of language disorders in children: Methods and directions for research* (chap. 6). (NINCDS Monograph 22, NIH Publication 79-440). Washington, DC: U. S. Government Printing Office, 1979.

Knox, C., & Roeser, R. Cerebral dominance in normal and dyslexic children. In R. W. Keith (Ed.), *Seminars in speech, language and hearing*, 1980, *1*, 181–194.

Lassen, N., Ingvar, D., & Skinhoj, E. Brain function and blood flow. *Scientific American*, October 1978, pp. 62–71.

Ling, A. Dichotic listening in hearing-impaired children. *Journal of Speech and Hearing Research*, 1971, *14*, 793–803.

McKeever, W., & VanDeventer, A. Dyslexic adolescents: Evidence of impaired visual and auditory language processing associated with normal lateralization and visual responsivity. *Cortex*, 1975, *11*, 361–378.

Millay, K., Roeser, R., & Godfrey, J. Reliability of performance for dichotic listening using two response modes. *Journal of Speech and Hearing Research*, 1977, *20*, 510–518.

Molfese, D. Left and right hemispheric involvement in speech perception: Electrophysiological correlates. *Perception and Psychology*, 1978, *23*, 237–243.

Mononen, L., & Seitz, M. An AER analysis of contralateral advantage in the transmission of auditory information. *Neuropsychologia*, 1977, *15*, 165–173.

Moscovitch, M. Right-hemisphere language. *Topics in Language Disorders*, 1981, *1*, 41–61.

Musiek, F., Wilson, D. & Pinheiro, M. Audiological manifestations in "split brain" patients. *Journal of the American Auditory Society*, 1979, *5*, 25–29.

Musiek, F., Wilson, D., & Reeves, A. Staged commissurotomy and central auditory function. *Archives of Otolaryngology*, 1981, *107*, 233–236.

Newell, D., & Rugel, R. Hemispheric specialization in normal and disabled readers. *Journal of Learning Disabilities*, 1981, *14*, 296–297.

Obrzut, J. E., & Hynd, G. W. *Neuropsychological Implications for Teaching the LD*, *Journal of Learning Disabilities*, 1983, *16*, 510–532.

Obrzut, J., Hynd, G., Obrzut, A., & Pirozzolo, F. Effects of directed attention on cerebral asymmetries in normal and learning-disabled children. *Developmental Psychology*, 1981, *17*, 118–125.

Orton, S. *Reading, writing and speech problems in children*. New York: Norton, 1937.

Porter, R., & Berlin, C. On interpreting developmental changes in the dichotic right-ear advantage. *Brain and Language*, 1975, *2*, 186–200.

Prior, M., & Bradshaw, J. Hemisphere functioning in autistic children. *Cortex*, 1979, *15*, 73–81.

Rasmussen, K., & Milner, B. *Clinical and surgical studies of the cerebral speech areas in man*. In K. Zulch, O. Oreutzfeldt, & K. Galbraith (Eds.), *Otfrid Foerster symposium on cerebral localization*. Heidelberg, Spring, 1975.

Richardson, J., & Firlej, M. Laterality and reading attainment. *Cortex*, 1979, *15*, 581–595.

Rosenberger, P., & Hier, D. Cerebral asymmetry and verbal intellectual deficits. *Annals of Neurology*, 1980, *8*, 300–304.

Schulman-Galambos, C. Dichotic listening performance in elementary and college students. *Neuropsychologia*, 1977, *15*, 577–584.

Seitz, M. Effects of response requirements and linguistic contexts on AER's to clicks. *Human Communication*, 1976, *1*, Summer.

Shankweiler, D., & Studdert-Kennedy, M. A continuum of lateralization for speech perception? *Brain and Language*, 1975, *2*, 212–225.

Sommers, R., & Starkey, K. Dichotic verbal processing in Down's syndrome children having qualitatively different speech and language skills. *American Journal of Mental Deficiency*, 1977, *82*, 44–53.

Sommers, R., & Taylor, M. Cerebral speech dominance in language-disordered and normal children. *Cortex*, 1972, *8*, 224–232.

Speaks, C., & Niccum, N. Variability of the ear advantage in dichotic listening. *Journal of the American Auditory Society*, 1977, *3*, 52–57.

Springer, S., & Eisenson, J. Hemispheric specialization for speech in language disordered children. *Neuropsychologia*, 1977, *15*, 287–293.

Springer, S., & Gazzaniga, M. Dichotic testing of partial and complete split brain subjects. *Neuropsychologia*, 1975, *13*, 341–346.

Studdert-Kennedy, M. Dichotic studies II: Two questions. *Brain and Language*, 1975, *2*, 123–130.

Thomson, M. A comparison of laterality effects in dyslexics and controls using dichotic listening tasks. *Neuropsychologia*, 1976, *14*, 243–246.

Wada, J., & Rasmussen, K. Intracarotid injection of sodium amytol for the lateralization of cerebral speech dominance. *Journal of Neurosurgery*, 1960, *17*, 266–288.

Wada, J., Clarke, R., & Hamm, A. Cerebral hemispheric asymmetry in humans. *Archives of Neurology*, 1975, *32*, 239–246.

Willeford, J. Assessing central auditory behavior in children: A test battery approach. In R. W. Keith (Ed.), *Central auditory dysfunction*. New York: Grune & Stratton, 1977.

Witelson, S., & Rabinovitch, M. Hemispheric speech lateralization in children with auditory-linguistic deficits. *Cortex*, 1972, *8*, 412–426.

Witelson, S. Early hemispheric specialization and interhemispheric plasticity: An empirical and theoretical review. In S. J. Segalowitz & F. A. Gruber (Eds.), *Language development and neurological theory*. New York: Academic Press, 1977.

2
IMPLICATIONS OF TEMPORAL PROCESSING FOR CHILDREN WITH LEARNING AND LANGUAGE PROBLEMS

Steven P. Bornstein
Ithaca College

Frank E. Musiek
Dartmouth-Hitchcock Medical Center

The development of a special auditory test battery for children has been based upon a need to evaluate children who manifest symptoms of auditory pathology but present normal results on standard audiological tests. Since these tests are relatively simple or contain redundant information, they primarily provide information about cochlear or eighth nerve function. The emergence of the awareness that neural encoding of acoustic stimuli within the central nervous system is of maximum importance has led to an interest in examining these children in more specific ways. The tests that have been developed are based on the fact that auditory neural pathways are multisynaptic and redundant (Jerger, 1973). Therefore, if a breakdown in this internal redundancy occurs, adequate pathways and neural interactions remain to properly encode simple acoustic stimuli such as pure tones and speech stimuli which contain multiple acoustic or linguistic cues. Subsequently it has been confirmed that with pathologies affecting central auditory nervous system function in adults, when a task becomes sufficiently complex or the extrinsic redundancy is reduced, neural encoding of acoustic stimuli is impaired leading to a perceptual impairment (Lynn & Gilroy, 1974; Noffsinger & Kurdziel, 1979).

Many of the tasks which were developed to identify site of central auditory nervous system pathology in adults have been used to assess performance of children with various communication problems. Although medically significant pathology affecting the auditory system may be present in children, the primary use of these tasks is to describe the child's performance and how it relates to behavior and communicative development. Performance difficulties on these tasks may reflect a dysfunction or a maturational delay of the central auditory nervous system, precluding adequate perception and hence optimum speech and language development. Chomsky (1967) postulated that development of linguistic rules will be impaired if the input signal is degraded. Alternatively, performance deficits may be a reflection of a more generalized linguistic deficit rather than a cause (Rees, 1981).

The purpose of this chapter is to discuss auditory temporality, which forms the theoretical base of many tests of central auditory nervous system function. Examination of the literature of central auditory assessment reveals that many behavioral tasks have been used. The use of many different tasks by numerous investigators reflects the lack of adequate theoretical bases for use with children, the minimal amount of methodological investigation into developing an efficient test battery, and the uncertainty as to how performance on these tasks relates to language and learning abilities. Discussions of the relationship of auditory temporality to speech perception and consideration of those tasks which are believed to reflect auditory temporal processing are presented, as well as discussion of those tasks which possibly may involve auditory temporal function and therefore are considered secondary. It is proposed that consideration of one aspect of performance at a time, in this case auditory temporal processing, leads to more effective assessment and remediation strategies. The neuroanatomic and neurophysiologic bases of central auditory function are of major importance (Luxon, 1981; Snow, Rintelmann, Miller, & Konkle, 1977) but are not considered due to the necessity for a separate treatment because of their enormous complexity.

The temporal nature of auditory–neural processing is important for auditory perception. Information encoded by both peripheral and central auditory system neurons is dependent upon the speed of neural transmission and the pattern of neural activity, which provide cues as to the interaction of the temporal, frequency, and intensity characteristics of the acoustic signal. The material presented in this chapter often focuses on data obtained with adults. While it is recognized that this data may not be related directly to children, it reflects the importance of temporal processing and the need for investigations of central auditory function with children.

THE TEMPORAL BASES OF SPEECH PERCEPTION

The importance of intact auditory temporal processing for auditory comprehension is supported by psychoacoustic, perceptual, and physiologic research (Aaronson, 1967; Efron, 1963; Hirsh, 1952, 1959; Masterton & Diamond, 1964; Neff, 1964; Swisher & Hirsh, 1972). The discrimination of rapid auditory patterns embedded in a speech background has been shown to be important for speech perception (Fujisaki, Nakamura, & Imoto, 1975; Klatt & Shattuck, 1975). Dorman, Cutting, & Raphael (1975) found that adults could identify the temporal order of vowels in running speech better when accompanied by the rapid changes in the acoustic spectrum known as formant transitions. Cole and Scott (1973) hypothesized that at rapid speech rates formant transitions preserve temporal order by connecting phonetic segments. In this regard, Cullinan, Erdos, Shaefer, and Tekieli (1977) found that adults could identify vowel temporal order with shorter vowel durations when formant transitions were present. Therefore the existence of a temporal processing deficit which precludes accurate perception of transitions may impair perception of the entire speech stream.

Identification of consonants as well as vowels, glides, and diphthongs is dependent upon transitions. Dellatre, Liberman, and Cooper (1955) identified second-formant transitions as perhaps the most important cue for place of articulation. Since these transitions occur within a time frame of less than 40 msec, the auditory system must be able to encode information over this brief time period. If it cannot, information as to the origin of the transition and the direction of the frequency change may not be perceived. In some cases, such as the /bʌ-wʌ/ distinction, the rate of formant transition has important phonemic importance (Liberman, Delattre, Gertsman, & Cooper, 1956). These findings have implications for children developing language. If transitions are not perceived, speech perception and hence the ultimate goals of comprehension and the development of linguistic and linguistically based skills will be impaired.

The pitch contour at the termination of a phrase may be defined as the rapid temporal change in the fundamental frequency. It has been shown that it is the most important acoustic cue for differentiating between a statement and a question (Fry, 1968). The duration of speech segments and the rate of spectral change also provide cues as to prosodic and emotional content (Fry, 1955).

The importance of duration cues for the identification of fricatives was demonstrated by Grimm (1966) and Liberman, Cooper, Shankweiler, & Studdert-Kennedy (1967). In addition, vowel duration is influenced by phonetic environment. For example, vowels are shorter when followed by a voiceless consonant. Also, vowel duration increases as manner of articulation following the vowel changes from plosives to nasals and then fricatives (Peterson & Lehiste, 1960). The influence of vowel duration on the identification of a following consonant is so strong that it may be considered a distinctive feature (Denes, 1955; House, 1961). Finally, a salient cue for the identification of an intervocalic stop is a brief silent interval as short as a few milliseconds, and the perception of an intervocalic stop consonant changes from a voiced to voiceless consonant as the silent closure interval increases (Bastian, Eimas, & Liberman, 1961; Lisker, 1957). If a child's auditory system cannot temporally process an ongoing signal interrupted for brief intervals in such a way as to prevent fusion, then speech perception will be impaired.

There are other cues which may influence vowel perception, particularly in ongoing speech and at short durations. Warren (1968) asked normal hearing adults to identify the temporal order of a repeating loop of four vowels. He found that without normal onset and decay characteristics and silent intervocalic intervals, performance was poor when vowel durations were 200 msec. Conditions where normal onset and decay characteristics as well as 50-msec intervocalic intervals were provided resulted in near perfect performance for vowels of 150 msec, indicating the importance of temporal cues to the process of speech perception. Recent research has indicated that methodological issues such as use of a repeating loop and listener training significantly influence the vowel duration necessary to identify temporal order (Kerivan, Alphonso, & Bornstein, 1979). For example, the use of a repeating loop of vowels rather than a single presentation significantly increases the vowel duration necessary for accurate identification. In spite of this, however, additional studies by Warren and Obusek (1972) and Warren and Warren (1970) support the view that there is a relationship between the vowel duration necessary to temporally order the vowel and the interaction of vowel rise and decay characteristics, and pauses between the vowels. The ability to make use of these duration cues would appear to be important for the maximum perception of the temporal order of conversational speech.

The ability to perceive and discriminate sounds of short duration also appears to be important, particularly since durations change as a function of linguistic environment. For example, in sentences the median duration has been found to be 70 msec for unstressed vowels and consonants and 130 msec for stressed vowels (Klatt, 1976), although phoneme and syllable durations have been shown to vary as a function of their position within a phrase (Klatt, 1975). Word duration also may be modified by the linguistic environment. For example, Goldhor (1976) found that nouns are longer when preceded by an adjective than in isolation.

Consonant durations may range from as short as 10 msec to 200 msec. Voiceless fricatives are approximately 40 msec longer than voiced fricatives. In general, bilabial stops are slightly longer than alveolar and velar stops (Klatt, 1976). Consonants are shortest in medial positions, longer in final positions, and longest in the initial position by approximately 10 to 30 msec (Oller, 1973). Umeda (1975) showed that consonants in the prestressed position are approximately 5 to 20 msec longer in duration compared to secondary stress positions. Vowels also may be identified in part by their duration, with /ɪ, ɛ, a, ʊ/ being shortest in duration (Peterson & Lehiste, 1966).

These results indicate that a temporal perceptual impairment would have negative linguistic implications for children. For example, duration cues play a role not only in phoneme identification, but in providing linguistic cues. The application of these normative parameters to tasks purporting to measure central auditory function has been pursued in recent years from several viewpoints.

PRIMARY TASKS OF AUDITORY TEMPORALITY

Time Altered Speech

Time compressed speech has been used most often as a monaural task. It appears to tax the ability of a listener to process rapid speech which has had nonphonetic acoustic structure removed. The inability to process speech elements which change rapidly in their acoustic structure may be expected to impair perception of the entire speech stream. It has been noted that adults with central nervous system dysfunction have difficulty understanding rapid speech in everyday situations (Albert & Baer, 1975; Gardner, Albert, & Weintraub, 1975; Wiedner & Laskey, 1976). Schuell (1953) noted that aphasic patients have a primary deficit with rapid conversational speech, while the comprehension of isolated words may be relatively unimpaired. Waas and Beedle (1972) cited studies which indicated that elderly hearing-impaired people improved their understanding when listening to a slow speaking rate. Waas and Beedle found that by time expanding speech, elderly subjects significantly improved their understanding of connected speech, compared with normal hearing subjects.

Blanchard and Prescott (1980) found that aphasic patients as a group improved their performance on the Revised Token Test to a significantly greater degree than normal subjects listening binaurally under various conditions of time expansion. However, differences were considered to be relatively small, with some patients showing no improvement. Landau, Goldstein, and Kleffner (1968) reported on a child with normal pure tone sensitivity and severe language disorder. They found that spoken language could be understood only if presented at a slow rate. A post-mortem study showed "severe damage to the primary projection pathways bilaterally with retrograde degeneration of the medial geniculate nuclei" (p. 919).

Temporally altered speech materials, either compressed or accelerated, have resulted in decreased speech intelligibility in the ear contralateral to temporal lobe lesions (Calearo & Lazzaroni, 1957; de Quiros, 1964; Korsan-Bengsten, 1973). Speech intelligibility performance using time compressed materials has been shown to decrease as a function of advanced age (Schon, 1970; Konkle, Beasley, & Bess, 1977) compared with the results expected for younger adults. These results may be due to degeneration in central auditory nervous system pathways. Schuknecht (1974) has described changes occurring in the central auditory nervous system as a function of age.

Despite the data which has been collected with normal-hearing children (Beasley, 1977; Beasley, Maki, & Orchik, 1976) further evaluation of time compressed materials with children presenting learning and language problems is needed, particularly as part of a test battery. Orchik and Oelschlaeger (1974) found diminished performance in children with articulation problems, but it was not clear if the problems were linguistically based. Manning, Johnston, and Beasley (1977) and Bornstein (1982) found that children who appeared to experience auditory perceptual difficulties scored significantly poorer on PB-K and WIPI words, respectively, at 0 and 60% compression, than a control group.

Depicted in Figure 2-1 are the results by Bornstein, who found that time compression was the most sensitive indicator of dysfunction in this group as a whole, although some exceptions not apparent in the mean data were observed. These results seem to indicate that a basic problem in processing undistorted auditory information existed, and became more evident as rate of presentation increased.

McCrosky and Thompson (1973) and Peck (1977) have presented evidence indicating that time expansion of speech improved auditory comprehension in language-disordered children and children suspected of having auditory processing difficulties. If these findings are found to be reliable and valid, the possible benefit of using artificially modified speech for remediative purposes begs investigation.

Temporal Sequencing

The theory that the ability to process and sequence rapid acoustic information is a primary defect with language-disordered children has been suggested (Bakker, 1970; Corkin, 1974; Doehring & Libman, 1974; Eisenson, 1968; Hardy, 1965; Monsees, 1961; Senf, 1969; Zurif & Carson, 1970). Impairment of temporal sequencing ability has been noted in adults with aphasia (Efron, 1963; Tallal & Newcombe, 1978), auditory agnosia (Albert, Sparks, Von Stockert, & Sax, 1972),

FIGURE 2-1
Mean scores for 15 children with learning problems, in the 9–10 year age range, on tasks assessing auditory function.

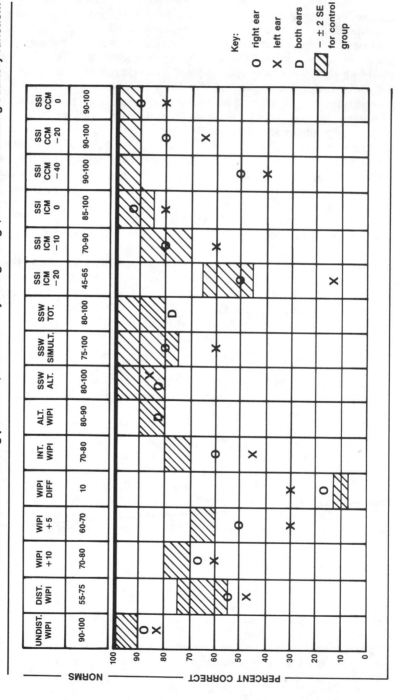

Figure 2-1. Test Abbreviations

UNDIST. WIPI	Word Intelligibility by Picture. Identification presented in Quiet.
DIST. WIPI	WIPI low-pass filtered below 800 Hz.
WIPI +10	WIPI presented against a multitalker babble at +10 Message to Competition Ratio.
WIPI +5	WIPI presented against a multitalker babble at +5 MCR.
WIPI Diff	The difference between WIPI +10 and WIPI +5.
INT. WIPI	WIPI in intelligibility at 60% time compression.
ALT WIPI	WIPI alternated between ears every 100 msec.
SSW Alt	Staggered Spondaic Word Test items in noncompeting conditions.
SSW Simult.	SSW Test items in competing conditions.
SSW Tot.	Total score on the SSW.
SSI ICM	Synthetic Sentence Identification with a competing message to the ipsilateral ear. The numbers denote the Message to Competition Ratio.
SSI CCM	Synthetic Sentence Identification with a competing message to the contralateral ear. The numbers denote the MCR.

bilateral temporal lobe lesions (Jerger, Weikers, Sharbrough, & Jerger, 1969), unilateral brain damage affecting auditory cortex (Hughes & Holtzapple, 1979; Swisher & Hirsh, 1972), and adults with unilateral temporal lobectomy (Sherwin & Efron, 1980). Many of the tasks used to assess temporal sequencing ability vary somewhat, but the basic paradigm requires subjects to identify the order of two tones differing in frequency with the onset of the second tone delayed in time. Although results vary depending upon the stimulus, the nature of the lesion, and whether the stimuli are presented to the same or opposite ears, normal hearing subjects can identify temporal order with onset differences ranging from 2 to 20 msec, whereas brain-damaged subjects without aphasia require onset differences of as much as 60 msec, and subjects with aphasia require 300 to 600 msec or greater. Other results from these studies may be summarized as follows:

1. Auditory cortical function is important for temporal order or sequence judgments;

2. The left or dominant hemisphere is primarily responsible for temporal sequencing. Lackner (1982), Lackner and Teuber (1973), and Swisher and Hirsh (1972) speculated that language may be "attracted" to the left hemisphere because of its predisposition for temporal sequencing;

3. There is a significant correlation between temporal ordering ability and linguistic skills.

A number of studies have been performed which provide indications of impaired temporal processing in children with language and learning problems (Tallal & Piercy, 1973, 1974, 1975; Lowe & Campbell, 1965) using paradigms requiring subjects to discriminate whether two successive sounds were the same or different, or to identify the order of two successive different sounds, as a function of the interval between the offset of one sound and the onset of the second. Stimuli have been pure tones, complex tones, or synthetic consonant–vowel syllables. Generally, a marked difference in the ability of language-disordered children compared with normal children has been found for interstimulus intervals less than approximately 300 msec, while performance has been similar using intervals greater than 300 msec. These results seem to indicate that sequencing disorders occur primarily when acoustic information is presented at a rapid rate. The necessity for providing an extended off time to correctly order the sequence or discriminate two different stimuli in children with language problems is consistent with diagnostic and therapeutic effects which have been found in adults with aphasia. Liles and Brookshire (1975), Lowe and Campbell (1965), Carpenter and Rutherford (1973), and Ebbin and Edwards (1967) have presented evidence which indicates that silent intervals improve performance, perhaps due to the allowance for a longer processing time.

Lackner compared the performance of 40 persons with penetrating wounds to either hemisphere or both hemispheres to a control group of 12 persons on three tasks requiring the identification of the order of phoneme sequences. The tasks differed as to whether they were all vowel sequences, a combination of consonant–vowel and vowel sequences, or all consonant–vowel sequences. All tasks used four elements in the sequence, and each element duration was fixed at 200 msec. A repeating loop of each sequence occurred for 32 sec, with all elements and sequences contiguous (Warren & Warren, 1970). Lackner found that persons who had penetrating wounds to the left hemisphere performed significantly poorer than the control group on all sequence tasks, with the poorest performance by persons who demonstrated residual dysphasia. The significance of this finding is that the difficulty occurred for stimuli considered to require linguistic analysis (CVs) as well as for stimuli considered to require more of an acoustic rather than linguistic analysis (vowels). Lackner concluded, in agreement with the work of Tallal, that a primary deficit in these adults resulted from an inability to resolve temporal order, independent of linguistic function. Although the repeating loop method may be criticized, as mentioned previously, this study is consistent with the theory that the left hemisphere's ability to process temporal information is the basis for its linguistic specialization. Furthermore, the types of sequencing errors which occurred in the left hemisphere damaged group indicated that primary auditory stream segregation occurred, which was consistent with the contention that the deficit was not in the ability to resolve the frequency components, but rather with the sequencing per se.

Although it is tempting to speculate that the inability to process auditory information presented rapidly is related to linguistically based disorders, as indicated by the results of studies involving interstimulus intervals, the effects of other variables need to be considered. In this regard, the work generated by Thomas Shriner showed the need to consider the complexity of the issue of temporal processing. Beasley and Shriner (1973), Beasley and Beasley (1973), and Beasley and Flaherty-Rintelmann (1976) found that the ability to recall sentences and sentential approximations decreased as the interstimulus interval between words increased from a normal speaking rate to 400 msec in both normal-hearing children and adults. However, Beasley and Shriner (1973) found that increasing the interstimulus interval between words could offset the deleterious effect of decreased word duration. In contrast to the theory that a deficit in processing rapid auditory information exists, these results suggest a difficulty with short-term memory, according to a model proposed by Aaronson (1967). This model of stimulus decay is consistent with the finding that many children with learning and language problems experience short-term memory disturbances. The work advanced by Shriner indicated that word duration, linguistic material, memory, stimulus length, and stimulus duration all play important roles in the rate at which auditory information is perceived most accurately. It is likely that difficulties processing rapid auditory information or with short-term memory are selectively impaired in different children or that they may coexist within the same individual. Auditory–temporal, linguistic, and memory processes need to be considered and investigated comprehensively in children with language and learning disorders. Specifically, there may be an optimal presentation rate for speech perception, whereby speech perception may be impaired if information is presented at more rapid or slower rates. In this regard, Plomp (1964) utilized a strict psychoacoustic paradigm which required two observers to identify the minimum silent interval they could perceive between two noise pulses. Using different sensation levels for the two pulses, he reasoned that the minimum time interval required would represent the rate of stimulus decay. According to the data obtained, the sensation of stimulus decay followed a straight-line function which reached its maximum value about 200–300 msec.

Pattern Perception

Pattern perception tasks and their results may be related to temporal sequencing, but they are different in one major respect. Pattern perception requires the ordering of more than two stimuli and requires a person to perceive and process the gestalt rather than individual components. In this respect, they may be more representative of conversational speech perception. Musiek and Guerkink (1980), Musiek, Guerkink, and Keitel (1982), and Pinheiro (1977) have shown that children with learning or suspected auditory processing difficulties have a marked impairment in the ability to report the order of three-element patterns, but that they can hum the response. Figure 2-2 shows the results obtained by Musiek et al., wherein two major points are worth noting. First, impairment of pattern perception was the most abnormal result of this test battery (although there were individual exceptions) reflecting the importance of this temporal skill to children's everyday performance. Second, the deficit occurred in both ears, leading these investigators to speculate that there is a need for interhemispheric interaction for adequate performance on these tasks. This speculation is supported by the similar findings of Musiek, Pinheiro, and Wilson (1980) with three adults who had undergone section of the corpus callosum. The right hemisphere presumably is necessary to recognize

FIGURE 2-2

Mean scores and standard deviations for the 22 children with auditory perceptual problems in this study for seven central auditory tests. (From Musiek, Guerkink, & Keitel, 1982; reproduced with permission.)

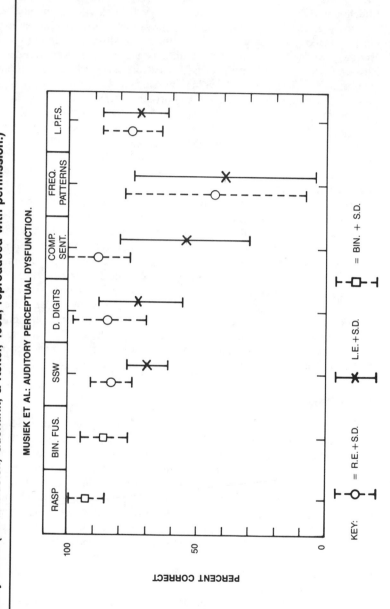

MUSIEK ET AL: AUDITORY PERCEPTUAL DYSFUNCTION.

Figure 2-2. Test Abbreviations

RASP	Rapidly Alternating Speech Perception: relatively simple sentences alternated between ears every 300 msec.
BIN. FUS.	Binaural Fusion: spondees filtered through a low bandpass (500–700 Hz) and high bandpass (1900–2100).
SSW:	Staggered Spondaic Word Test.
D. Digits	Dichotic Digits.
Comp. Sent.	Competing Sentences: primary signal in test ear at 35-dB SL and competing sentence in nontest ear at 50-dB SL.
Freq. Patterns	Frequency Patterns: three-element patterns using two different frequencies.
LPFS	Low-Pass Filtered Speech: CNC monosyllables with high-frequency cutoff frequency of 500 Hz with rejection rate of 18 dB/octave.

the pattern gestalt while the left hemisphere contributes temporal sequencing and verbal mediation. The fully developed corpus callosum is highly myelinated and therefore would appear to be specialized for the purpose of rapid interhemispheric interaction. It is tempting to speculate that inadequate or delayed development of the corpus callosum might result in a breakdown of the temporal processing capability of the auditory system, which is necessary for the perception, sequencing, and labeling of acoustic information.

Musiek et al. (1982) also found a greater left ear deficit than expected. They concluded that their results may reflect "inept transfer of auditory information from the right to the left hemisphere" (p. 255). Selnes (1974) reported that Alpers and Grant (1931) observed "the most striking thing in the mental picture is the inability of patients with a callosal tumor to concentrate and to focus and to maintain attention for even a brief time" (p. 121). This "disinhibited" type of behavior often is seen in children and the possibility needs to be considered that it is associated with corpus callosum dysfunction. Furthermore, Selnes reported that Unterharnscheidt, Jacnik, and Gott (1968) found that language delay frequently accompanied callosal agenesis. Drake (1968) provided a post-mortem report on a 12-year-old male with what was considered a mild learning disorder including dyslexia. Although many problems were present, difficulties with sequencing were prominent. The neuropathological report revealed several anomalies including a thinning of the corpus callosum. The reader is referred to this article for a comprehensive overview of issues related to learning disabilities, as well as medical, psychological, educational, developmental, and neurological details of this particular child. Kracke (1975) hypothesized that children with language disorders experienced a deficit in perceiving a pattern gestalt. She found that language-disordered children had a deficit perceiving duration patterns compared with a control group and children with peripheral hearing impairment. Furthermore, the responses given seemed to indicate that they were using an element-by-element strategy to process the patterns rather than attending to the pattern as a whole or as a gestalt. Kracke speculated that the inability to structurally organize incoming patterns "makes speech a confusing conglomerate of noises" (p. 50). The distractible and confused behavior of many children with learning and language disorders in classroom settings is consistent with this hypothesis.

Perception of Rapid Spectral Changes

Tasks of two-tone sequences and pattern perception require the auditory system to encode information in such a way that abrupt differences in frequency, duration, or intensity can be detected over time. While they have relevance to the role of auditory factors in speech perception, the ability to perceive contiguous changes in the speech spectrum is more important and relates to the previous discussion of perceptual streaming. Tallal and Piercy (1974, 1975) found that language-disordered children had difficulty discriminating consonant–vowel stimuli which contained rapid formant transitions, while discrimination of steady-state vowels with the same total duration was unimpaired. Furthermore, children with language disorders experienced difficulty discriminating consonant–vowel stimuli with 43-msec formant transitions, while performance was equivalent to that of normal language children when the formant transitions were extended to 95 msec. The 95-msec transition stimuli were still perceived as normal speech, suggesting the research potential of remediation approaches.

Tallal, Stark, and Curtiss (1976) and Stark and Tallal (1979) used tasks which covaried interstimulus intervals and the rate of formant transitions. They found that difficulties with stimuli having short interstimulus intervals or rapid formant transitions were related to speech production abilities. Stark and Tallal (1981) found deficits on these tasks to be significantly correlated with language disorders.

Detection and Frequency Discrimination of Short Duration Stimuli

The effect of stimulus duration on detection is a known auditory phenomenon (Zwislocki, 1960). In general, the integration of energy over time occurs within 200 msec, resulting in the effect that for every tenfold decrease in stimulus duration, threshold increases 10 dB. Since detection is necessary before perception, an impairment in the ability to detect acoustic structure of the extremely short duration speech sounds would interfere with speech perception. This would have significant learning and language implications for a child developing language. The work of Baru, Gersuni, and Tonkonogii (1964), Gersuni (1965), and Baru and Karaseva (1972) showed that in patients with temporal lobe lesions involving the auditory cortex, sensitivity to stimuli greater than 200 msec duration was unaffected, while sensitivity to stimuli 10 to 20 msec in length was markedly elevated, sometimes on the order of 50 dB in the ear contralateral to the lesion, compared with the ipsilateral ear. The patient with bilateral temporal lobe lesions described by Jerger et al. (1969) also showed a similar effect. Conversely, Cranford (1979) and Cranford and Igareshi (1977) did not find this alteration of the threshold duration function in cats with lesions involving auditory cortex. Also, Pederson (1967) found variable and equivocal results in adults with cortical pathology. Furthermore, temporal integration performance did not seem to be related to speech discrimination ability, and therefore the utility of this task for the central auditory assessment of adults was questioned. Olsen, Rose, and Noffsinger (1974) did not find an abnormal increase in threshold with decreasing stimulus duration for adults with eighth nerve dysfunction.

Cranford et al. (1982) reported on 10 persons with cortical pathology, 7 of whom had pathology affecting auditory cortex. In general, they did not find any alteration in the detection of brief tones. When an abnormal elevation for the detection of a brief tone in the contralateral ear occurred, it reflected an active neuropathologic process. They reasoned that after the acute phase of a cortical pathology, this function returns to normal levels. Further, they found that frequency discrimination for short duration stimuli was severely impaired, but that frequency discrimination for long duration stimuli was unimpaired. The deficit always was present in the contralateral ear, and sometimes was reflected bilaterally. Also, recovery of function did not occur, as it did for detection. The stimulus duration which resulted in impaired performance varied among patients, but generally was less than 200 msec. A similar deficit in frequency discrimination using short duration stimuli was found in cats (Cranford, 1979).

Hochman, Thal, and Maxon (1977) did not find a significant difference in the temporal integration function of children with language disorders and children with no apparent problems. Interestingly, they did find that the absolute threshold for both long and short duration signals was greater for the children with language disorders. This ability deserves further investigation particularly as it relates to speech perception ability. Pinheiro (1977), for example, reported that children with learning problems often show a loss of sensitivity at 8000 Hz for stimuli with durations greater than 200 msec.

Interrupted Speech

The ability to perceive speech with periodic interruptions may be related to the auditory system's ability to fill in temporal gaps, although perception may be more dependent upon cognitive and linguistic functions for interrupted speech. The ability to understand interrupted speech depends upon the number of interruptions and the relationship of the speech duration to silent intervals. In short, intelligibility of monosyllabic words increases from approximately 50 to 90% as interruptions increase from 1 to 10 per sec in normal hearing persons. A 15 to 20% reduction in scores for the ear contralateral to a unilateral temporal lobe lesion compared with the ipsilateral ear has been demonstrated (Antonelli, 1970, Bocca, 1958; Calearo & Antonelli, 1963). In cases of brainstem dysfunction, the contralateral ear or both ears have been shown to be affected (Bocca, 1963, 1967; Calearo & Antonelli, 1968; Jerger, 1970). Korsan-Bengsten (1973) found that only lesions involving or close to auditory cortex resulted in reduced speech intelligibility scores in the contralateral ear for interrupted speech. Furthermore, she found that in her test battery, interrupted speech and time compressed speech, the two temporally based tasks, were the most sensitive indices of dysfunction. She also found decreased performance on interrupted speech tasks in elderly subjects, perhaps due to degeneration within the central auditory nervous system. Of interest was the finding that elderly subjects increased their scores 25 to 30% with practice while younger subjects did not. This may reflect that the ability to process temporally distorted speech may be amenable to remediation.

SECONDARY TASKS OF AUDITORY TEMPORALITY

Many of the tasks presented in this section are related to binaural phenomena. While the ability to perform these tasks may be related to temporal auditory encoding, due to preservation of the timing relationship between ears, the relationship is not clear. Furthermore, the exact role this ability plays in speech perception has not been determined, and for this reason they have been considered secondary tasks.

Sound Localization and Lateralization

The abilities to localize a source in the sound field and to judge the perceived spatial location within the head when listening under earphones are related binaural phenomena. Sound localization serves an important function for protective and speech purposes. A speech signal must be localized and attended before meaningful extraction of information can occur. Sound localization may be related to many phenomena such as detection of short duration stimuli, discriminating speech in a noise background, or listening to competing speech, where location of the primary source must occur. Devens, Hoyer, and McCroskey (1978) found that children with learning problems had significantly greater difficulty than normal children while manually tracking an acoustic stimulus moving in a geometric pattern for a speech signal and white noise, but not a pulsed or continuous square wave. Jerger et al. (1969) found that their patient with bilateral temporal lobe lesions could not accurately localize a free field sound source, with errors sometimes being as great as 180°. In addition, for stimuli greater than 100 msec duration, the stimuli seemed to move in an arc, both for sound field presentation and stimuli presented binaurally under earphones. These investigators speculated that this finding could be explained by the different temporal integration functions for each ear, in that at the onset of stimulation the stimulus would be lateralized to the ear receiving the louder stimulus, which was the ear with the shallower function. However, as the stimulus increased in duration, the loudness in the ear with the steeper function would increase, thereby causing perception of movement of the stimulus toward that ear. In this regard, Tolkmitt (1970) found that the ability of normal adults to localize a moving sound source was improved by increasing stimulus duration. Similarly, Thurlow and Mergerer (1970) stated that stimulus duration was an important factor in localization and suggested that a minimum duration of 2 sec was necessary for maximum localization ability.

The behaviors of many children with learning and language problems suggest that they have difficulty localizing sound. Rapid head movements and the appearance of searching for a sound source often are seen. During this searching process, speech intelligibility may be lost. The distractiveness and confusion of background noise conditions may be related to this disability. Other investigators have reported that adults with brain damage have difficulty localizing a sound in the free field (Oster, 1973; Sanchez-Longo, Forster, & Auth, 1957). Goldstein, Brown, and Hollander (1975) reported a case of auditory agnosia where localization of sound and reproduction of rhythmic sound patterns were impaired.

Several investigators have demonstrated that cats with unilateral ablation involving auditory cortex have difficulty with sound localization (Cranford, Ravizza, Diamond, & Whitfield, 1971; Cranford & Oberholtzer, 1976; Whitfield, Cranford, Ravizza, & Diamond, 1972). For example, when two identical sounds originated from different loudspeakers, animals without lesions could localize to the speaker which produced the sound first by a few milliseconds. However, animals with lesions could localize only when the sound began first from the speaker on the side opposite the intact hemisphere. Cranford, Stream, Rye, and Slade (1982) found this same effect with one of their adult patients with brain damage affecting auditory cortex, as did Hochster and Kelly (1981) with children who had unilateral temporal lobe epilepsy.

Sound localization for low-frequency signals is based upon interaural time differences (Teas, 1962). Various physiological mechanisms of sound localization have been proposed (Jeffress, 1948; Rose et al., 1966). Sound localization is related to the lateralization of stimuli under earphones. In general, as a broadband signal to one ear is delayed in time by approximately 2.5 msec, two separate sounds are perceived. At time delays less than 2.5 msec a fused percept occurs. Lackner and Teuber (1973) found that in adults with penetrating wounds to the left temporal lobe, a significantly greater time delay needed to be presented for the perception of two stimuli. These investigators hypothesized that the left temporal lobe is responsible for temporal acuity which forms the base for specialization of linguistic analysis. They speculated that a performance deficit on this task "might underlie at least some forms of difficulties in the detection of those extremely rapid transitions that occur within and between acoustic events in speech" (p. 413). Interestingly, Milner and Teuber (1968) have reported that persons under the influence of LSD require time differences 5 to 10 times that of normal to perceive two separate clicks presented dichotically rather than as a fused percept.

Lateralization based on interaural intensity cues is based in part on the preservation of neural impulse rate at levels within the central auditory nervous system. Pinheiro and Tobin (1969, 1971) found that in subjects with unilateral cerebral disease or trauma, a greater interaural intensity difference needed to be presented under earphones to shift the fused percept to the ear ipsilateral to the lesion compared with the contralateral ear. Also, the necessity to consider stimulus duration as a factor was shown by the increase in the interaural intensity difference with a 76-msec stimulus compared with a 506-msec stimulus. They reported that of 40 patients with neurologic disorder tested, this greater interaural intensity difference occurred in patients with symptoms implicating only temporal or parietal lobe areas. These investigators hypothesized that performance on this task may be mediated by cortical or immediately subcortical structures.

A variation of the procedure used by Pinheiro and Tobin which determines the intensity level of two dichotic stimuli presented simultaneously to achieve a midline percept has been used in patients with cochlear, brainstem, and cerebral pathology (Bosatra & Russolo, 1976; Jerger, 1960; Matzker, 1962; Nordlund, 1964). It is known as simultaneous binaural median plane localization (SBMPL). Carhart (1973) reported that patients with brainstem lesions have extreme difficulty on the SBMPL. Bocca and Antonelli (1974) did not find a disturbance in the ability of five subjects with unilateral cerebral lesions to make a simultaneous binaural medial plane localization. Unimpaired performance also was found by Hodgson (1967) in a patient after left hemispherectomy. Barr, Mullin, and Harbert (1977) reported that when two tones of slightly different frequency were presented dichotically to aphasic patients they were not able to hear the expected phenomenon of binaural beats. Furthermore, they were unable to lateralize the percept. They hypothesized that one reason for this disturbance may be due to the exertion of pressure on brainstem structures.

Masking Level Differences

Jeffress (1972) postulated that correlation processes within the central nervous system are responsible for the occurrence of masking level differences (MLDs). MLDs refer to the improvement in threshold or speech intelligibility when the relationship between ears of either speech or noise presented simultaneously and binaurally is shifted 180° out of phase. Summarizing studies with adults, it appears that patients with cortical pathology have normal MLDs while those with brainstem dysfunction, multiple sclerosis, or presbycusis have reduced MLDs (Cullen & Thompson, 1974; Olsen, Noffsinger, & Carhart, 1976). Alternatively, Bocca and Antonelli (1974) did not find any disturbance in the MLDs of elderly subjects, whereas subjects with cerebral lesions showed reduced MLDs, particularly when the leading ear was contralateral to the damaged hemisphere. Sweetow and Reddel (1978) found that children with suspected auditory perceptual problems demonstrated reduced MLDs for pure tones but not speech. The interaction and comparison of stimuli within the central nervous system is necessary for auditory figure-ground relationships and localization ability. The disinhibition and behavior problems manifested by many children may be related to a breakdown in performing this function. The relationship between MLDs and other aspects of auditory perception was demonstrated by Quaranta and Cervellera (1974). Their data showed a correlation between poor performance on time compressed, frequency-distorted speech, and small MLDs in patients with various loci of central nervous system dysfunction.

Hannley, Jerger, and Rivera (1983) examined the release of masking for a 500-Hz tone in 20 persons with multiple sclerosis and found reduced MLDs for the group as a whole. However, overlap was noted with a normal control group in those persons who demonstrated the presence of Wave III during auditory brainstem response (ABR) testing. Significantly reduced MLDs were found in those persons who showed prolongation of Wave III, and the lowest MLDs were found for those persons in whom both the absence of Wave III and abnormal acoustic reflex results were found. Lynn, Gilroy, Taylor, and Leiser (1981) found that in 26 persons with confirmed brainstem and cerebral lesions, abnormal speech MLDs were found only when there was involvement of the pontomedullary level. These results support the premise that important temporal processing between ears occurs in the lower brainstem, probably by superior olivary complex structures.

DIRECTIONS FOR FUTURE RESEARCH AND SUMMARY

The most obvious need with all of the tasks discussed is extensive collection of normative data and reliability studies with children. Furthermore, the effectiveness of these procedures and the false-positive rate as part of a test battery to identify children with learning and language problems needs to be evaluated. Spitzer (1983) has provided a strong rationale for establishing the sensitivity and specificity of tests purporting to measure function of the central auditory nervous system. The fact that a majority of work has been performed with adults and that the results have been equivocal in terms of effectiveness and identification of site of lesion makes their use with children questionable. Most important, the exact relationship of performance on these tasks to speech perception needs clarification. One may infer that a deficit in temporal processing does exist. However, several other questions remain. Is the deficit monaural or binaural? Do left ear deficits reflect impairment in the rapid transmission of information between hemispheres? What is the relationship of interstimulus interval and stimulus duration particularly as they relate to the interaction of auditory, linguistic, and memory factors?

Several other measures of auditory temporality also deserve investigation. Abnormalities in the ability to detect intensity changes over time have been demonstrated in adults with cortical pathology (Hodgson, 1967; Jerger et al., 1969), in contrast to the findings of Swisher (1967). Abnormal auditory adaptation has been reported in children with speech and language disorders (Costello & McGee, 1967) and adults with brainstem pathology (J. Jerger & S. Jerger, 1975; S. Jerger & J. Jerger, 1975; Noffsinger, Olsen, Carhart, Hart, & Sahgal, 1972). Impairment in the ability to discriminate duration differences have been reported in cases of cortical pathology (Baru & Karaseva, 1972). Needham and Black (1970) found that persons with aphasia demonstrated poor performance on tasks of temporal and intensity discrimination. Also, Faires and Lankford (1976) found that children with cerebral palsy performed more poorly than a control group matched for mental age on duration and frequency discrimination tasks. Faires and Lankford reported that Edmondson (1953) found duration discrimination ability to be most significantly related to language recovery in aphasic patients, compared with other tasks on the Seashore Test of Musical Abilities. Difficulties discriminating temporal cues (Carpenter & Rutherford, 1973) and categorically judging segmental duration cues (Sasanuma, Tatsumi, Kiritani, & Fujisaki, 1973) also have been reported in adults with aphasia. Normal hearing adults are able to detect gaps when the interstimulus interval is greater than approximately 3 msec. The ability to hear the gaps in speech appears to be related to the perception of stop phonemes in a consonant cluster (Marcus, 1978). Chapman, Symmes, and Halstead (1955) reported that mild, non-localized brain damage in adults resulted in an impairment of this ability. Gap detection probably is related to forward masking effects, and both phenomena deserve investigation with children in order to provide information about the normal maturation of auditory function, and the relationship of deficits on these tasks to speech perception. Finally, the investigation cited earlier by Cranford et al. (1982) indicated that frequency discrimination as a function of stimulus duration may be an important indicator of central auditory nervous system dysfunction.

Despite the number of studies discussed in this chapter, relatively little systematic research has been performed on the basic psychoacoustic processes, such as gap detection and forward masking, in adults and children suspected of central auditory nervous system dysfunction. Tasks not only of purported central auditory function, but those believed to reflect cochlear processes need to be performed, such as frequency selectivity and discrimination of frequency and intensity differences over time. It may be that tasks assumed to test cochlear function may require eighth nerve and central auditory nervous system function as well. Also, it should be considered that subtle forms of cochlear dysfunction may exist despite the presence of normal-hearing sensitivity. The number of children with suspected auditory processing problems is a primary educational concern. Clearer delineation of basic auditory skills and their relation to normal and disordered language development needs to occur.

REFERENCES

Aaronson, D. Temporal factors in perception and short-term memory. *Psychological Bulletin*, 1967, *67*, 130–144.

Albert, L., & Baer, D. Time to understand: A case study of word deafness with reference to the role of time in auditory comprehension. *Brain*, 1973, *97*, 373–384.

Albert, M., Sparks, R., Von Stockert, T., & Sax, D. A case study of auditory agnosia: Linguistic and non-linguistic processing. *Cortex*, 1972, *8*, 427–443.

Alpers, B., & Grant, F. The clinical syndrome of the corpus callosum. *Archives of Neurology and Psychiatry*, 1931, *25*, 67–86.

Antonelli, A. Sensitized tests: Results in brain-stem lesions and diffusive central nervous system disease. In. C. Rojskaer (Ed.), *Speech audiometry* (2nd Danavox Symposium, pp. 130–139), 1970.

Bakker, D. Temporal order perception and reading retardation. In D. Bakker & P. Satz (Eds.), *Specific reading disability: Advances in theory and method*. Rotterdam: Rotterdam University Press, 1970.

Barr, D., Mullin, T., & Harbert, P. Application of binaural heat phenomenon with aphasic patients. *Archives of Otolaryngology,* 1977, *103,* 192–194.

Baru, A., Gersuni, G., & Tonkonogii, I. The importance of detection of acoustic stimuli of different duration in the diagnosis of temporal brain lesions. *Zh. Nevropat I Psikiat,* 1964, *64,* 481–485.

Baru, A., & Karaseva, T. *The brain and hearing: Hearing disturbance associated with local brain lesions.* New York: Consultant Bureau, 1972.

Bastian, J., Eimas, P., & Liberman, A. Identification and discrimination of a phonemic contrast induced by a silent interval. *Journal of the Acoustical Society of America,* 1961, *33,* 842 (A).

Beasley, D., & Freeman, B. Time-altered speech as a measure of central auditory processing. In R. Keith (Ed.), *Central auditory dysfunction.* New York: Grune & Stratton, 1977.

Beasley, D., & Flaherty-Rintelmann, A. Children's perception of temporally distorted sentential approximations of varying length. *Audiology,* 1976, *15,* 315–325.

Beasley, D., Maki, J., & Orchik, D. Children's perception of time-compressed speech using two measures of speech discrimination. *Journal of Speech and Hearing Disorders,* 1976, *41,* 216–225.

Beasley, D., & Shriner, T. Auditory analysis of temporally distorted sentential approximation. *Journal of Auditory Communication,* 1973, *12,* 262–271.

Blanchard, S., & Prescott, T. The effects of temporal expansion upon auditory comprehension in aphasia. *British Journal of Communication Disorders,* 1980, *15,* 115–129.

Bocca, E. Clinical aspects of cortical deafness. *Laryngoscope,* 1958, *68,* 301–309.

Bocca, E. Distorted speech tests. In B. Graham (Ed.), *Sensorineural hearing processes and disorders.* Boston: Little, Brown, 1967.

Bocca, E., & Antonelli, A. Masking level difference: Another tool for the evaluation of peripheral and cortical defects. *Audiology,* 1976, *15,* 480–487.

Bocca, E., & Calearo, C. Central hearing processes. In J. Jerger (Ed.), *Modern developments in audiology.* New York: Academic Press, 1963.

Bornstein, S. *Audiological contribution to the management of children with language and learning problems.* Paper presented at the Twelfth Annual Mid-South Conference on Communication Disorders, Memphis, February, 1982.

Bosatra, A., & Russolo, M. Directional hearing, temporal order and auditory pattern in peripheral and brain stem lesions. *Audiology,* 1976, *15,* 141–147.

Burgener, G., & Mouw, J. Part I: Study one, minimal hearing loss effect on academic/intellectual performance of children. *Hearing Instruments,* 1982, *33,* 14–18.

Calearo, C., & Antonelli, A. "Cortical" hearing tests and cerebral dominance. *Acta Otolaryngologica,* 1963, *56,* 17–26.

Calearo, C., & Antonelli, A. Audiometric findings in brainstem lesions. *Acta Otolaryngologica,* 1968, *66,* 305–319.

Calearo, C., & Lazzaroni, A. Speech intelligibility in relation to the speed of the message. *Laryngoscope,* 1957, *67,* 410–419.

Carhart, R. Updating special hearing tests in neuro-otologic diagnosis. *Archives of Otolaryngology,* 1973, *97,* 88–92.

Carpenter, R., & Rutherford, D. Acoustic cue discrimination in adult aphasia. *Journal of Speech and Hearing Research,* 1973, *16,* 367–374.

Chapman, L., Symmes, D., & Halstead, W. Auditory flutter fusion in patients with cortical ablation. *Journal of Comparative and Physiological Psychology,* 1955, *48,* 421–425.

Chomsky, N. The formal nature of language. In E. Lenneberg (Ed.), *Biological foundation of language.* New York: Wiley, 1967.

Corkin, S. Serial-oral deficits in inferior readers. *Neuropsychologia,* 1974, *12,* 347–354.

Costello, M., & McGee, T. Language impairment associated with abnormal auditory adaptation. In A. Graham (Ed.), *Sensorineural hearing processes and disorders.* Boston: Little, Brown, 1967.

Cranford, J. Detection versus discrimination of brief tones by cats with auditory cortex lesions. *Journal of the Acoustical Society of America,* 1979, *65,* 1573–1575.

Cranford, J., & Igareshi, M. Effects of auditory cortex lesions on temporal summation in cats. *Brain Research,* 1977, *136,* 559–564.

Cranford, J., & Oberholtzer, M. Role of neocortex in binaural hearing in the cat: II. The "precedence" effect in sound localization. *Brain Research,* 1976, *111,* 235–239.

Cranford, J., Ravizza, R., Diamond, I., & Whitfield, I. Unilateral ablations of the auditory cortex in the cat impairs and localization. *Science,* 1971, *72,* 286–288.

Cranford, J., Stream, R., Rye, C., & Slade, T. Detection versus discrimination of brief duration tones. *Archives of Otolaryngology,* 1982, *108,* 350–357.

Cullinan, W., Erdos, E., Schaefer, R., & Tekieli, M. Perception of temporal order of vowels and consonant–vowel syllables. *Journal of Speech and Hearing Research,* 1977, *20,* 742–751.

Delattre, P., Liberman, A., & Cooper, F. Acoustic loci and transitional cues for consonants. *Journal of the Acoustical Society of America,* 1955, *27,* 769–773.

Denes, P. Effect of duration on the perception of voicing. *Journal of the Acoustical Society of America,* 1955, *27,* 761–764.

Devens, J., Hoyer, E., & McCroskey, R. Dynamic auditory localization by normal and learning disability children. *Journal of the American Audiology Society,* 1978, *3,* 172–178.

Doehring, D., & Libman, R. Signal detection analysis of auditory sequence discrimination by children. *Perceptual Motor Skills,* 1974, *38,* 163–169.

Drake, W. Clinical and pathological findings in a child with a developmental learning disability. *Journal of Learning Disabilities,* 1968, *1,* 9–25.

Dorman, M., Cutting, J., & Raphael, L. Perception of temporal order in vowel sequences with and without formant transitions. *Journal of Experimental Psychology: Human Perception and Performance,* 1975, *104,* 121–129.

Ebbin, J., & Edwards, A. Speech sound discrimination of aphasics when intersound interval is varied. *Journal of Speech and Hearing Research,* 1967, *10,* 120–125.

Edmondson, H. *The Seashores measure of musical talents as a prognostic guide in language rehabilitation for persons with aphasia.* Unpublished doctoral dissertation, University of Michigan, 1953.

Efron, R. Temporal perception, aphasia, and deja vu. *Brain,* 1963, *86,* 403–424.

Eisenson, J. Developmental aphasia: A speculative view with therapeutic implications. *Journal of Speech and Hearing Disorders,* 1968, *33,* 3–13.

Faires, W., & Lankford, S. Auditory frequency and intensity discrimination ability of cerebral palsied children. *British Journal of Disorders of Communication,* 1976, *11,* 73–80.

Frith, V. Studies in pattern detection in normal and autistic children: I. Immediate recall of auditory sequences. *Journal of Abnormal Psychology,* 1970, *76,* 413–420.

Fry, D. Duration and intensity as physical correlates of linguistic stress. *Journal of Acoustical Society of America*, 1955, *27*, 765–768.

Fry, D. Experiments in the perception of stress. *Language and Speech*, 1958, *1*, 126–152.

Fry, D. Prosodic phenomena. In B. Malmberg (Ed.), *Manual of phonetics.* Amsterdam: North-Holland, 1968.

Fujisaki, H., Nakamura, K., & Imoto, T. Auditory perception of duration of speech and nonspeech stimuli. In G. Fant & M. Tatham (Eds.), *Auditory analysis and perception of speech.* New York: Academic Press, 1975.

Gardner, H., Albert, M., & Weintraub, S. Comprehending a word: The influence of speech and redundancy on auditory comprehension in aphasia. *Cortex*, 1975, *11*, 155–162.

Gersuni, G. Organization of afferent inflow and the process of external signal discrimination. *Neuropsychologia*, 1965, *3*, 95–110.

Gersuni, G., Baru, E., & Karaseva, T. Role of auditory cortex in discrimination of acoustic stimuli. *Neuroscience Translations*, 1971, *1*, 370–382.

Gersuni, G. Sensory processes at the neuronal and behavioral levels. New York: Academic Press, 1971.

Goldhor, R. *Sentential determinates of duration in speech.* Unpublished master's thesis, MIT, 1976.

Goldstein, M., Brown, M., & Hollander, J. Auditory agnosia and cortical deafness: Analysis of a case with three-year follow ups. *Brain and Language*, 1975, *2*, 324–332.

Grimm, W. Perception of segments of English-spoken consonant–vowel syllables. *Journal of the Acoustical Society of America*, 1966, *40*, 1454–1461.

Hannley, M., Jerger, J., & Rivera, V. Relationships among auditory brainstem responses, masking level differences and the acoustic reflex in multiple sclerosis. *Audiology*, 1983, *22*, 20–33.

Hardy, W. On language disorders in young children: A reorganization of thinking. *Journal of Speech and Hearing Disorders*, 1965, *32*, 3–10.

Hirsh, I. Certain temporal factors in audition. *Science*, 1952, *116*, 523 (A).

Hirsh, I. Auditory perception of temporal order. *Journal of the Acoustical Society of America*, 1959, *31*, 759–767.

Hochman, R., Thal, D., & Maxon, A. Temporal integration in dysphasic children. *Journal of the Acoustical Society of America,* 1977, *62,* 97.

Hochster, M., & Kelly, J. The precedence effect and sound localization by children with temporal lobe epilepsy. *Neuropsychologia,* 1981, *19,* 49–54.

Hodgson, W. Audiological report of a patient with left hemispherectomy. *Journal of Speech and Hearing Disorders,* 1967, *32,* 39–45.

Horenstein, S., LeZak, R., & Pitts, W. Temporal tone discrimination in auditory aphasia. *Transactions of the American Neurology Association,* 1966, *91,* 251–253.

House, A. On vowel duration in English. *Journal of the Acoustical Society of America,* 1961, *33,* 1174–1178.

Hughes, L., & Holtzapple, P. Temporal order judgments of speech and noise stimuli by normal and brain-injured subjects. In J. Wolf & D. Klatt (Eds.), *Speech communication papers.* New York: Acoustical Society of America, 1979.

Jeffress, L. A place theory of sound localization. *Journal of Comparative and Physiological Psychology,* 1948, *41,* 35–39.

Jeffress, L. Binaural signal detection. Vector theory. In J. Tobias (Ed.), *Foundations of modern auditory theory,* Vol. 2. New York: Academic Press, 1972.

Jerger, J. Observations on auditory lesions in the central auditory pathways. *Archives of Otolaryngology,* 1960, *71,* 797–806.

Jerger, J. Auditory tests for disorders of the central auditory mechanism. In W. Fields & B. Alford (Eds.), *Neurological aspects of auditory and vestibular disorders.* Springfield, IL: Thomas, 1970.

Jerger, J. Diagnostic audiometry. In J. Jerger (Ed.), *Modern developments in audiology* (2nd ed.). New York: Academic Press, 1973.

Jerger, J., Weikers, N., Sharbrough, F., & Jerger, S. Bilateral lesions of the temporal lobe. A case study. *Acta Otolaryngologica,* 1969, *258* (supplement), 1–51.

Jerger, S., & Jerger, J. Extra- and intra-axial brainstem auditory disorders. *Audiology,* 1975, *14,* 93–117.

Karaseva, T. The role of the temporal lobe in human auditory perception. *Neuropsychologia,* 1972, *10,* 227–231.

Kerivan, J., Alphonso, P., & Bornstein, S. Identification of temporal order in vowel sequences. In J. Wolf & D. Klatt (Eds.), *Speech communication papers presented at the 97th meeting of the Acoustical Society of America.* New York: Acoustical Society of America, 1979.

Klatt, D. Vowel lengthening is systematically determined in connected discourse. *Journal of Phonetics,* 1975, *3,* 129–140.

Klatt, D. Linguistic uses of segmental duration in English: Acoustic and perceptual evidence. *Journal of the Acoustical Society of America,* 1976, *59,* 1208–1221.

Klatt, D., & Shattuck, S. Perception of brief stimuli that resemble rapid formant transitions. In G. Fant & M. Tatham (Eds.), *Auditory analysis and perception of speech.* New York: Academic Press, 1975.

Konkle, D., Beasley, D., & Bess, F. Intelligibility of time-altered speech in relation to chronological aging. *Journal of Speech and Hearing Research,* 1977, *20,* 108–115.

Korsan-Bengsten, M. Distorted speech audiometry. *Acta Otolaryngologica,* 1973, *310* (supplement), 7–75.

Kracke, I. Perception of rhythmic sequences by aphasic and deaf children. *British Journal of Disorders of Communication,* 1975, *10,* 43–52.

Kurdziel, S., Rintelmann, W., & Beasley, D. Performance by cortical lesion patients on 40 and 60% time-compressed materials. *Journal of the American Audiology Society,* 1976, *2,* 3–7.

Lackner, J. Alterations in resolution of temporal order after cerebral injury in man. *Experimental Neurology,* 1982, *75,* 501–509.

Lackner, J., & Teuber, H. Alterations in auditory fusion thresholds after cerebral injury in man. *Neuropsychologia,* 1973, *11,* 409–415.

Landau, W., Goldstein, R., & Kleffner, F. Congenital aphasia: A clinic–pathologic study. *Neurology,* 1960, *19,* 915–921.

Lehiste, I., Olive, J., & Streeter, L. Role of duration in disambiguating syntactically ambiguous sentences. *Journal of the Acoustical Society of America,* 1976, *60,* 1199–1202.

Liberman, A., Delattre, P., Gertsman, L., & Cooper, F. Tempo of frequency change as a cue for distinguishing classes of speech sounds. *Journal of Experimental Psychology,* 1956, *52,* 127–137.

Liberman, A., Cooper, F., Shankweiler, D., & Studdert-Kennedy, M. Perception of the speech code. *Psychology Review,* 1967, *74,* 431–461.

Liles, B., & Brookshire, R. The effects of pause time on auditory comprehension of aphasic subjects. *Journal of Communication Disorders,* 1975, *8,* 221–235.

Lisker, L. Closure duration and the intervocalic voiced–voiceless distinction in English. *Language,* 1957, *33,* 42–49.

Lowe, A., & Campbell, R. Temporal discrimination in aphasoid and normal children. *Journal of Speech and Hearing Research,* 1965, *18,* 313–314.

Luxon, L. The anatomy and pathology of the central auditory pathways. *British Journal of Audiology,* 1981, *15,* 31–41.

Lynn, G., Benitez, J., Eisenbray, A., Gilroy, J., & Wilner, H. Neuroaudiological correlates in cerebral hemisphere lesions: Temporal and parietal lobe tumors. *Audiology,* 1972, *11,* 115–134.

Lynn, G., Gilroy, J. Effects of brain lesions on the perception of monotic and dichotic speech stimuli. In M. Sullivan & J. Ercolani (Eds.), *Proceedings of a symposium on central auditory processing disorders,* University of Nebraska Medical Center, 1974.

Lynn, G., & Gilroy, J. Neuro-audiological abnormalities in patients with temporal lobe tumors. *Journal of Neurological Sciences,* 1972, *17,* 167–184.

Lynn, G., Gilroy, J., Taylor, P., & Leiser, R. Binaural MLD's in neurological disorders. *Archives of Otolaryngology,* 1981, *103,* 192–194.

Manning, W., Johnston, K., & Beasley, D. The performance of children with auditory perceptual disorders on a time-compressed speech discrimination measure. *Journal of Speech and Hearing Disorders,* 1977, *42,* 77–84.

Marcus, S. Distinguishing between split and slit—An invariant timing cue in speech perception. *Perception and Psychophysics,* 1978, *23,* 58–60.

Masterton, R., & Diamond, I. Effects of auditory cortex ablation on discrimination of small binaural time differences. *Journal of Neurophysiology,* 1964, *27,* 15–36.

Matzker, J. The sound location test. *International Audiology,* 1962, *1,* 248–249.

McCroskey, R., & Thompson, N. Comprehension of rate-controlled speech by children with learning problems. *Journal of Learning Disabilities,* 1973, *6,* 621–627.

Milner, B., & Teuber, H. Alteration of perception and memory in man: Reflection on methods. In L. Weiskrantz (Ed.), *Analysis of behavioral change.* New York: Harper & Row, 1968.

Monsees, E. Aphasia in children: Diagnosis and evaluation. *Journal of Speech and Hearing Disorders,* 1961, *26,* 83–86.

Musiek, F., & Guerkink, N. Auditory perceptual problems in children: Considerations for the otolaryngologist and audiologist. *Laryngoscope,* 1980, *90,* 962–971.

Musiek, F., Guerkink, N., & Keitel, S. Test battery assessment of auditory perceptual dysfunction in children. *Laryngoscope,* 1982, *92,* 251–258.

Musiek, F., Pinheiro, M., & Wilson, D. Auditory pattern perception in split brain patients. *Archives of Otolaryngology,* 1980, *106,* 610–612.

Needham, E., & Black, J. The relative ability of aphasic persons to judge the duration and intensity of pure tones. *Journal of Speech and Hearing Research,* 1970, *8,* 129–136.

Neff, W. Temporal pattern discrimination in lower animals and its relation to language perception in man. In A. deReuck & M. O'Connor (Eds.), *Disorders of language.* Boston: Little, Brown, 1964.

Noffsinger, D., & Kurdziel, S. Assessment of central auditory lesions. In W. Rintelmann (Ed.), *Hearing assessment.* Baltimore: University Park Press, 1979.

Noffsinger, D., Olsen, W., Carhart, R., Hart, C., & Sahgal, V. Auditory and vestibular aberrations in multiple sclerosis. *Acta Otolaryngologica,* 1972, *303* (supplement), 1–63.

Nordlund, B. Directional audiometry. *Acta Otolaryngologica,* 1964, *57,* 1–18.

Oller, D. The effect of position in utterance on speech segment duration in English. *Journal of the Acoustical Society of America,* 1973, *54,* 1235–1247.

Olsen, W., Rose, D., & Noffsinger, D. Brief-tone audiometry with normal, cochlear, and eighth nerve tumor patients. *Archives of Otolaryngology,* 1974, *99,* 185–189.

Olsen, W., Noffsinger, D., & Carhart, R. Masking level differences encountered in clinical populations. *Audiology,* 1976, *15,* 287–301.

Orchik, D., & Oelschlaeger, M. Time compressed speech discrimination in children and its relationship to articulation. *Journal of the American Audiology Society,* 1974, *3,* 37–41.

Oster, G. Auditory beats in the brain. *Scientific American,* 1973, *229,* 94–102.

Peck, D. *The effects of presentation rates on the auditory comprehension of learning-disabled children.* Paper presented to the convention of the American Speech–Language–Hearing Association, Chicago, 1977.

Pedersen, C. Brief-tone audiometry. *Scandinavian Audiology,* 1976, *5,* 27–33.

Peterson, G., & Lehiste, I. Duration of syllabic nuclei in English. *Journal of the Acoustical Society of America,* 1960, *51,* 1296–1303.

Pinheiro, M., & Tobin, H. The interaural intensity difference as a diagnostic indicator. *Acta Otolaryngologica,* 1971, *46,* 1482–1487.

Pinheiro, M. Tests of central auditory function in children with learning disabilities. In R. Keith (Ed.), *Central auditory dysfunction.* New York: Grune & Stratton, 1977.

Plomp, R. Rate of decay of auditory sensation. *Journal of the Acoustical Society of America,* 1964, *36,* 277–282.

Quaranta, A., & Cervellera, G. Masking level difference in normal and pathological ears. *Audiology,* 1974, *13,* 428–431.

Rees, N. Saying more than we know: Is auditory processing disorder a meaningful concept? In R. Keith (Ed.), *Central auditory and language disorders in children.* San Diego: College–Hill Press, 1981.

Rose, J., Galambos, R., & Hughes, J. Organization of frequency sensitive neurons in the cochlear nuclear complex of the cat. In G. Rasmussen & W. Windle (Eds.), *Neural mechanisms of the auditory and vestibular systems.* Springfield, IL: Thomas, 1960.

Rose, J., Gross, N., Geisler, C., & Hind, J. Some neural mechanisms in the inferior colliculus of the cat which may be relevant to localization of a sound source. *Journal of Neurophysiology,* 1966, *29,* 283–314.

Sanchez-Longo, L., & Forster, F. Clinical significance of impairment of sound localization. *Neurology,* 1958, *8,* 119–125.

Sanchez-Longo, L., Forster, F., & Auth, T. A clinical test for sound localization and its applications. *Neurology,* 1957, *7,* 655–663.

Sasanuma, S., Tatsumi, I., Kiritani, S., & Fujisaki, H. Auditory perception of signal duration in aphasic patients. *Research Institute of Logopedics and Phoniatrics, Annual Bulletin,* 1973, *7,* 67–72.

Schon, T. The effects on speech intelligibility of time compression and expansion on normal-hearing, hard of hearing, and aged males. *Journal of Auditory Research,* 1970, *10,* 263–268.

Schuell, H. Aphasic difficulties understanding spoken language. *Neurology*, 1953, *3*, 176–184.

Schuknecht, H. *Pathology of the ear.* Cambridge, MA: Harvard University Press, 1974.

Selnes, O. The corpus callosum: Some anatomical and functional considerations with special reference to language. *Brain and Language*, 1974, *1*, 111–139.

Senf, G. Development of immediate memory for bisensory stimuli in normal children and children with learning disabilities. *Developmental Psychology*, 1969, *1*, 1–28.

Sherwin, I., & Efron, R. Temporal ordering deficits following anterior temporal lobectomy. *Brain and Language*, 1980, *11*, 159–203.

Snow, J., Rintelmann, W., Miller, J., & Konkle, D. Central auditory imperception. *Laryngoscope*, 1977, *87*, 1450–1471.

Spitzer, J. *A central auditory evaluation protocol: A guide for training and diagnosis of lesions of the central system.* Unpublished manuscript, 1983.

Stark, R., & Tallal, P. Perceptual and motor deficits in language-impaired children. In R. Keith (Ed.), *Central auditory and language disorders in children.* San Diego: College–Hill Press, 1981.

Stark, R., & Tallal, P. Analysis of stop consonant production errors in developmentally dysphasic children. *Journal of the Acoustical Society of America*, 1979, *66*, 1703–1712.

Sweetow, R., & Reddel, R. The use of masking level differences in the identification of children with perceptual problems. *Journal of the American Audiology Society*, 1978, *4*, 52–56.

Swisher, L., & Hirsh, I. Brain damage and the ordering of two temporally successive stimuli. *Neuropsychologia*, 1972, *10*, 137–152.

Swisher, L. Auditory intensity discrimination in patients with temporal lobe damage. *Cortex*, 1967, *2*, 179–183.

Tallal, P., & Newcombe, F. Impairment of auditory perception and language comprehension in dysphasia. *Brain and Language*, 1978, *5*, 13–24.

Tallal, P., & Piercy, M. Developmental aphasia: The perception of brief vowels and extended consonants. *Neuropsychologia*, 1975, *13*, 69–74.

Tallal, P., & Piercy, M. Developmental aphasia: Rate of auditory processing and selective impairment of consonant perception. *Neuropsychologia,* 1974, *12,* 83–94.

Tallal, P., & Piercy, M. Developmental aphasia: Impaired rate of nonverbal processing as a function of sensory modality. *Neuropsychologia,* 1973, *11,* 389–398.

Tallal, P., & Piercy, M. Defects of nonverbal auditory perception in children with developmental aphasia. *Nature (London),* 1973, *241,* 468–469.

Tallal, P. Rapid auditory processing in normal and disordered language development. *Journal of Speech and Hearing Research,* 1976, *19,* 561–571.

Tallal, P., Stark, R., & Curtiss, B. The relation between speech perception impairment and speech production impairment in children with developmental dysphasia. *Brain and Language,* 1976, *3,* 305–317.

Teas, D. Lateralization of acoustic transients. *Journal of the Acoustical Society of America,* 1962, *34,* 1460–1465.

Teuber, H., & Diamond, S. Effects of brain wounds implicating right or left hemisphere in man. In V. Mountcastle (Ed.), *Interhemispheric relations and cerebral dominance.* Baltimore: Johns Hopkins Press, 1962.

Thurlow, W., & Mergerer, J. Effects of stimulus duration on localization of sound. *Journal of Speech and Hearing Research,* 1970, *13,* 826–838.

Tolkmitt, F. Processing limits and organizational tendencies. *Journal of Experimental Psychology,* 1970, *86,* 171–180.

Umeda, N. Vowel duration in American English. *Journal of the Acoustical Society of America,* 1975, *58,* 434–455.

Unterharnscheidt, F., Jacnik, D., & Gott, H. Derbalkenmangel. *Monographien Aus Dem Gesamtgebiete der Neurologie und Psychiatrie,* 1968, *128,* 1–232.

Waas, B., & Beedle, R. Responses to time-expanded speech in presbycusic and normal hearing males. *Ohio Journal of Speech and Hearing,* 1972, *7,* 33–41.

Warren, R. Relation of verbal transformation to other perceptual phenomena. In *IEE/NPL Conference of Pattern Recognition* (Conference Publication 42), Institute of Electrical Engineers, Teddington, England, 1968.

Warren, R., & Obusel, C. Identification of temporal order within auditory sequences. *Perception and Psychophysics,* 1970, *12,* 86–90.

Warren, R. M., & Warren, R. Auditory illusions and confusions. *Scientific American,* 1970, *233,* 30–36.

FIGURE 3-1.
Schematic diagram of central auditory nervous system. Patterned after R. R. Gacek. (From *Foundations of Modern Auditory Theory* (pp. 239–262, Vol. II), edited by J. B. Tobias, 1972, New York, Academic Press. Reprinted by permission.)

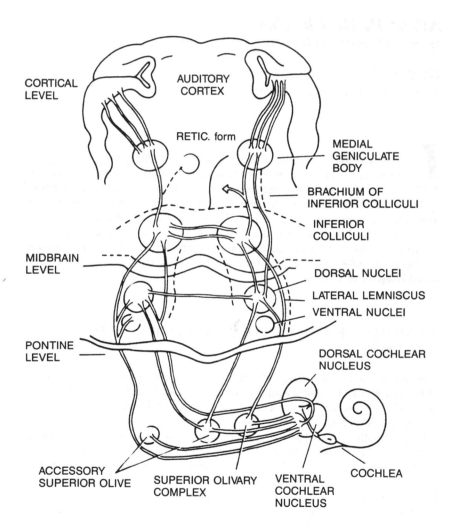

Fibers from the superior olive continue to course rostrally, some terminating on the lateral lemniscus, others ascending on the inferior colliculus. Thus, the inferior colliculus may receive second- , third- , or fourth-order neurons. From the inferior colliculus other fibers course to the medial geniculate body and from there to the auditory cortex.

Whitfield (1967), Dublin (1976), and Durrant and Lovrinic (1977) discussed the physiologic importance of the integrity of the brainstem. The auditory nuclei, located in the central auditory pathway, have a critical role in processing information relating to acoustic events such as intensity and frequency. Also, due to the contra-lateral pathways resulting from the many decussating fibers, the auditory nuclei provide binaural cues concerning time and phase of acoustic signals, two parameters vitally important in localization tasks.

There are many various auditory nuclei within the brainstem and not all nuclei within a given nuclear complex react in the same way to acoustic stimuli. Durrant and Lovrinic (1977) indicated that because of the redundancy in the auditory path-way informational processing of certain stimuli may be carried out at different brainstem levels. In addition, Whitfield (1967) and Durrant and Lovrinic (1977) reported that, at the higher auditory brainstem levels, neurons appear to be more specialized and are able to respond to more specific features of the auditory stimulus, enhancing the systems' ability to process more complex sounds such as speech.

HISTORICAL INFORMATION

The development of auditory brainstem response measurement is the most recent application of auditory evoked potentials that date back as early as Wever and Bray's (1930) investigation concerning the cochlear microphonic. Advances in signal averaging capabilities since the 1950s are primarily responsible for the significant advances in evoked potential measurement (Davis, 1976).

Auditory evoked potentials are classified according to the latencies at which they occur following stimulus onset. Table 3-1 lists the classifications of these responses according to Davis (1976). The earliest of these potentials comprise the auditory brainstem response or ABR.

Evoked potentials occurring in the first 10 msec following stimulus onset were first reported in humans by Sohmer and Feinmesser (1967). These investigators were able to identify four successive waves occurring about 1 msec apart, when electrophysiologic recordings were made with electrodes placed on the earlobe and nasion. They reported that the first two waves were probably due to the firing of the auditory nerve, and speculated that the remaining waves were either the result of repeated firing of the auditory nerve or activity in brainstem auditory nuclei. Subsequent investigations (Jewett, 1970; Jewett, Romano, & Williston, 1970; Jewett & Williston, 1971) provided additional data more clearly defining these early responses as originating in the brainstem.

Jewett (1970), in a subsequent study, obtained ABR measurements on eighteen anesthetized cats. A recording electrode consisting of .25-mm stainless steel wire was placed at various points on the brainstem. Four waves were observed by repeated

TABLE 3-1
Auditory Evoked Potentials

	CLASS	PROBABLE SOURCE	LATENCY (MSEC)	BEST RESPONSE	ERA
ECOCHG	FIRST	ORGAN OF CORTI (CM = EXTERNAL HAIR CELLS) N VIII	0 / 1-4	SP (DC) CM (AC) AP (N_1)	? **
	FAST	N VIII, BRAIN STEM	2-12	P_6	**
	MIDDLE	NEUROGENIC: CORTEX I MYOGENIC: "SONOMOTOR"	12-50	P_{35}	* ?
VERTEX POTENTIALS	SLOW	CORTEX II (WAKING) CORTEX III (ASLEEP)	50-300 200-800	N_{90}—P_{180}—N_{250} SUSTAINED POTENTIAL (DC) P_{200}—N_{300}:$\overrightarrow{N_{600}P}$	** ? *
	LATE	CORTEX IV (EXPECTATION)	250-600 DC SHIFT	P_{300} CNV	?

Note. From "Principles of Electric Response Audiometry" by H. Davis, 1976, *The Annals of Otology, Rhinology and Laryngology, 85*(3), p. 3, Suppl. 28. Reprinted by permission.

averaging techniques and labeled P_1, P_2, P_3, P_4, and P_5, as seen in Figure 3-2. The results indicated that P_1 was coincidental with the potential recorded at the round window and it was concluded this wave most probably reflected activity generated by the acoustic nerve. Wave P_2 was shown to be generated in the area of the cochlear nucleus, while P_3 was most prominent in the vicinity of the superior olive. P_4 was thought to reflect activity near the inferior colliculus, but the nature of the response suggested that this wave reflected activity from different brainstem sources. The final wave in the complex, Wave P_5, was reported as being generated in the inferior colliculus or just rostral to it.

In an effort to determine more clearly the primary origins of these far-field potentials, Buchwald and Huang (1975) performed lesion experiments on 10 adult cats. Their findings indicated that Wave I was associated with the acoustic nerve and Wave II required the integrity of the cochlear nucleus. Wave III was shown to depend on the medial superior olivary nucleus, while the ventral nucleus of the lateral lemniscus and the inferior colliculus served as the generator sites for Waves IV and V, respectively.

As a result of those initial studies, the schema represented in Figure 3-3 illustrates the most widely accepted opinion associating individual wave responses with suspected generator source. This figure, however, represents a rather simplistic view of a highly complex anatomical structure and while there are data to support the one-to-one relationship (Starr & Achor, 1975), with the exception of Wave I, evidence concerning brainstem generators remains inconclusive. Recently, for example, Moller, Jannetta, and Moller (1982) recorded compound action potentials intracranially in humans and reported the origin of both Wave I and Wave II to be associated with the auditory nerve.

Regardless of the source of generation for this brainstem response, these auditory evoked potentials can provide meaningful information relative to peripheral and central auditory function. The remaining portion of this chapter is devoted to the clinical application of this response as it relates to auditory assessment in a pediatric population.

CLINICAL UTILITY OF ABR IN THRESHOLD ESTIMATION

One routine use of ABR measurements is in assessment of peripheral auditory function, particularly as it relates to hearing sensitivity. When using the ABR in this manner, the wave most often selected for observation is Wave V. This wave has been shown to be the most prominent and easiest to reproduce in the electrophysiologic response (Jewett & Williston, 1971; Picton, Woods, Baribeau-Braun, & Healy, 1977; Starr & Achor, 1975). Equally important, however, is the latency of Wave I. This is particularly true in responses obtained on neonates, where Wave I has been shown to be the more sensitive indicator of middle ear abnormality (Mendelson, Salamy, Lenoir, & McKean, 1979; Fria & Sabo, 1980). Also, as is seen later, the interval between Waves I and V can be important to differential diagnosis. Thus, while Wave V tends to be the easiest to replicate and gives the best

FIGURE 3-2.
Illustration of four waves generated by an electrophysiologic response. From *Electroencephalography and Clinical Neurophysiology*, Vol. 28, by D. Jewett, 1970, Amsterdam/New York, Elsevier. Reprinted by permission.

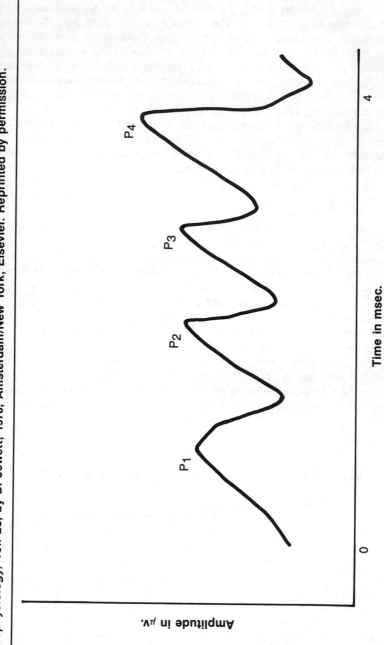

FIGURE 3-3.
Representation of the suggested relationships between individual ABR components and structures comprising the ascending auditory pathway. From "Detection and Localization of Occult Lesions with Brainstem Auditory Responses" by J. J. Stockard, J. E. Stockard, and F. W. Sharbrough, 1977, *Mayo Clinic Proceedings, 52,* pp. 761–769. Reprinted by permission.

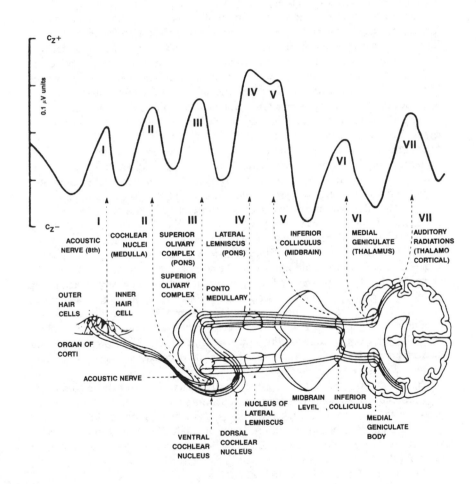

estimate of threshold, information concerning the latency of Wave I should be derived whenever possible.

Typically, assessment of auditory function via auditory evoked potentials requires the use of latency–intensity curves. As the intensity of the sound increases, a greater amount of energy is propagated to the cochlea causing the electrophysiologic response to occur earlier in time, thus producing a reduction in response latency. Thus, a direct relationship exists between the latency of the electrophysiologic response and the amount of energy reaching the cochlear receptors.

Through the use of latency–intensity functions a basis for distinguishing between the various types of hearing loss can be established (Finitzo-Hieber, 1982, Galambos & Hecox, 1977, 1978; Picton et al., 1977). A comparison of the functions in Figure 3-4 illustrates how individuals with conductive (3-4A) and sensorineural (3-4B) hearing impairment can be differentiated from those demonstrating normal auditory function. In a conductive hearing loss, since less sound energy reaches the cochlea, the latency of the response is prolonged by an amount proportional to the conductive component. This latency increase would be an equal amount at each intensity level. In a sensorineural impairment, however, the latency of the response is prolonged by the amount of time necessary for a sufficient stimulus to activate a responsive area of the basilar membrane. Thus, at stimulus levels that approximate threshold, less sound energy reaches the cochlea resulting in a prolongation of the response or perhaps an absence of the response in cases of severe hearing impairment. At suprathreshold levels the latency of the response is reduced with each increase in stimulus intensity and eventually will approximate normal latencies unless the impairment is of a severe or profound nature, as illustrated in Figure 3-4C.

Figure 3-5 illustrates normative data from several investigations and shows the systematic increase in Wave V latency with corresponding decrease in signal intensity. It can be seen from this figure that, on the average, the latency of this wave increases from approximately 5.8 msec at 80 dB HL to 8.5 msec at 10 dB HL. Galambos and Hecox (1978) report an increase in the response latency of this wave to be approximately 40 μsec for every 1 dB decrease in stimulus intensity. Taken a step further, this translates into a 0.4 msec change in response for 10 dB change in signal intensity. They report the change to be slightly shorter at high intensities and longer at intensities nearer threshold values. Furthermore, they indicate that a slope exceeding 60 μsec per dB is usually indicative of a patient demonstrating recruitment, while a slope of less than 30 μsec per dB is consistent with severe high-frequency sensorineural loss.

The practice of comparing latency–intensity functions is the more commonly used procedure in audiologic assessment. It provides the examiner with information pertinent to the type of hearing loss, that is, sensorineural or conductive and in the latter instance some estimate of the degree of conductive component. Galambos and Hecox (1978), however, suggested using bone conducted ABR measurements to establish cochlear sensitivity.

Mauldin and Jerger (1979) examined ABR latencies to air and bone conducted signals in 4 normal listeners and 11 hearing-impaired subjects with conductive hearing losses. Bone conduction responses were obtained with a Radioear B-70A oscillator. They reported that for normal listeners, latencies for bone conducted signals were approximately 0.5 msec longer than for air conducted signals and

FIGURE 3-4.
The suggested relationship between a normal Wave V latency–intensity function and conductive, sensorineural, and severe sensorineural hearing loss. From "The Auditory Brainstem Response: Background and Clinical Applications," by T. J. Fria, 1980, *Maico Hearing Instruments: Monographs in Contemporary Audiology*, 2(2). Reprinted with permission.

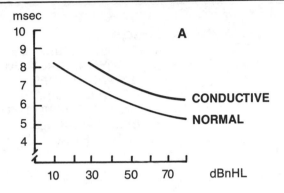

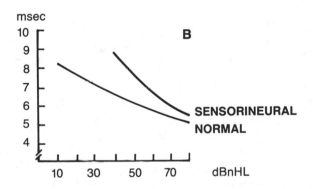

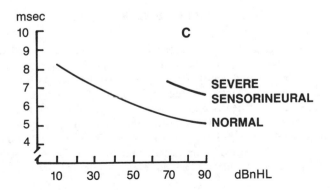

FIGURE 3-5.
The click-elicited latency–intensity functions for Waves V and I obtained on normal hearing adults in several normative investigations. From "The Auditory Brainstem Response: Background and Clinical Applications" by T. J. Fria, 1980, *Maico Hearing Instruments: Monographs in Contemporary Audiology, 2*(2). Reprinted with permission.

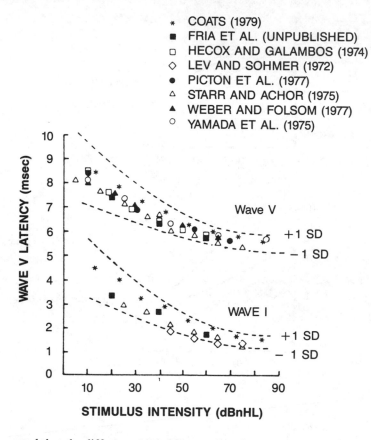

suggested that the difference probably was related to the reduced amount of high-frequency energy present when a click is delivered through a bone oscillator. For the hearing-impaired population, they reported that comparisons of air and bone conduction latency–intensity functions provided a good estimate of degree of conductive impairment. Following several correlational analyses it was concluded that both ABR bone conduction thresholds and the predictive accuracy of air-bone gaps related best to the PTA_2 (pure-tone average of 1000, 2000, and 4000 Hz).

Hicks (1980) reported similar success in determining cochlear sensitivity through ABR procedures. In this instance, however, a high pass noise was delivered through a bone oscillator and bone conduction thresholds were derived on the basis of the amount of noise necessary to mask an air conducted response at 5 dB above the ABR threshold. On a small sample of subjects, Hicks was able to demonstrate agreement between behavioral bone conduction thresholds and derived bone conduction thresholds to be within ±5 dB.

Mauldin and Jerger (1979) point out several advantages in using ABR thresholds obtained through bone conduction stimulation as opposed to air conduction stimulation in estimating the degree of conductive hearing loss. One such advantage, discussed later, is that frequently central auditory pathologies result in a prolonged Wave V latency and with no other audiologic information the determination between peripheral and central dysfunction could be confused. Also, while some would contend that impedance or oto-admittance measurements would document the existence of conductive pathology, it is not always possible to obtain those results. This is particularly true in populations exhibiting craniofacial anomalies resulting in conditions such as aural atresia.

One major advantage in using ABR measurements in the assessment of hearing sensitivity is that the results do not depend on a voluntary response from the patient and are not affected by sleep or sedation (Brackmann, 1977; Hecox & Galambos, 1974). The predictive accuracy of this procedure in the identification of hearing loss has been reported as being quite high in a number of investigations (Jerger & Hayes, 1976; Jerger & Mauldin, 1978; Mokotoff, Schulman-Galambos, & Galambos, 1977; Moller & Blegvad, 1976; Smith & Simmons, 1982).

Jerger and Mauldin (1978) correlated ABR Wave V latency and threshold data to several audiometric indices in 275 ears with sensorineural hearing loss of differing degrees and configurations. They concluded that the ABR response to clicks correlates best with high-frequency sensitivity in the 1000–4000 Hz region (PTA$_2$) and was most accurately predicted when a multiplication factor of 0.6 was applied to the ABR threshold. They indicated that the results of such a prediction may be in error by as much as 15 to 16 dB and consequently may limit the success of determining audiometric threshold by ABR measurements alone. This study showed that with stimulus levels of 70–90 dB HL the latency of the ABR was prolonged approximately 0.2 msec for a 30 dB increase in the audiometric contour between 1000 and 4000 Hz. Finally, it was concluded that although both absolute sensitivity and audiometric contour were related to latency prolongation the more important of the two measures was audiometric contour.

The conclusion by Jerger and Mauldin (1978) that audiometric contour had the greatest impact upon response latency supported the earlier work of Moller and Blegvad (1976). They also reported that patients with flat audiometric configurations demonstrated reduced ABR latencies when compared to patients with gradually sloping and steeply sloping audiograms. Moller and Blegvad also concluded that use of wide spectrum clicks in ABR generated activity in the basal portion of the cochlea. As a result, they advised against the use of unfiltered clicks as a sole indication of hearing sensitivity.

The influence of high-frequency hearing sensitivity upon ABR latency and threshold is a typical finding, as the results of several additional studies (Coats, 1978; Coats & Martin, 1977; Davis, 1976) have indicated a similar relationship. In an effort to achieve more frequency specificity a number of experiments have been conducted examining the ABR using tone "pips" or "bursts" (Bauch, Rose, & Horner, 1980; Clemis & Mitchell, 1977; Suzuki & Horiuchi, 1977). This type of signal has a slower rise and fall time associated with its stimulus envelope, thus providing for more frequency selectivity in the associated response.

Kodera, Yamane, Yamada, and Suzuki (1977) obtained ABR responses using tone pips with 5 msec rise and fall times for three frequencies (500, 1000, and 2000 Hz). They found that in normal hearing listeners, ABR thresholds ranged from 10 to 20 dB SL. For hearing-impaired subjects threshold values were found to be somewhat higher, but it was concluded that on the average the correspondence with conventional pure tone results was good and ABR using similar stimuli could be used as an objective measure to determine auditory threshold with those frequencies.

Picton, Ouellette, Hamel, and Smith (1979) compared tone pips notched in noise to tone pips in estimating ABR thresholds. The notched noise served to mask the frequency spread of energy that results from the brief stimulus (tone pip) used to elicit the response. Their results indicated that thresholds obtained with tone pips notched in noise were more frequency specific and on the average within 20 dB of thresholds obtained via conventional techniques.

Certain sacrifices are made, however, when using stimuli with slow rise and fall times. Because the ABR is so dependent upon synchronous firing of the neural elements within the brainstem, the slower fall times associated with tone pips typically result in an increased response latency (Davis, 1976; Weber & Folsom, 1977). Also, because of the high pass filter settings that are often necessary to obtain frequency specificity to low tone stimuli, the morphology of the response is altered (Stapells & Picton, 1981).

IDENTIFICATION OF HEARING LOSS IN INFANTS AND CHILDREN

The importance of early identification of hearing loss has prompted many clinics to incorporate the use of ABR in their hearing screening programs. With the ABR identifiable by 27–30 weeks gestational age, there have been several studies indicating that this measure is a viable alternative to conventional screening procedures for assessing hearing, particularly in intensive care units (Finitzo-Hieber, 1982; Frye-Osier, Hirsch, Goldstein, & Weber, 1982; Starr, Amlie, Martin, & Sanders, 1977; Zubick, Fried, Feudo, Epstein, & Strome, 1982). In addition, Salamy, Mendelson, Tooley, and Chaplin (1980) demonstrated that children who were born "at risk" but not having severe auditory hearing loss or major neurological impairment could be differentiated from healthy newborns during the first postnatal year. In general their results showed that the infants at risk had increased response latencies and reduced amplitudes for Waves I, II, and V, regardless of age.

Galambos, Hicks, and Wilson (1982) used ABR to screen 890 infants in an intensive care unit. Fifteen percent (141) of those infants failed the hearing screening measurement. Of the 43% who returned for follow up evaluations, over half (N=33) were found to have bilateral hearing loss of varying degree. That represents a total of 3.7% of the original 890 infants screened. Sixteen (1.8%) have graduated from the intensive care and wear hearing aids. Based upon their findings, Galambos et al. suggest that approximately 2% of infants discharged from intensive care units may have severe to profound hearing loss that is not reversible and they argue for the use of ABR for screening of high-risk children.

Mokotoff et al. (1977) reported ABR results on 81 infants and children divided into two groups based on audiologic history. One group consisted of 38 patients who had previous evaluations and whose results were either inconsistent or inclusive. A second group of 43 children were directly referred for evaluation, but no previous audiologic information was available for that group. For the first group of 38, ABR results supported the suspicion of normal peripheral function in 8 out of 8 cases, but was able to support the impression of substantial hearing loss in only 15 out of 23 cases. In eight of those children, ABR findings suggested normal peripheral auditory function. Of the 39 individuals in that sample of 81 who were considered to have abnormal ABRs, 19 subsequently returned for reevaluation. In all instances audiologic results supported the impression obtained from the initial ABR measurements. In the remaining 42 subjects, ABR results indicated normal hearing, but follow-up audiologic information was insufficient to draw any conclusions concerning test reliability.

While ABR appears to be a sensitive index of hearing acuity, as well as maturation of auditory brainstem function, its application as an instrument for mass screening of infants has been questioned from a cost-effectiveness standpoint. This issue was addressed by Schulman-Galambos and Galambos (1979). They examined ABR results in 220 normal term infants less than 72 hours of age, 72 infants in neonatal intensive care units (NICU) and 325 NICU graduates. Their results showed no hearing abnormalities for the normal term infants. Of the 72 infants in intensive care, they reported 4 (seven ears) to have severe sensorineural hearing loss. The results for the infants who had graduated from NICUs revealed an additional four children with severe sensorineural hearing impairment. It also was reported that all abnormal ABR findings were subsequently confirmed through follow-up audiologic measures.

Because of the low yield, Schulman-Galambos and Galambos (1979) concluded that mass screening of newborns using ABR techniques probably was not cost effective. They strongly recommended screening of all infants associated with NICUs as they estimated the incidence of hearing loss in that population to approximate 1 in 50. They proposed a strategy that called for ABR screening in the following cases: (1) infants who failed behavioral screening, (2) high-risk infants, (3) graduates of intensive care units. They also recommended audiologic follow-up for all infants screened with ABR.

Finally, there is evidence to indicate that variability is somewhat greater in premature infants, and it has been suggested that ABR assessments not be conducted until the infant is at least 39 weeks gestational age, or full term (Finitzo-Hieber, 1982).

Because of the increased variability seen in premature infants and the maturational effects on the ABR it is important for each clinic to establish its own normative data for neonatal screening purposes. Typically, clinics based their normative data on response latency (usually Waves I and V) for various gestational ages. Weber

(1982) points out two problems with that procedure. The first, he notes, is that in premature infants the amplitude of Wave V is often reduced making identification of this wave difficult. Second, he points out that the infant's gestational age is often determined through maternal interview or informal assessments by the physician, raising questions concerning the accuracy of the reported age.

As an alternative procedure, Weber (1982) proposes that determination of ABR latency norms be based on the interwave interval rather than gestational age. Weber developed four sets of latency norms using 130 newborn infants in intensive care nurseries. These sets of normative data included (1) Wave V latencies for different conceptual age (conceptual age was defined as gestational age and postnatal age), (2) Wave III latencies for conceptual age, (3) Wave V latencies for different I–V intervals, and (4) Wave III latencies for different I–III intervals. To predict the accuracy of each of these four measures an additional 131 infants were evaluated. Results indicated that brainstem maturation was best predicted using Wave III with the I–III interval as the estimator. The poorest indicator was the Wave V latency based on conceptual age.

Several other factors of a nonpathologic nature may influence the outcome or interpretation of ABR testing. These variables, to be discussed in the following section, must be taken into consideration to reduce variability and thus improve overall reliability of ABR with children.

NONPATHOLOGIC CONDITIONS AFFECTING ABR

There are several subject and stimulus variables which can influence both the amplitude and latency of the ABR. We have already discussed how stimulus intensity has a direct effect upon latency, in that the less intense the signal the greater the response latency.

Another important consideration is the relationship between patient age and response latency. An investigation by Liberman, Sohmer, and Szabo (1973) provided one of the first reports concerning this particular variable in ABR testing. They showed that in a group of 19 normal infants the most consistently observed response was Wave I, occurring at about 1.8 msec, and that the remaining waves in the ABR complex were either prolonged or absent. They concluded that this probably was due to a delay in myelinization or a product of conductive hearing loss.

In a subsequent study (Hecox & Galambos, 1974), ABR results were examined in 35 children aged 3 weeks to 3 years. As signal intensity was reduced from 60 to 10 dB SL, the expected increase in Wave V latency was found. It was also noted, however, that for very young infants, response latency was increased relative to older children and that the latency approached adult values by 12–18 months.

Similar findings have been reported by other investigators (Salamy et al., 1975; Starr et al., 1977; Despland & Galambos, 1980). Age related changes for Waves I and V from two investigations are shown in Figure 3-6. It can be seen from the figure that Wave I reached adult values more rapidly than did Wave V in each of those studies. Finitzo-Hieber (1982), Salamy, Birtley-Fenn, and Bronshvag (1979), and Salamy and McKean (1976) reported that Wave I reached adult values by 6

FIGURE 3-6.
Maturation of Waves I and V latency as they relate to babies born at different gestational ages and assessed longitudinally. From "Auditory Brainstem Response: Its Placement in Infant Audiological Evaluations" by T. Finitzo-Hieber, 1982, Thieme-Stratton: *Seminars in Speech, Language and Hearing, 3*(1). Reprinted by permission.

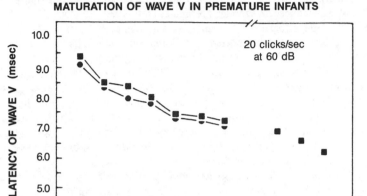

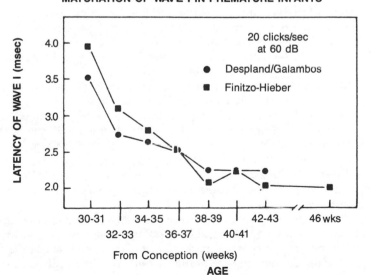

weeks to 3 months of age. Those findings are in agreement with previously published findings (Salamy, McKean, & Buda, 1975).

Differences in the rate of maturation for both Wave I and Wave V results in changes in the I–V interwave latency. Salamy and McKean (1976), Starr et al. (1977), and Schulman-Galambos and Galambos (1979), all report a reduction in the I–V interval during the first year of life.

Another factor that seems to influence the latency of Wave V is subject gender. In adults there have been a number of investigations showing that the response of Wave V was reduced in females (Jerger & Hall, 1980; Stockard, Stockard, & Sharbrough, 1978; Stockard, Stockard, Westmoreland, & Corfits, 1979).

Similar effects have been reported in children, but the results have not been as consistent. For example, Beagley and Sheldrake (1978), Seitz, Weber, and Jacobson (1980), and O'Donavon, Beagley, and Shaw (1980) all report the latency of Wave V to be significantly reduced for females. O'Donavon et al. (1980), however, reported significant latency differences in children aged 8 to 11 years, but not in those aged 5 to 7 years. Another investigation (De Chicchis, 1981) found no significant differences in response latency for a group of children aged 8 to 12 years. Finally, Stockard et al., (1979) reported no significant difference in response latencies when comparing male to female newborns.

In addition to the effects of age and gender upon response latency, there are several additional stimulus variables which have been shown to influence ABR results. Among these are stimulus phase and rate, as well as amplifier filter settings.

Depending upon the phase of the click stimulus, the initial movement of the earphone diaphragm will be one of either outward or inward motion. This, in turn, will determine the initial direction of tympanic membrane movement. Rarefaction clicks cause the initial movement of the tympanic membrane to be outward, while condensation clicks produce an initial inward motion. Stockard et al. (1979) examined the effect of the click stimulus on the ABR in 77 normal full term neonates and compared the response to a group of normal hearing adults. They found that Wave I was more sensitive to stimulus phase than were the latter components that comprised the ABR. As a result, significant changes in the I–V interwave latency were found. Also, the I–V latency differences were larger in the newborns than in the adults.

The effect of stimulus rate also was examined in the Stockard et al. (1979) study. They indicated that increasing the rate of rarefaction clicks from 10 to 80 per second produced increases in the interwave latency for both infants and adults. They reported, however, that the average adult change was .45 msec, while the average newborn change was .89 msec, a result that was statistically significant.

Stockard, Stockard, and Sharbrough (1978) recommended band pass filter settings to be 100–3000 Hz. They indicated that raising the low-frequency cutoff or lowering the high-frequency cutoff caused the ABR to be reduced in amplitude and prolonged with respect to peak latency.

Despite the necessary precautions concerning physiologic and technical variables, ABR remains a significant advancement in assessing hearing sensitivity in young children. However, before concluding this section, it is important to emphasize one major point. ABR does not measure hearing sensitivity in the same manner as more conventional audiometric procedures. It is a measure that provides information concerning peripheral auditory function and brainstem integrity. Worthington and Peters (1980) provide an excellent example of this distinction. They showed that it was possible for a child to have normal peripheral hearing, but an abnormal ABR, due to the inability of the neuronal units to fire synchronously within the brainstem. Likewise, a neurological disorder at the level of the cortex might inhibit a child's ability to process the auditory signal, but the normal brainstem function would result in a normal ABR. Worthington and Peters (1980) stress the need for corroborative behavioral data whenever possible.

CENTRAL AUDITORY ASSESSMENT

Although ABR has been shown to be useful as an indicator of peripheral hearing loss, the major emphasis in many clinics has been the use of ABR in the identification of retrocochlear lesions. There is an abundance of published research which supports the sensitivity of ABR in detecting retrocochlear pathology, although the vast majority deals with adult subjects. This section deals with the general use of ABR in differential diagnosis and reviews the few studies which relate specifically to the pediatric population. For a more complete review of the diagnostic efficiency of ABR in identifying retrocochlear pathology, the reader is referred to the work of Fria (1980).

Diagnostic criteria applied to the ABR vary among clinics. Frequently used parameters include (1) absolute Wave V latency, (2) absolute and relative amplitude for Waves I and V, (3) I–III and I–V interwave latency, and (4) interaural Wave V latency difference (ILD). Fria (1980) points out the hazard of relying too heavily on the ILD. He indicated that due to the effects of peripheral hearing loss, interpretation based on the ILD can be misleading. It also should be pointed out that because of the nonpathologic factors discussed earlier, it is extremely important that normative data be established for each clinical facility and applied to its particular patient population.

Retrocochlear lesions may be extrinsic or intrinsic to the brainstem, at the level of midbrain or cortical. It should be pointed out, however, that the ABR in itself cannot be specific in identifying the type of pathology, nor can it be specific about location because of the multiple generator sources. Abnormal findings should be incorporated in a battery of measurements to provide the most specific site of lesion information.

Lesions extrinsic to the brainstem characteristically result in one of three conditions: (1) Wave I being reduced in amplitude and prolonged in latency with none of the subsequent waves present in the response; (2) absence of all the waves; (3) a prolongation of Wave I latency, but with later waves prolonged by a greater amount (Hashimoto, Ishiyama, Totsuka, & Mizutani, 1979; Selters & Brackmann, 1977; Starr & Achor, 1975; Terkildsen, Huis In't Veld, & Osterhammel, 1977). The accuracy of ABR to detect such lesions has been reported as being greater than 90% (Clemis & McGee, 1979; Glasscock, Jackson, Josey, Dickens, & Wiet, 1979; House & Brackmann, 1979).

Selters and Brackmann (1977) examined the ABR in 46 cases of acoustic tumor. They reported that in cases involving tumors less than 2.5 cm, 30% of the patients exhibited no ABR, while tumors larger than 2.5 cm resulted in no response 80% of the time. They reported further that of 21 cases in which Wave V was identifiable, the (ILD) for Wave V ranged from 0.4 to 3.2 msec. That represented a significant deviation from the 0.1 to 0.2 msec ILD typical for the nontumor group.

Lesions intrinsic to the brainstem usually reflect a different ABR morphology. Generally, Waves I and II are unaffected while the later waves are either absent, or occur at increased latencies (Starr & Achor, 1975; Starr & Hamilton, 1976; Stockard & Rossiter, 1977). For example, Gilroy and Lynn (1978) reported ABR results in patients exhibiting olivopontocerebellar degeneration. They found a prolongation in the interval between Waves I and V in all instances. In two of the cases the interval between Waves I and III was prolonged, while the III–V interval was normal; in a third patient the III–V interval was prolonged.

Stockard, Stockard, and Sharbrough (1977) demonstrated the usefulness of ABR in the detection of subclinical lesions in 100 patients with multiple sclerosis (MS). Thirty of those patients had been diagnosed as having definite MS, thirty as having a probable MS, and forty as having possible MS. Response abnormalities were reported in 93% of patients with definite MS, 77% of those with probably MS, and 35% with possible MS. The abnormalities were reflected in both amplitude and latency of the response, but increased response latency occurred more frequently.

Nodar, Hahn, and Levine (1980) reported abnormal ABR findings in seven children with brainstem neoplasms. In an attempt to assess the diagnostic value of the individual waves within the response, these investigators estimated the site of lesion based on the ABR for later correlation with roentgenographic and surgical findings. They reported that the ABR was a good indicator for determining site of lesion as well as degree of involvement. In general, when the lesion was at the level of the pons or extended rostrally, Wave I was preserved and appeared at normal latencies. Subsequent waves, however, were either prolonged significantly or absent and frequently reduced in amplitude when compared to responses from the uninvolved side. In children whose lesions extended to the lower brainstem region, the latency of Wave V was prolonged, but earlier waves were generally indistinct or not identifiable. Wave form morphology was often very poor in those instances.

ABR measurements also have been shown to be effective in identifying brainstem dysfunction in children with less localized lesions such as autism, minimal brain damage, and psychomotor retardation. For example, Sohmer and Student (1978) compared ABR findings in three groups of children having different psychopathologies to a group of normal children. The three experimental groups were comprised of 13 children with autistic traits, 16 children diagnosed as having minimal brainstem damage, and 10 children diagnosed as having psychomotor retardation. The results of the investigation showed that each of the experimental groups demonstrated an increased absolute latency for Wave I compared to the control group. Furthermore, the differences were found to be significant when the normal children were compared to the minimally brain-damaged and psychomotor retarded children. Although it was apparent that latencies for subsequent wave were also increased for the experimental groups, statistical significance was not reached. Brainstem transmission time also was reported as being prolonged for each of the experimental groups, as evidenced by the significantly increased I–V interwave interval observed for the children with various brainstem pathology.

Gillberg, Rosenhall, and Johansson (1983) compared ABR results obtained in 31 children identified as being psychotic and 31 normal children. Of the 31 psychotic children, 24 were reported as being autistic while the remaining 7 were diagnosed as having other psychoses. Thirty-three percent of the children with infantile autism showed abnormal ABR findings, with the most frequently observed abnormality being a significantly prolonged Wave V as well as a prolonged I–V interwave interval. All of the children identified as having other psychoses showed normal ABR results. Similar findings have been reported by Rosenblum, Arick, Krug, Stubbs, Young, and Pelson (1980).

SUMMARY

Without question, ABR has been a valuable addition to the audiologic battery. It offers several advantages in that the auditory measurement is not dependent upon a voluntary response from the patient and the results are relatively unaffected by sedation or level of awareness. Furthermore, ABR can provide information relative to peripheral as well as central auditory function.

ABR is not without its limitations, however, and recognition of those limitations can only improve its clinical efficacy. It is important to remember that ABR does not replace conventional methods in assessing hearing sensitivity, but only supplements them. Furthermore, as previously discussed, several technologic, as well as physiologic factors can influence the outcome of the ABR and any interpretation should be made in light of those variables. The value of ABR to a pediatric diagnostic battery is unquestionable, but only if care is exercised in its administration and interpretation.

REFERENCES

Ades, H. Central auditory mechanisms. In J. Field, H. Magoun, & V. Hall (Eds.), *Handbook of physiology: Neurophysiology* (Vol. 1, pp. 583–613), 1959. Baltimore: Williams & Wilkins.

Bauch, C. D., Rose, D. E., & Horner, S. G. Brainstem responses to tone pip and click stimuli. *Ear and Hearing,* 1980, *1*(4), 181–184.

Beagley, H. A., & Sheldrake, J. B. *British Journal of Audiology,* 1978, *12,* 69–77.

Brackmann, D. E. Electric response audiometry in a clinical practice. *Laryngoscope,* 1977, *87,* Suppl. 5.

Buchwald, J. S., & Huang, G. M. Farfield acoustic response: Origins in the cat. *Science*, 1975, *189*, 382–384.

Clemis, J. D., & McGee, T. Brainstem electric response audiometry in differential diagnosis of acoustic tumors. *Laryngoscope*, 1979, *89*, 31–42.

Clemis, J. D., & Mitchell, C. Electrocochleography and brainstem responses used in the diagnosis of acoustic tumors. *Journal of Otolaryngology*, 1977, *6*, 447–459.

Coats, A. C. Human auditory nerve action potentials and brainstem evoked responses: Latency–intensity functions in detection of cochlear and retrocochlear abnormality. *Archives of Otolaryngology*, 1978, *104*, 709–717.

Coats, A. C., & Martin, J. L. Human auditory nerve action potentials and brainstem evoked responses: Effects of audiogram shape and lesion location. *Archives of Otolaryngology*, 1977, *103*, 605–622.

Davis, H. Principles of electric response audiometry. *Annals of Otology, Rhinology and Laryngology*, 1976, *85*, Suppl. 28(3).

De Chicchis, A. *Binaural interaction in human auditory brainstem response.* Unpublished doctoral dissertation, Memphis State University, 1981.

Despland, P. A., & Galambos, R. The auditory brainstem response (ABR) evaluates risk-factors for hearing loss in newborn. *Pediatric Research*, 1980, *14*, 159–163.

Dublin, W. B. *Fundamentals of sensorineural auditory pathology.* Springfield, IL: Thomas, 1976.

Durrant, J., & Lovrinic, J. *Bases of hearing science.* Baltimore: Williams & Wilkins, 1977.

Finitzo-Hieber, T. Auditory brainstem response: Its placement in infant audiological evaluations. *Seminars in Speech, Language and Hearing*, 1982, *3*(1), 76–85.

Fria, T. J. The auditory brainstem response: Background and clinical applications. *Monographs in Contemporary Audiology*, 1980, *2*(2).

Fria, T. J., & Sabo, D. Auditory brainstem responses in children with otitis media with effusion. *Annals of Otology, Rhinology and Laryngology*, 1980, *68*, 200–206, Suppl. 3, Pt. 2.

Frye-Osier, H. A., Goldstein, R., Hirsch, J. E., & Weber, K. Early and middle-AER components to clicks as response indices for neonatal hearing screening. *Annals of Otology, Rhinology and Laryngology*, 1982, *91*(3), 272–276.

Gacek, R. R. Neuroanatomy of the Auditory System. In J. B. Tobias (Ed.), *Foundations of modern auditory theory,* 1972, (pp. 239–262, Vol. II). New York: Academic Press.

Galambos, R. Neural mechanisms of audition. *Physiological Reviews,* 1954, *34,* 497–528.

Galambos, R., & Hecox, K. Clinical applications of the brainstem evoked potentials. In J. E. Desmedt (Ed.), *Auditory evoked potentials in man: Psycho-pharmacology correlates of evoked potentials,* 1977, (pp. 1–9). Basel: Karger.

Galambos, R., & Hecox, K. Clinical applictions of the auditory brainstem response. *Otolaryngologic Clinics of North America,* 1978, *11*(3), 709–721.

Galambos, R., Hicks, G., & Wilson, M. J. Hearing loss in graduates of a tertiary intensive care nursery. *Ear and Hearing,* 1982, *3*(2), 87–90.

Gillberg, C., Rosenhall, U., & Johansson, E. Auditory brainstem responses in children. *Journal of Autism and Developmental Disorders,* 1983, *13*(2), 181–195.

Gilroy, J., & Lynn, G. E. Computerized tomography and auditory-evoked potentials. *Archives of Neurology,* 1978, *35,* 143–147.

Glasscock, M. E., Jackson, C. E., Josey, A. F., Dickens, J. R. E., & Wiet, R. J. Brainstem evoked response audiometry in a clinical practice. *Laryngoscope,* 1979, *89,* 1021–1035.

Hashimoto, I., Ishiyama, Y., Totsuka, G., & Mizutani, H. Diagnostic significance of brainstem auditory evoked responses in acoustic neuromas and other posterior fossa lesions. *Neurologia Medico-Chirurgica (Tokyo),* 1979, *19,* 605–615.

Hecox, K., & Galambos, R. Brainstem auditory evoked responses in human infants and adults. *Archives of Otolaryngology,* 1974, *99,* 30–33.

Hicks, G. Auditory brainstem response: Sensory assessment by bone conduction masking. *Archives of Otolaryngology,* 1980, *106,* 392–395.

House, J. W., & Brackmann, D. E. Brainstem audiometry in neurotologic diagnosis. *Archives of Otolaryngology,* 1979, *105,* 305–309.

Jerger, J., & Hall, J. Effects of age and sex on auditory brainstem response. *Archives of Otolaryngology,* 1980, *106,* 387–391.

Jerger, J., & Hayes, D. The cross-check principle in pediatric audiometry. *Archives of Otolaryngology,* 1976, *102,* 614–620.

Jerger, J., & Mauldin, L. Prediction of sensorineural hearing level from the brainstem evoked response. *Archives of Otolaryngology,* 1978, *104,* 456–461.

Jewett, D. Volume conducted potentials in response to auditory stimuli as detected by averaging in the cat. *Electroencephalography and Clinical Neurophysiology,* 1970, *28,* 609–618.

Jewett, D., Romano, H. N., & Williston, J. S. Human auditory evoked responses: Possible brainstem components detected on the scalp. *Science,* 1970, *167,* 1517–1518.

Jewett, D., & Williston, J. Auditory evoked farfields averaged from the scalp of humans. *Brain,* 1971, *94,* 681–696.

Kodera, K., Yamane, H., Yamada, O., & Suzuki, J. Brainstem response audiometry at speech frequencies. *Audiology,* 1977, *16,* 469–479.

Liberman, A., Sohmer, H., & Szabo, G. Cochlear audiometry: Electrococh-leography during the neonatal period. *Developmental Medicine and Child Neurology,* 1973, *15,* 8–13.

Lorente de No, R. Anatomy of the eighth nerve. *Laryngoscope,* 1933, *43,* 327–359.

Mauldin, L., & Jerger, J. Auditory brainstem responses to bone conducted signals. *Archives of Otolaryngology,* 1979, *105,* 656–661.

Mendelson, T., Salamy, A., Lenoir, M., & McKean, C. Brainstem evoked potential findings in children with otitis media. *Archives of Otolaryngology,* 1979, *105,* 17–20.

Mokotoff, B., Schulman-Galambos, C., Galambos, R. Brainstem auditory evoked responses in children. *Archives of Otolaryngology,* 1977, *103,* 38–43.

Moller, K., & Blegvad, B. Brainstem responses in patients with sensorineural hearing loss. *Scandinavian Audiology,* 1976, *5,* 115–127.

Moller, A. R., Jannetta, P., & Moller, M. B. Intracranially recorded auditory nerve response in man. *Archives of Otolaryngology,* 1982, *108,* 77–82.

Nodar, R. H., Hahn, J., & Levine, H. L. Brain stem auditory evoked potentials in determining site of lesion of brain stem gliomas in children. *Laryngoscope,* 1980, *90,* 258–266.

O'Donavon, C. A., Beagley, H. A., & Shaw, M. Latency of brainstem response in children. *British Journal of Audiology,* 1980, *14,* 23–29.

Picton, T. W., Ouellette, J., Hamel, G., & Smith, A. D. Brainstem evoked potentials to tone pips in notched noise. *Journal of Otolaryngology,* 1979, *8,* 289–314.

Picton, T., Woods, D. L., Baribeau-Braun, J., & Healey, T. M. Evoked potential audiometry. *Journal of Otolaryngology,* 1977, *6,* 90–119.

Rosenblum, S. M., Arick, J. R., Krug, D. A., Stubbs, E. G., Young, N. B., & Pelson, R. O. Auditory brainstem evoked responses in autistic children. *Journal of Autism and Developmental Disorders,* 1980, *10,* 215–225.

Salamy, A., & McKean, C. M. Postnatal development of human brainstem potentials during the first year of life. *Electroencephalography and Clinical Neurophysiology,* 1976, *40,* 418–426.

Salamy, A., Birtley-Fenn, B. C., & Bronshrag, M. Ontogenesis of human brainstem evoked potential amplitude. *Developmental Psychobiology,* 1979, 12(5), 519–526.

Salamy, A., McKean, C. M., & Buda, F. B. Maturational changes in auditory transmission as reflected in human brainstem potentials. *Brain Research,* 1975, *96,* 361–366.

Salamy, A., Mendelson, T., Tooley, W. H., & Chaplin, E. R. Contrasts in brainstem function between normal high-risk infants in early postnatal life. *Early Human Development,* 1980, 4(2), 179–185.

Schulman-Galambos, C., & Galambos, R. Brain stem evoked response audiometry in newborn hearing screening. *Archives of Otolaryngology,* 1979, *105,* 86–90.

Seitz, M., Weber, B., & Jacobson, J. *Sex differences in auditory brainstem responses.* Paper presented at the 8th annual meeting of the International Neurological Society, San Francisco, 1980.

Selters, W. A., & Brackmann, D. E. Acoustic tumor detection with brainstem electric response audiometry. *Archives of Otolaryngology,* 1977, *103,* 181–187.

Smith, L. E., & Simmons, F. B. Accuracy of auditory brainstem evoked response with hearing level unknown. *Annals of Otology, Rhinology and Laryngology,* 1982, 91(3), 266–267.

Sohmer, H., & Feinmesser, M. Cochlear action potentials recorded from the external ear in man. *Annals of Otology, Rhinology and Laryngology,* 1967, *76,* 427–435.

Sohmer, H., & Student, M. Auditory nerve and brain stem evoked responses in normal, autistic, minimal brain dysfunction and psychomotor retarded children. *Electroencephalography and Clinical Neurophysiology,* 1978, *44,* 380–388.

Stapells, D. R., & Picton, T. W. Technical aspects of brainstem evoked potential audiometry using tones. *Ear and Hearing,* 1981, 2(1), 20–29.

Starr, A., & Achor, J. Auditory brainstem responses in neurological disease. *Archives of Neurology*, 1975, *32*, 761–768.

Starr, A., Amlie, R. N., Martin, W. H., & Sanders, S. Development of auditory function in newborn infants revealed by auditory brainstem potentials. *Pediatrics*, 1977, *60*(6), 831–839.

Starr, A., & Hamilton, A. E. Correlation between confirmed sites of neurological lesions and abnormalities of far-field auditory brainstem responses. *Electroencephalography and Clinical Neurophysiology*, 1976, *41*, 595–608.

Stockard, J. J., Stockard, J. E., & Sharbrough, F. W. Nonpathologic factors influencing brainstem auditory evoked potentials. *The American Journal of EEG Technology*, 1978, *18*, 197–209.

Stockard, J. J., & Rossiter, V. S. Clinical pathological correlates of brainstem auditory response abnormalities. *Neurology*, 1977, *27*, 316–325.

Stockard, J. J., Stockard, J. E., & Sharbrough, F. W. Detection and localization of occult lesions with brainstem auditory responses. *Mayo Clinic Proceedings*, 1977, *52*, 761–769.

Stockard, J. E., Stockard, J. J., Westmoreland, B. F., & Corfits, J. L. Brainstem auditory-evoked responses: Normal variation as a function of stimulus and subject characteristics. *Archives of Otolaryngology*, 1979, *36*, 823–831.

Suzuki, T., & Horiuchi, K. Effect of high pass filter on auditory brainstem responses to tone pips. *Scandinavian Audiology*, 1977, 123–126.

Terkildsen, K., Huis In't Veld, F., & Osterhammel, P. Auditory brainstem responses in the diagnosis of cerebellopontine angle tumors. *Scandinavian Audiology*, 1977, *6*, 43–47.

Weber, B. A. Comparison of auditory brainstem response latency norms for premature infants. *Ear and Hearing*, 1982, *3*(5), 257–262.

Weber, B. A., & Folsom, R. C. Brainstem Wave V latencies to tone pip stimuli. *Journal of the American Auditory Society*, 1977, *2*(5), 182–184.

Wever, E. G., & Bray, C. W. The nature of the acoustic response: The relation between sound and frequency of impulses in the auditory nerve. *Journal of Experimental Psychology*, 1930, *13*, 373–387.

Whitfield, I. *The auditory pathway.* Baltimore: Williams & Wilkins, 1967.

Worthington, D., & Peters, J. Quantifiable hearing and no BER: Paradox or error? *Ear and Hearing,* 1980, *1,* 281-285.

Zubick, H. H., Fried, M. P., Feudo, P., Jr., Epstein, M. F., & Strome, M. Normal neonatal brainstem auditory evoked potentials. *Annals of Otology, Rhinology and Laryngology,* 1982, *91,* 485-487.

4
COMMENTS ON THE ORIGIN OF SHORT LATENCY AUDITORY EVOKED POTENTIALS

Theodore J. Glattke
University of Arizona

Cheryl A. Runge
Stanford University Medical Center

*T*he short-latency auditory brain stem response (ABR) has been found to have important application as an aid for the identification of hearing loss and neurological disorders. Examples of responses obtained from a young adult with normal hearing are illustrated in Figure 4-1. Each tracing consists of the mean of samples of electric activity coincident with the presentation of 2000 click stimuli at the stimulus sensation level indicated on the left. Stimuli that are close to the threshold of audibility elicit a response consisting of a biphasic voltage fluctuation with a latency of 8 to 8.5 msec. As the stimulus sound pressure level (SPL) is increased to moderate levels, the response takes the form of multiple succinct maxima and minima. The response peaks are identified with Roman numerals (I, II,..., VII) in the manner of Jewett (1970). The first five waves oscillate about a relatively slow voltage shift, or "pedestal," so that the fifth peak and subsequent voltage minimum dominate the response.

Soon after the initial publications of descriptions of the response in humans (Jewett, Romano, & Williston, 1970; Jewett & Williston, 1971), there appeared a number of publications that supported a concept of a single-source generator for each of the voltage fluctuations forming the response to high-intensity stimulation. In addition, several authors during the middle and late 1970s advanced the notion that the multiple peaks represented sequential activation of various structures in the afferent auditory system.

The sequential activation scheme assigns probable generators as follows: Wave I—auditory nerve; Wave II—cochlear nucleus; Wave III—superior olivary complex; Waves IV/V—lemniscal pathways and inferior colliculi. The response components subsequent to Wave V are associated with thalamic and cortical origins (Stockard, Stockard, & Sharbrough, 1977). The investigations that supported the isolated sequential generator hypothesis were correlative in nature, and included the following:

FIGURE 4-1
Auditory brainstem responses obtained from a normal listener at the
stimulus sensation levels indicated to the left of each tracing. The 0-dB
level tracing corresponds with a control (no stimulus) condition.

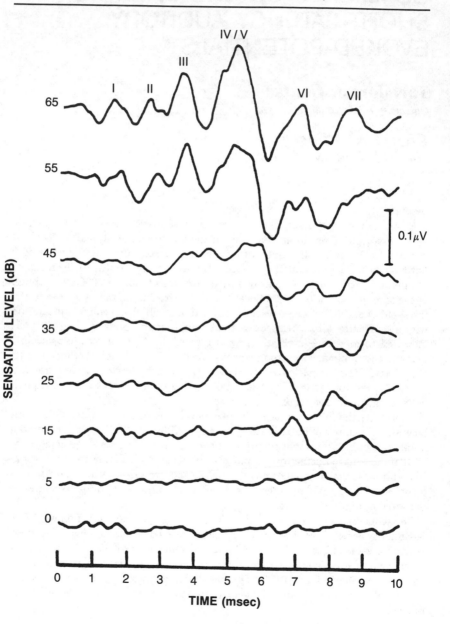

1. Examination of the coincidence between surface-recorded potentials and responses detected by electrodes placed within auditory nuclei or fiber tracts (e.g., Lev & Sohmer, 1972).

2. Descriptions of the effects of acute experimental lesions placed within the auditory system (e. g., Buchwald & Huang, 1975).

3. Evaluation of clinical impressions, X-ray, or other objective findings for patients whose ABRs also had been studied (e. g., Stockard et al., 1977).

If the ABR were to offer an indication of isolated and sequentially activated structures within the auditory system, its sensitivity and precision for site-of-lesion testing would be unparalleled among measures of evoked potential and several of the modern X-ray techniques. Unfortunately, more recent experimental findings have cast doubt on both the isolated generator and sequential-activation ideas. The purpose of this chapter is to review the more recent data and to suggest some of their implications with regard to clinical interpretation. The studies to be considered include both response coincidence and experimental lesion approaches, as well as those involving the use of novel recording techniques.

INVESTIGATIONS OF RESPONSE COINCIDENCE

Achor and Starr (1980a) and Runge (1980) have reported studies of the coincidence between electrical fields detected by surface and indwelling electrodes in cat. The technique employed by Achor and Starr (1980a) involved the use of a large number of intracranial recording sites and a stimulus of fixed intensity. The analysis technique employed by Achor and Starr permitted the construction of graphical representations of the spatial–temporal distributions of the electrical fields detected by the indwelling electrodes. Runge's (1980) method involved the use of a limited number of intracranial recording sites and the manipulation of stimulus SPL and interstimulus interval. Her technique permitted the investigation of the temporal stability of the intracranial recordings relative to the surface-recorded ABR peaks.

Both investigations replicated the findings of Wickelgren (1968) and earlier investigators who had demonstrated sustained electric activity within the various nuclei along the auditory system neuraxis in response to click stimulation. As a consequence, it was not possible to demonstrate that a single intracranial site contributes to an individual surface ABR peak to the exclusion of other intracranial sites. Figure 4-2 provides an illustration of examples of responses obtained by Runge (1980). The surface record was sampled from electrodes placed in the scalp midline 5 mm anterior to the vertex (noninverting preamplifier input), in the soft tissue overlying the bulla ipsilateral to the stimulus ear (inverting amplifier input), and the dorsal neck (common). The round window record was obtained with a fine wire loop electrode placed in the niche adjacent to the membrane itself to reduce the contribution of the cochlear microphonic. The other indwelling recordings were obtained at histologically confirmed sites with bipolar stainless steel wire electrodes (125 μm diameter) fixed to a 22-gauge hypodermic tube carrier and positioned by conventional stereotaxic methods. The stimulus consisted of a click formed by a 100-μsec rectangular pulse led to an insert earphone–earpiece placed in the pinna

FIGURE 4-2
Surface ABR and indwelling electrode records obtained from cat or click stimuli. The surface ABR peaks are numbered P1,...,P5. The other recording sites are as follows: DNLL—dorsal nucleus of the lateral lemniscus; SOC—superior olivary complex, "S" segment; CN—anteroventral cochlear nucleus; RW—round window. All indwelling electrodes were ipsilateral to the stimulus ear.

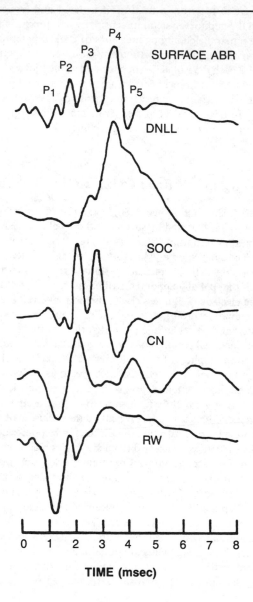

ipsilateral to the intracranial recording sites. The responses are the computed means of electric activity coincident with 200 replications of the click at a peak equivalent SPL of 86.5 dB (re: 20 μPa).

The first evidence of electric activity in the surface record corresponds with the cochlear microphonic. The later major peaks, noted as P1 through P5, are associated with neural sources. The intracranial records are complex. The round window response is characterized by two succinct negative peaks followed by a slow positive component that extends more than 4 msec beyond the second negative peak. The principal contributor to this response is the auditory nerve, although very small voltages corresponding to the cochlear microphonic and summating potential are reflected in the initial portion of the record. The cochlear nucleus response is multiphasic, reaching its initial negative peak approximately 300 μsec after the initial peak of the round window response. Sustained activity is apparent as a series of peaks extending to 6 msec after stimulus onset. The superior olivary complex response has two major and several smaller peaks that overlap the response obtained from the cochlear nucleus. The major peaks of the recording obtained from the dorsal nucleus of the lateral lemniscus overlap the superior olivary complex activity and they are followed by a relatively slow voltage drift back to the recording baseline. The probability that the intracranial records illustrated in Figure 4-2 represent "far field" voltages detected from distant generator sites is low because of the use of the bipolar indwelling electrodes. The polarity of the maxima and minima of the intracranial recordings is arbitrary and was selected to reveal possible correlates to the surface-recorded response.

As is apparent from inspection of the illustration, the surface-recorded peaks are coincident with electric activity at two or more intracranial sites. The intracranial recordings do reflect sequential activation of brain stem structures, but it is not possible to relate the voltage fluctuations detected by the indwelling electrodes to the surface ABR in any more than a casual way. The sustained activity associated with each of the structures overlaps the onset of activity from more rostral electrode sites.

More recent evidence of this type was presented by Møller, Jannetta, and Møller (1981, 1982), Møller, Jannetta, Bennett, and Møller (1981), and by Møller and Jannetta (1982) for human subjects. Their reports compared the surface-recorded ABR to intracranial recordings obtained from the surface of the auditory nerve in individuals who were undergoing vascular decompression surgery. Møller, Jannetta, Bennett, and Møller (1981) noted that the major peak of the whole-nerve response occurred at a time that was much later than the whole-nerve response peak detected at promontory, ear canal, or surface sites in human subjects. The multiphasic whole-nerve response detected by Møller et al. coincided with Waves II and III and the negative 'trough" between these two waves. In their second report, they concluded that the generator of "the second (vertex negative) peak" of the ABR is the "intracranial portion of the auditory nerve" (Møller, Jannetta, & Møller, 1981).

According to the reasoning of Møller et al. the first peak in the surface-recorded ABR is identical to the auditory nerve response as detected by distal recording electrodes such as those commonly used for electrocochleography or ABR recordings. The later ABR peaks (II and perhaps III) also are due to auditory nerve activity.

The auditory nerve response appears as several distinct peaks because the internal auditory meatus acts as an insulator that precludes the electric activity of the nerve from detection on the surface during the time period that the activity passes through the meatus. Møller et al. estimated the travel time of conduction along the auditory nerve in humans to be 1 to 1.5 msec, in agreement with the interval between the first two peaks of the surface-recorded ABR. Their study did not include simultaneous recordings from other intracranial sites, and so their observations do not permit the exclusion of additional sites as contributors to Wave II. However, based upon their observations, the auditory nerve does appear to be a major contributor to the generation of both Wave I and Wave II of the ABR.

Hashimoto, Ishiyama, Yoshimoto, and Nemoto (1981) conducted similar studies with patients who were undergoing neurosurgical procedures. They observed that the intracranial recording of the auditory nerve response coincided with the surface-recorded negative trough between Waves I and II. Small positive voltages detected in the auditory nerve response corresponded with the peaks of Waves I and II recorded from the surface. The Hashimoto et al. observation is different from that of Møller et al. in that Hashimoto et al. noted best alignment of the auditory nerve response with Waves I and II, rather than II and III. The difference may obtain from the fact that Hashimoto and his co-workers used click stimuli, while Møller et al. used 2000-Hz tone bursts to elicit their responses. The use of lower frequency stimuli is known to modify the intervals among response peaks (Coats, Martin, & Kidder, 1979). The use of the 2000-Hz stimulus by Møller et al. may be the reason for the apparent delay of their whole-nerve response latency in comparison with the results of Hashimoto et al. Another factor that may contribute to the differences between the two sets of observations is that Hashimoto et al. used a "reference" recording site that was on the surface of the skull. Hence, some of the whole-nerve response components detected by them may have been derived from distant generators that produce voltages detected by surface electrodes.

Probing elsewhere in thalamic, midbrain, and brainstem locations with stereotaxic electrodes, Hashimoto et al. explored intracranial electrical activity from within the fourth ventricle and therein noted a multiphasic short-latency response that appeared very similar to that recorded on the surface of the skull between the vertex and periauricular recording sites. As the electrode was retracted toward the superior surface of the brain via the cerebral aqueduct, the indwelling recording became dominated by a large positive-going peak that reversed polarity as the electrode passed between pons and midbrain. Hashimoto and his co-workers consider this to be the correlate to Wave V and associate it with midbrain structures, specifically the inferior colliculi. However, recent observations by Møller and Jannetta (1982) indicated that the intracranial recording of the activity of the inferior colliculus is delayed relative to Wave V of the surface recording.

In summary, the recent observations obtained from both laboratory animals and human subjects suggest that the first four to five fast components of the ABR represent a composite of several sources. Contributions from the auditory nerve appear to extend well into the first two or three waves of the surface record. According to the observations of Achor and Starr (1980a) and Møller and Jannetta (1982), responses from the inferior colliculus are initiated after the major ABR response peak (P4 in cats, Wave V in humans). While Hashimoto's observations are not in entire agreement with those of Møller and Jannetta, they do underscore the probable complexity of the origin of the response components.

INVESTIGATIONS OF EXPERIMENTAL LESIONS

The lesion studies of Goldenberg and Derbyshire (1975) and Achor and Starr (1980b) provide some important insights into the complexity of the origins of the ABR. A major finding of Goldenberg and Derbyshire was that destruction of the inferior colliculus in cat failed to alter the surface ABR. This finding was not reproduced exactly by Achor and Starr, but the latter authors did fail to demonstrate changes of P4 after placing lesions in the inferior colliculus. (P4 in cat is considered to be analogous to Wave V in human subjects.) They noted only inconsistent or no changes in the characteristics of P5. One important difference between the earlier work of Buchwald and Huang (1975) and the Achor and Starr study (1980b) was that some of the animal preparations in the latter study were allowed to recover from the acute effects of the surgery required to induce the lesions. Achor and Starr (1980b) reported that some of the lesion-induced effects were transient. For example, they reported that an acute lesion in the anterior (upper) portion of the lateral lemniscus was associated with a marked attenuation of the negative trough between P3 and P4 in the cat surface-recorded response. Recordings obtained after the animal recovered from surgery indicated that the response returned to 75% of its prelesion amplitude. They also observed that a single response peak (e.g., P3) could be eliminated without obliterating the subsequent peaks, although the later peaks were attenuated.

Other general findings of Achor and Starr (1980b) included the following:

1. Single discrete lesions are likely to affect more than one surface-recorded response peak;

2. Lesions in various locations along the auditory brainstem pathways may have similar effects on the surface-recorded ABR;

3. The principal effect of discrete lesions is an alteration of the response amplitude.

Taken together, the observations of Achor and Starr suggest not only a complicated scheme of generation of the surface-recorded potentials, but also poor precision when the ABR is employed as a site-of-lesion diagnostic instrument for lesions involving the brainstem and midbrain. As they note, an important implication of the reversible effects of some of their acute lesions is that the response may recover independently of the lesion, leading one to conclude that the neural pathology underlying a response aberration is resolving when, in fact, it is not. Additionally, their observation that response amplitude changes, and not alterations of response latencies, accompanied their lesions has important implications for the clinical interpretation of ABR results.

OTHER INVESTIGATIONS

Other approaches to determining the possible sites of origin of the various components of the ABR have involved sophisticated analyses of responses obtained from other than the conventional recording sites. Many locations where electrodes might be placed on the head to record the ABR are electrically "active" and reveal short-latency responses to auditory stimulation. The conventional waveform is due to a standard differential preamplifier's interaction with the electrical fields detected at the periauricular and vertex recording sites. Ino and Mizoi (1980) have presented a vector analysis of the ABR based on recordings obtained simultaneously in three planes. This technique involved placement of three pairs of electrodes (vertex–chin, forehead–inion, and right–left external meati). Their analysis technique allowed them to examine the temporal and the spatial development of the response components in three planes that were approximately orthogonal. Their analysis of Wave I supported the general conclusion that it was due to the auditory nerve. They suggested that Wave II was derived partly from the auditory nerve and also from brainstem sources. The vector for Wave III was distributed over a broad spatial area, suggesting a number of possible contributors near the midline of the caudal brainstem. Finally, they noted that the vector associated with Wave V was oriented superior, rostral, and contralateral to the stimulated ear. From this observation, they inferred that its origin lay in the lemniscal pathways and midbrain.

Kevanishvili (1980) examined the ABR waveform of human subjects using simultaneous recordings from paired electrodes (parasagittal central vs. mastoid) ipsilateral and contralateral to the stimulated ear. Examining the amplitudes and latencies of the various response components, Kevanishvili noted that responses detected ipsilateral to the stimulated ear were generally of greater amplitude than when they were detected from contralateral electrodes. The exception to this was Wave II, which did not reveal a change of amplitude. He also noted that Wave V had a shorter latency when recorded ipsilateral to the stimulus ear. Kevanishvili's observations led him to hypothesize a sublemniscal origin of the ABR through Wave V.

Prasher (1980) responded to Kevanishvili's suggestions with a counterhypothesis based on consideration of possible nonneural and neural sources for the differences noted by Kevanishvili. Prasher argued that the electrical conduction properties of the skull and its contents could have been responsible for some of the earlier observations. Prasher also suggested that some of Kevanishvili's observations could be supported by alternate neural transmission pathways involving the superior olivary complex and inferior colliculi. Kevanishvili (1981) reexamined his hypothesis after conducting additional studies using noncephalic reference electrodes in conjunction with his near-sagittal and mastoid sites. The amplitude asymmetries noted by him in 1980 were less distinct when the noncranial reference site was used, suggesting a complex interaction among the mastoid–parasagittal sites. Kevanishvili concluded that his sublemniscal hypothesis remained reasonable in the face of his latter observations.

CONCLUSIONS

Overall, the recent observations on human subjects cited above tend to support some degree of skepticism regarding the isolated generator concept. They are not sufficient to determine the exact locus of production of each of the response components, but do support the hypothesis of probable multiple generators for the response components subsequent to Wave I.

Several of the studies cited previously have direct implications for clinical analysis of ABR findings, in addition to their contributions to determining the complex origin of the response. The findings of Achor and Starr (1980a), Runge (1980), and Møller and Jannetta (1982) are in agreement with Kevanishvili's general hypothesis. They suggest that midbrain lesions involving the inferior colliculi may not be detected by conventional ABR measurements. Jerger, Neely, and Jerger (1980) report findings from one patient that are in agreement with this. In spite of widespread damage to the inferior colliculi and thalamic nuclei, ABR findings were normal for stimulation of one ear and revealed only a modest reduction in the amplitude of Wave V for stimulation of the other. Achor and Starr's (1980b) lesion studies suggest that measures of response amplitude may be as critical as the response latency measures that are favored by most clinical investigators. A report that echoes the finding of Achor and Starr is that of Parving and his co-workers (1981) who examined ABRs of multiple sclerosis patients. They noted significant waveform variations in one-half of their patients. Wave V was poorly defined and was followed by a sustained baseline shift that might be interpreted as a prolonged Wave V in some circumstances. Careful measurements revealed the presence of a small voltage fluctuation corresponding with the expected Wave V latency, but obscured by the larger aberrant response component.

In summary, the ABR remains elusive as to its exact origin. The concept of isolated, sequential generators for the individual fast components of the response is not supported by recent measurements obtained from both animal and human subjects. Relationships among response component amplitudes, while difficult to quantify, may emerge as important diagnostic indices, improving the precision with which ABR techniques may be used to locate disorders involving the auditory nervous system.

REFERENCES

Achor, L. J., & Starr, A. Auditory brainstem responses in the cat. I. Intracranial and extracranial recordings. *Electroencephalography and Clinical Neurophysiology*, 1980a, *48*, 154–173.

Achor, L. J., & Starr, A. Auditory brainstem responses in the cat. II. Effects of lesions. *Electroencephalography and Clinical Neurophysiology*, 1980b, *48*, 174–190.

Buchwald, J. S., & Huang, C. -M. Far-field acoustic responses: Origins in the cat. *Science*, 1975, *189*, 382–384.

Coats, A. C., Martin, J. L., & Kidder, H. R. Normal short-latency electro-physiological filtered click responses recorded from vertex and external auditory meatus. *Journal of the Acoustical Society of America*, 1979, *68*, 1671–1675.

Goldenberg, R. A., & Derbyshire, A. J. Averaged evoked potentials in cats with lesions of the auditory pathway. *Journal of Speech and Hearing Research,* 1975, *18,* 420–429.

Hashimoto, I., Ishiyama, Y., Yoshimoto, T., & Nemoto, S. Brainstem auditory-evoked potentials recorded directly from human brainstem and thalamus. *Brain,* 1981, *104,* 841–859.

Ino, T., & Mizoi, K. Vector analysis of auditory brainstem responses (BSR) in human beings. *Archives of Otology-Rhinology-Laryngology,* 1980, *226,* 55–62.

Jerger, J., Neely, J. G., & Jerger, S. Speech, impedance, and brainstem response audiometry in brainstem tumors: Importance of a multiple test strategy. *Archives of Otolaryngology,* 1980, *106,* 218–233.

Jewett, D. L. Volume conducted potentials in response to auditory stimuli as detected by averaging in the cat. *Electroencephalography and Clinical Neurophysiology,* 1970, *28,* 609–618.

Jewett, D. L., & Williston, J. S. Auditory evoked far fields averaged from the scalp of humans. *Brain,* 1971, *94,* 681–696.

Jewett, D. L., Romano, M. N., & Williston, J. S. Human auditory evoked potentials: Possible brainstem components detected on the scalp. *Science,* 1970, *167,* 1517–1518.

Kevanishvili, Z. Sh. Sources of the human brainstem auditory evoked potential. *Scandinavian Audiology,* 1980, *9,* 75–82.

Kevanishvili, Z. Sh. Considerations of the sources of brainstem auditory evoked potentials on the basis of bilateral asymmetry of its parameters. *Scandinavian Audiology,* 1981, *10,* 197–202.

Lev, A., & Sohmer, H. Sources of averaged neural responses recorded in animal and human subjects during cochlear audiometry. *Archiv for Klinische und Experimentelle Ohrn- Nasen- und Kehlkopfheilkunde,* 1972, *201,* 79–90.

Møller, A. R., & Jannetta, P. *Neural generators of the brainstem auditory evoked potential.* Abstracts of the Fifth Midwinter Research Meeting, Association for Research in Otolaryngology, 1982, St. Petersburg Beach, Florida.

Møller, A. R., Jannetta, P., & Møller, M. B. Neural generators of brainstem evoked potentials. Results from human intracranial recordings. *Annals of Otology, Rhinology and Laryngology,* 1981, *90,* 591–596.

Møller, A. R., Jannetta, P., & Møller, M. B. Intracranially recorded auditory nerve response in man. New interpretations of BSER. *Archives of Otolaryngology,* 1982, *108,* 77–82.

Møller, A. R., Jannetta, P., Bennett, M., & Møller, B. M. Intracranially recorded responses from the human auditory nerve: New insights into the origin of brainstem evoked potentials (BSEPs). *Electroencephalography and Clinical Neurophysiology,* 1981, *52,* 18-27.

Parving, A., Elberling, C., & Smith, T. Auditory electrophysiology: Findings in multiple sclerosis. *Audiology,* 1981, *20,* 123-142.

Prasher, D. K. Alternative hypotheses concerning the sources of the human brainstem auditory evoked potentials. *Scandinavian Audiology,* 1980, *9,* 75-76.

Runge, C. A. *Intracranial and surface recordings of the auditory brainstem response in the cat.* Master's thesis, University of Arizona, Tucson, 1980.

Stockard, J. J., Stockard, J. E., & Sharbrough, F. W. Detection and localization of occult lesions with brainstem auditory responses. *Mayo Clinic Proceedings,* 1977, *52,* 761-769.

Wickelgren, W. O. Effect of state of arousal on click-evoked responses in cats. *Journal of Neurophysiology,* 1968, *31,* 757-767.

5
THE INTERPRETATION OF SELECTIVE ADAPTATION FOR SPEECH

Gisela Wilson
University of Wisconsin

Raymond G. Daniloff
University of Vermont

*T*o offer an alternative to motor theory and engineering matching-filter accounts of the speech perception process, Abbs and Sussman (1971) proposed that the elementary stages of speech processing might involve a feature detector network similar to those found in auditory and visual systems (e.g., Hubel & Wiesel, 1962; Kay & Matthews, 1972; Whitfield & Evans, 1965). There was evidence suggesting that these networks possessed the ability to make biologically significant distinctions between stimuli (Capranica, Frishkopf, & Nevo, 1973; Lettvin, MaTurana, McColloch, & Pitts, 1959; Wollberg & Newman, 1972) and it seemed both logical and parsimonious for speech perception to proceed via a similar network.

In the absence of acoustically invariant cues, the retrieval of linguistic features appeared to invoke exotic perceptual mechanisms (Liberman, Cooper, Shankweiler, & Studdert-Kennedy, 1967). Feature detectors selectively tuned to speech offered an economical account of the auditory system's ability to extract phonemically relevant cues from their acoustically "smeared" environment. For those supporting the view that acoustically invariant cues do exist in the speech signal (Stevens, 1975), the detectors were a means for "simply and economically" extracting these cues. The detector network also offered a simple explanation for the categorical perception abilities demonstrated by infants assuming the detectors were present at birth (Cutting & Eimas, 1975; Eimas, 1974, 1975; Eimas, Siqueland, Jusczyk, & Vigorito, 1971). In their search for such sensorineural networks, numerous investigators applied the psychophysical method of adaptation to the study of speech perception.

In the physiological sense, adaptation (or fatigue) refers to a gradual and temporary reduction in the sensitivity of neurons caused by the continued presentation of a stimulus (Barlow & Hill, 1963; Evans, 1971). Once the stimulus is removed, the discharge rate of the neurons in question recovers to prestimulation levels. If a second presentation of the stimulus is made before the end of this recovery period, neuronal sensitivity and responsiveness will be depressed. This neuronal behavior generally is assumed to be the basis of the "aftereffects" observed in psychophysical research. Briefly, in vision, prolonged exposure to a grid of lines tilted at some critical angle will cause a grid of straight lines to appear tilted in the opposite direction (Campbell & Maffei, 1971). In this case, it is assumed that a critical perceptual balance has been destroyed—a balance created by cells functioning in a mutually opposed fashion. Thus, the perception of a straight line might be determined by the equal excitability of two opposed tilt detectors; when the response of one detector is depressed, the response of the opposed detector will be the predominant influence on some higher order integrator (often assumed to be a single cell).

Extending the above rationale to the detection of linguistic features, Eimas and Corbit (1973) examined the influence of adaptation on identification and discrimination functions obtained for two different series of stop + vowel syllables systematically varied along their voice onset time (VOT) dimension. The two test series consisted of syllables ranging from /ba/ to /pa/ and from /da/ to /ta/. Comparing subjects' pre- and post-adaptation performance, Eimas and Corbit found that repeated presentations of a stimulus taken from the extreme ends of either test series produced a significant change in their subjects' placement of the phoneme boundary. Specifically, adaptation with either the /pa/ or /ta/ extremes caused fewer items to be placed in the voiceless category, while adaptation with either /ba/ or /da/ caused fewer items to be placed in the voiced category. Adaptation moved the boundary toward the adaptor. Furthermore, this effect was obtained even if the adaptor was not from the same phonemic dimension as the test series (bilabial or alveolar). That is, /ga/ was nearly as effective an adaptor of the /ba–da/ dimension as either /ba/ or /da/.

Eimas and Corbit concluded that they had tapped a feature specific level of perceptual analysis. They speculated that this analysis was performed by a set of opposed detectors whose combined receptive fields corresponded to a stimulus range overlapping that of the VOT continuum. They presumed that the repeated presentations of the adaptor had fatigued one of these detectors, reducing its contribution to a higher order integrator whose decision criterion was based upon which detector (voiced or voiceless) had produced the largest input. Subsequent research (for reviews see Ades, 1976; Cooper, 1975) has shown that adaptation influences the boundaries of feature dimensions such as place of articulation; (Ades, 1974a, 1974b; Cooper, 1974a; Cooper & Blumstein, 1974; Pisoni & Tash, 1975; Sawusch, 1976, 1977a, 1977b; Tartter & Eimas, 1975) and manner of articulation (Cole & Cooper, 1975; Cooper, Ebert, & Cole, 1976; Diehl, 1976).

The results of these studies have been interpreted as providing support for feature detectors and, in addition, have been used to determine the network's neuronal configuration. Despite physiological evidence of neuronal adaptation, the relationship between perceptual experience and single-unit activity remains vague, and conclusions regarding the detecting mechanisms remain premature. Cautionary remarks to this effect are not uncommon in the visual pattern recognition literature (e.g., Campbell & Kulikowski, 1966; Uttal, 1971; Weisstein, 1973). The above authors imply that while the assumptions made by a feature detector model are plausible for simple, one-dimensional visual operations, they are questionable for more complex stimuli such as speech. Furthermore, ongoing research has revealed that the linguistic feature detector network based on feature detector pairs and straightforward integrator circuits is inadequate. Apparently, the network includes either complex acoustic cue detectors (Blumstein, Stevens, & Nigro, 1977), complex linguistic detectors (Eimas & Miller, 1978), or some combinations of the two. Multiple levels of detectors, both peripheral and central (Ades, 1974b; Diehl, 1975; Foreit, 1977; Sawusch, 1977b; Sawusch & Pisoni, 1978), and detectors specially tuned to a speech–nonspeech contrast (Remez, 1979, 1980) also must exist. Although psychophysical methods permit speculation concerning the mechanisms mediating perceptual experience, these methods are a tool and not an actual description of the anatomical organization of the mechanisms involved. As Uttal (1971) notes, the reductionistic transformation of psychophysical method from tool to theory regularly tempts the psychologist. Students of speech perception employing the adaptation paradigm have not resisted this temptation; it is useful, therefore, to determine whether other perceptual mechanisms might offer a reasonable explanation of adaptation data.

EVIDENCE CONCERNING LINGUISTIC FEATURE DETECTORS

One strength of the feature detector model lay in the assumption that adaptation influenced linguistic feature detectors. Thus, if such detectors were speech specific, then the phonetic similarity of the adaptor to the test series would be a prerequisite for an adapting effect. If detectors were acoustical then acoustic similarity, and not phonetic similarity, would determine the adaptability of the test series. There is much evidence to support the latter alternative indicating that, in fact, the detectors under examination do not operate on a purely linguistic decision criterion.

Evidence for the above conclusion has been gathered from two popular extensions of the adaptation procedure: (a) crossed-series adaptation and (b) contingent adaptation. Crossed-series adaptation refers to the production of a significant boundary shift with an adaptor phoneme different from the phoneme whose allophones comprise the test series, but one sharing the distinctive feature varied in the test series. For instance, in the Eimas and Corbit (1973) study, the /pa/ adaptor produced a significant shift in the voicing boundary separating /da/ and /ta/.

Crossed-series adaptation usually is employed to show that each distinctive feature is analyzed by the same set of detectors regardless of the phoneme's allophonic context. In contrast, contingent adaptation demonstrates the existence of different detector pairs for the same feature. The pair of detectors activated by the speech waveform depends upon the outcome of a lower level decision concerning the presence or absence of one of the phoneme's other features. Consider the following example. If an alternating sequence of /ba/ and /pa/ syllables from the ends of the VOT continuum is presented during the adaptation period, one would expect both detectors (voiced and voiceless) to be adapted equally. Neither detector would bias the decision made by the integrator, and the phoneme boundary for a /ba/–/pa/ continuum would remain unaffected. Upon replacement of the /ba/ adaptor with /bi/, if these VOT detectors are not allophonically sensitive, that is, make the voicing decision independently of vowel context, the phoneme boundary would be unshifted if a /bi/ adaptor were used for the /ba/–/pa/ continuum. However, if the VOT detectors were vowel sensitive (e.g., one VOT detector set for /a/ allophones of /b–p/ and another set for /i/), there would be a shift in the boundary. Fewer items in the /ba/–/pa/ continuum would be identified as /pa/ because the /bi/ adaptor would not have affected the /ba/ detector quite so strongly.

Employing the crossed-series procedure, Ades (1974a) attempted to adapt the VOT detectors for word-final stops with their word-initial counterparts. Linguistic detectors would be expected to adapt regardless of differences between the adaptor and test series in syllable position and acoustic waveform. However, Ades found the adaptation effect failed to transfer across syllable position. In a similar vein, other authors (Cooper, 1974b; Miller & Eimas, 1976; Sawusch & Pisoni, 1978) using the contingent adaptation technique found the effect to be vowel-context dependent for both VOT and place of articulation. In a further study, Sawusch and Nusbaum found that a /da/ - /ga/ continuum was readily adapted by a /ska/ syllable wherein the /k/ resembled /d/ acoustically, and /g/ phonemically. /Ska/ resembled /d/ in its adapting effects, suggesting that acoustic similarity at an acoustic-processing level is crucial to adaptation. To preserve the linguistic nature of the detector model, it became necessary to modify the detector network. Thus, an initial level of analysis distinguishing phonemes on the basis of positional and vocalic cues was followed by a consonantal analysis performed by allophone selective detectors. The alternative to this complex network was to suggest that acoustic similarity, and not phonemic identity, determined an adaptor's ability to produce an effect (Ades, 1974b, 1976; Bailey, 1975, cited in Cooper, 1979). The absence of adaptation in the above studies was then easily explained by the adaptor's spectral difference from the test series.

To determine which of the above alternatives, namely allophonic differences in vocalic context or acoustic dissimilarity of the allophones comprising the adaptor and test series, was responsible for the contingencies observed in earlier studies, Howell (1980) manipulated the phoneme class of diphthongs independently of spectral similarity. Because different diphthongs (having identical transitions) failed to produce a contingent effect, Howell concluded that the vowel contingencies seen in earlier studies "are best explained by feature detectors which extract spectral information about formant transitions, independent of the identity of the following vowel" (p. 41). Similarly, Diehl (1976), Sawusch (1977a), and Tartter and Eimas (1975) successfully employed acoustically similar, nonspeech stimuli to adapt a syllable continuum, further indicating that spectral overlap of adaptor and stimulus continuum was an important prerequisite to adaptation. Thus, the linguistic feature detector model in its strictest (and most valuable) sense must be rejected since the acoustic characteristics (and not phonetic identity) of a sound determined which set of detectors was activated. This conclusion gains further strength from other contingent effects which have been obtained for fundamental frequency (Ades, 1977) and intonation contour (Elman, 1980).

SINGLE VERSUS MULTIPLE LEVEL FEATURE DETECTOR MODELS

Although the conclusion that adaptation was spectrally specific rather than speech specific allowed a one-level model to be retained, there were other reasons to suggest that adaptation affected a multiple level detector arrangement. These included adaptor dependent differences in the magnitude of the adaptation effect for crossed series (Eimas & Corbit, 1973; Eimas, Cooper, & Corbit, 1973) and contingent procedures (Ades, 1974a; Sawusch, 1977b), as well as the possibility of an integrative site that also was adaptable (Diehl, 1975; Foreit, 1977; Sawusch, 1977b; Sawusch & Pisoni, 1978). Also, the presence of only a partial interaural transfer of the adaptation effect when adaptors were presented monotically to one ear and the test series to the other ear (Ades, 1974b; Sawusch, 1977b) supports this contention.

Cooper (1979) and Sawusch (1977b) suggested that the nature of a feature detector's responsiveness might account for the observed differences in the magnitude of adaptation for different adaptors. They proposed that feature detectors most sensitive to consonant cues within one band of frequency (of undetermined range, to date) may respond, but with less vigor, to consonant cues within adjacent frequency bands. A syllable spectrally distant from the test series /da/-/ta/, such as /bi/ might slightly adapt the detector most sensitive to /a/ stop allophones. If presented an adaptor segment of /bi/ alternating with /pa/, the /bi/ would influence /da/ less than /pa/ would influence /ta/. However, this explanation is unable to resolve questions raised concerning the adaptability of the integrative site and the partial interaural transfer of adaptation seen in several studies. These data suggest that, in fact, adaptation may well affect a hierarchy of two levels of acoustic feature processing. Either the higher level, sequential acoustic detectors or the integrative, linguistic detectors could be susceptible to adaptation. To this point, the assumption has been that there is a single relevant acoustic cue for each linguistic feature and therefore the motivation for an integrative, multiply cued detector must appeal to phonetic facts. Indeed, the work of Cooper (1974b) and others (Diehl, 1975; Diehl & Rosenberg, 1977) indicates that multiple cues participate in adaptation.

For example, VOT is but one of a complex of acoustic cues influencing the perception of the voicing feature (e.g., Lisker, 1975; Slis & Cohen, 1969; Stevens & Klatt, 1974; Winitz, LaRiviere, & Herriman, 1975). Cooper (1974b) investigated whether feature detectors other than VOT could be adapted. He sought to determine whether boundary shifts obtained with short-lag and long-lag VOT adaptors also could be obtained with adaptors varying only in their transition durations. One adaptor had a transition duration of 40 msec (indicative of voicelessness). The VOT value was the same for both adaptors and both were heard as /da/ (although the adaptor with the short transition was somewhat ambiguous). On a /pa/-/ba/ continuum in which VOT and transition duration covaried, the long-transition adaptor produced a significant shift of the phoneme boundary toward the voiced end of the continuum. The ambiguous short-transition adaptor produced an insignificant boundary shift toward the voiceless end of the test series. Cooper concluded that the feature detectors were sensitive to the transition duration cue.

Because duration had less adapting power than VOT, transition duration alone appeared ineffective as the sole cue mediating the detection of the voicing feature. Cooper proposed that an integrative site was necessary to weigh the detector output for both cues. The essence of these conclusions for a VOT continuum was supported by the work of Diehl and Rosenberg (1977) who replicated Cooper's results.

Extending the logic of the above experiment to place of articulation, Diehl (1975) examined the adapting effects of burst and transition cues. If an integrative site was being adapted, a significant shift in the phoneme boundary separating /bɛ/ and /dɛ/ would be obtained even when the adaptor and test series were cued by different acoustic information. The results supported this hypothesis. Diehl further observed that when the burst and transitions were heard alone, that is, not recognized as speechlike, they produced no adaptation. Diehl's results supported Cooper's (1974) conclusions that an integrative site was necessary, following an initial lower level acoustic detector site. However, in contrast to Diehl's (1975) results, other investigators have shown that the nonspeechlike burst and transition cues are effective adaptors of speech continua, although their efforts are typically smaller than those produced using complete syllables as adaptors (Diehl, 1976; Pisoni & Tash, 1975; Sawusch, 1977a; Tartter & Eimas, 1975). To account for the partial effects of nonspeech adaptors, it was suggested that while these cues excited the lower level acoustic cue detectors, the resulting activity was insufficient to activate the integrative phonetic detectors. Similarly, because these adaptors were fragments of a phonetic segment, they also may have excited the phonetic detectors, although to a lesser degree. Either explanation allowed the phonetic nature of the integrative site to be preserved, although other investigators (Ades, 1976; Cutting, Rosner, & Foard, 1976; Sawusch, 1977b) have been skeptical of the linguistic nature of the integrative mechanism.

Ades (1976) suggested that most conflicting results could be explained by resorting to a single-level acoustic detector model. Relying on the evidence that feature detectors were sensitive to multiple cues for each feature decision, Ades dispensed with the notion of opposed detector pairs for each feature. Instead he posited detectors for each of the multiple acoustic cues which cue any given phonetic feature. These cues were then amalgamated at a higher integrative level for a phonetic judgment, but this level was not adaptable. Objections to this account were raised on the basis of results which showed that burst-cued adaptors affected the perception of place of articulation in test syllables cued only by transitional information (e.g., Diehl, 1975)—results which suggested that the integrative level was adaptable. While this dilemma could be resolved if one chose to view burst and transition cues as being conjunctive, possessing similar spectral shapes (Blumstein & Stevens, 1979, 1980), and thus capable of exciting the same detectors (Ades, 1976; Ganong, 1978), Ades' (1976) proposal must be rejected on other grounds. The results of several investigations (Ades, 1974b; Miller, 1975; Sawusch, 1977b; Sawusch & Pisoni, 1978) examining the extent to which certain adaptation effects transfer interaurally cannot be explained without recourse to the two-level model.

Sawusch (1977b) reported data suggesting two sites were being separately adapted. Resorting to the notion of spectral specificity as a requirement for the adaptation effect, he manipulated the spectral similarity between the pairs of adaptors in two ways, using paired adaptors taken from opposing ends of /bæ/–/dæ/ test series. First, some of the adaptors were reduced to chirps by removing the steady-state portions of the vowel segments. Then, the formants of one or both the syllable and chirp pairs were logarithmically scaled upward at least one critical bandwidth higher than their counterparts. Both the high and low adaptors produced significant boundary shifts in the normal (unscaled), full-syllable test series. However, the high (scaled) adaptors only had approximately half the adapting effect produced by adaptors in the same frequency range as the test series. To explain this difference in a second experiment, Sawusch (1977b) presented adaptors and test stimuli to opposite ears. If the one-level, spectral-spreading hypothesis (discussed earlier with reference to conflicting vowel-contingent and crossed-series results) was correct, there would be no interaural transfer from the high-frequency adaptors. Based on the two-level model, one would hypothesize either no interaural transfer of the adapting effect of chirps or that such transfer would be less than for the full-syllable adaptors. Further, if both levels of neural processing occur beyond the point of binaural fusion, one might expect 100% transfer for all conditions.

Surprisingly, none of these hypotheses accounts for Sawusch's results. He found that the less potent, high-frequency adaptors produced equal monaural and interaural effects, whereas the effect of the monaurally more potent, low-frequency adaptors suffered a decrement when presented in the interaural procedure. Furthermore, the chirp adaptors produced nearly the same effect as the full-syllable adaptors in the interaural mode. The low-frequency monaural effect which did not fully transfer suggested the existence of a peripheral set of detectors whose responses to speech stimuli were spectrally specific. Additionally, there seemed to be a higher level of integrative detectors whose response was spectrally *non*specific. This was indicated by the essentially complete interaural transfer of the high-frequency adaptors' effects and by the equal strength of the low- and high-frequency adaptors once the peripheral contribution had been eliminated. However, the question regarding the nature of the integrative mechanism remained unanswered.

The results of other investigations of the nature of feature detectors (e.g., Blumstein et al., 1977; Cutting et al., 1976; Samuel & Newport, 1979) generally were compatible with Sawusch's (1977b) conclusions. Briefly, nonspeech adaptors were shown to adapt both nonspeech continua (Cutting et al., 1976) and speech continua (Samuel & Newport, 1979) at both the spectrally specific and nonspecific sites, thereby supporting the contention that the integrative sites tapped operated on *both* acoustic and phonetic information. Because this level did not distinguish between speech and nonspeech, it seemed necessary to conclude that both detector levels functioned on an acoustic basis. A description of this network was offered by Blumstein et al.:

> A two-stage auditory process prior to the identification of a phonetic feature. In the initial stage, the auditory system produces some kind of display of amplitude, frequency, and time. This display is represented as a pattern of excitation of a set of neural elements....At the second stage, it is postulated that a number of selective filters operate on this display, the output of a given filter being maximal when the input display exhibits a particular property or configuration. (1977, p. 1310).

EVIDENCE LEADING TO THE REJECTION OF THE FEATURE DETECTOR NETWORK

The feature detector model in its present state seems tenable and is similar to descriptions of speech processing derived apart from the adaptation paradigm (e.g., Bondarko, Zagorujko, Kozevnikov, Molcanov, & Čistovič, 1970). However, the combined results of several studies (discussed below) cannot successfully be integrated into the present detector framework, forcing either the postulation of yet another level of detectors or the rejection of the detector model.

Remez (1979) wished to examine whether a categorically perceived speech-nonspeech continuum might be adaptable. He suggested that if separate networks mediated the perception of acoustic and linguistic stimuli then the boundary separating his test series would not be adaptable. Furthermore, even if acoustic and linguistic data were processed by the same detectors, he felt there could not be opposed detectors arranged specifically to make the speech–nonspeech distinction. Using the extreme endpoints of an /a/-buzz test series, Remez successfully altered his listeners' placement of the category boundary. After extending these findings to a /ba/-buzz continuum (Remez, 1980), Remez concluded that because this sound distinction was not biologically relevant (i.e., not specific to speech), a feature detector account of this effect was unacceptable. This conclusion can be debated, however, by arguing that the distinction between speech and nonspeech is the most fundamental and necessary one in speech perception and therefore biologically significant. To explain Remez's results (1979, 1980) within the feature detector model, it would be necessary to add an additional level of detectors tuned to the speech–nonspeech contrast. The remaining acoustic analyses would then be performed by either acoustic or linguistic detectors, which would include two separate networks, existing in parallel and responsible for similar feature decisions, depending on the decision (speech or nonspeech) reached by the first set of detectors. Although this proposal adds to the complexity of the feature detector model, it is plausible and supported by other, more recent data.

Testing the Stevens and Klatt (1974) hypothesis that the voiced–voiceless distinction is a consequence of the auditory system's limited ability to perceive temporal order (Hirsh, 1959; Hirsh & Sherrick, 1961), Pisoni (1980) found that a two-tone adaptor set differing in the onsets of the individual spectral components was able to adapt the boundary of similar stimuli varied along the onset dimension. However, two-tone adaptors were ineffective when VOT-varying speech stimuli were employed as the test series. Similarly, Remez, Cutting, and Studdert-Kennedy (1980) revealed that a nonspeech "plucked-string–bowed-string" continuum could be adapted using its extreme end point stimuli as adaptors; however, these adaptors were unsuccessful in altering the perception of a phonetic affricate–fricative continuum even though the test series was varied along the same parameter—stimulus rise time. By postulating an initial level of detectors, the absence of crossed-series adaptation in the above studies can be easily explained because the adaptors would have been processed by detectors separate from those analyzing the speech stimuli. A third study (Ades, 1977) showed contingent adaptation effects for fundamental frequency. This supports the suggestion of an additional level of detectors, if one accepts that this level mediates the process of source assignment for speech from different speakers, as well as the more general speech–nonspeech contrast.

Thus, the detector model now must possess a *minimum* of three distinct levels of analysis: the first level, sensitive to the source of the stimuli; the second level, sensitive to spectrally specific acoustic information; and finally, the third level, responsible for integrating this information from the lower levels to make a final feature decision. Furthermore, this arrangement makes it necessary to propose that there exist a number of independent, identical feature-processing channels to analyze speech arising from different speakers and nonspeech versus speech waveforms. Pisoni (1980) and Remez et al. (1980) reject this triple-stage model because of its complexity and suggest the perception of the features they examined must be, instead, a function of the auditory system's limitations. However, complexity should not be the sole reason for rejecting the feature detector model as it has been developed by the adaptation paradigm. It is not because the model is unable to explain why other investigators (e.g., Diehl, 1976; Samuel & Newport, 1979; Sawusch, 1977a, 1977b; Tartter & Eimas, 1975) found significant adaptation effects for speech using nonspeech adaptors. Because the perception of these adaptors should have been mediated by the nonspeech detector network, it should have been impossible for these adaptors to affect the category boundary separating a speech continuum. This conflict forces the conclusion that other perceptual mechanisms must mediate the adaptation phenomena observed in speech research. The feature detector network cannot successfully predict the occasions during which adaptation will be successful.

There are further grounds for rejecting the notion of feature detectors, independent of the adaptation literature. In his detailed review of evidence for feature detectors, Diehl (1981) suggested that despite their seeming parsimony for perception of isolated syllables—a case where only immediately surrounding cues influence the phonemic decision—the detector network cannot account for changes in identification caused by the more global properties of running speech (e.g., *rate*, Ainsworth, 1974; *language*, Elman, Diehl, & Buchwald, 1977; *and speaker source*, Ladefoged & Broadbent, 1957). In a similar vein, the detector mechanism model has difficulty accounting for the phonemic restoration illusion observed by Warren (1970) and Warren and Obusek (1971). Finally, it should be noted that one of the initial reasons for proposing the feature detector network was to account for the categorical perception of speech. Yet, in recent years this concept also has come under close scrutiny (Studdert-Kennedy, 1980). Certainly, if categorical perception of speech is demonstrated by chinchilla (Kuhl & Miller, 1975, 1978) it is difficult to accept that categorical perception demonstrated by infants (e.g., Eimas, 1974, 1975; Eimas, Siqueland, Jusczyk, & Vigorito, 1971) is mediated by sets of heritable, adaptable detectors for speech.

ALTERNATIVE ACCOUNTS OF ADAPTATION

Without doubt, the adaptation technique taps the auditory system's sensitivity to the multiple cues within the speech signal. Because the feature detector model fails to predict in many instances when an adaptor will successfully alter listeners' perception of phoneme boundaries, alternative explanations of the adaptation data have been generated.

Over the past decade numerous alternatives to the feature detector account have been considered (a complete discussion of these is found in Simon & Studdert-Kennedy, 1978). Among these are variations of Helson's (1964, 1971) adaptation level theory, the perceptual retuning hypothesis tested by Cole and Cooper (1977) and Ainsworth (1977), auditory contrasts examined by Diehl, Elman, and McCusker (1978) and Simon and Studdert-Kennedy (1978), and the response bias account discussed by Cooper et al. (1976), Diehl et al. (1978), and Elman (1978). These proposals have in common their suggestion that contrast- and context-dependent operations are active in linguistic feature processing. They vary in the nature of the influence hypothesized for the effect of adaptation upon phonemic judgments and the amount of influence attributed to prior linguistic experience. For example, adaptation level theory proposes that when subjects are asked to classify the syllables comprising a typical adaptation test series, they base their decision on a reference point which results from the mean and distribution of the stimuli. In this case, prior linguistic experience is given little weight in comparison to the range and central tendency of the adaptor–test series distribution. This account, however, does not accurately predict the changes in identification produced by adaptation, because the obtained boundary shifts are typically smaller than those predicted from adaptation level theory.

A second alternative, the perceptual retuning hypothesis (Ainsworth, 1977; Cole & Cooper, 1977), also is unsuccessful in predicting the outcomes of adaptation experiments. Under this hypothesis, the repeated presentations of the adaptor cause subjects to view this syllable as the best exemplar of its phonemic category. During the identification task, because subjects use the adaptor as a reference, the criteria for admitting a test syllable into the same category are more stringent. However, Ainsworth (1977) has demonstrated that adaptation affects the perception of the adaptor itself, a result contradictory to the retuning hypothesis.

A third alternative hypothesis accounts for selective adaptation as a case of response bias. Quite possibly, the adapting effects are caused by changes in the criteria subjects use to label phones. The response bias account proposes that the perceptual mechanism under study detects phonemes and their features on the basis of both their established probabilities of occurrence, and the acoustic cues that they present. The more contextual information provided regarding the phones to be labeled, the more these probabilities will be predetermined. Thus, the labeling process is a result of the unconscious weighting of the chances that a given linguistic event has occurred. Assuming a 50% probability for each category's occurrence, subjects attempt to retain this balance during adaptation by moving the phoneme boundary closer to the adaptor's category. Extreme shifts of boundary do not occur because the subject comes to the task with a great deal of prior linguistic experience, limiting the movement of the boundary.

The response bias explanation was discounted originally because it was thought that the discrimination technique, used in conjunction with the identification technique, provided an adequate check of potential changes in subjects' labeling criteria. However, the notion that "a specialized processor...has stripped the signal of all normal sensory information" (Liberman, Mattingly, & Turvey, 1972, p. 320) suggested that the discrimination procedure may not free consonants from the labeling process. Therefore, some investigators (Cooper et al. 1976; Wood, 1976) explored the categorical "phoneme-boundary effect" and adaptation with a more sensitive technique—an analysis of signal detectability (for a short review of this technique see Swets, 1971; a lengthier account, Egan, 1975). Originally formulated to examine sensory thresholds, signal detectability allows experimental effects to be separated into components of changes in the criteria used in the decision process. The earliest studies using this technique suggested that the phoneme boundary and adaptation effects were caused by changes in neuronal sensitivity (Cooper et al., 1976; Wood, 1976). Recently, however, investigators have questioned these findings. Diehl et al. (1978) pointed out that the Cooper et al. results did reveal a decrease in sensitivity, but the assumptions put forth by the feature detector model were clearly not met. The feature detector account predicts a monotonic decrease in sensitivity which should have been most evident for the detector responding to the adaptor. However, the decreases in the Cooper et al. data were not uniform, and the test items closest to the adaptor were not the ones to be the most dramatically affected.

In another study more closely meeting the requirements of an analysis of signal detectability, Elman (1979) replicated the finding that some component of the "phoneme-boundary effect" seemed to be caused by changes in sensitivity (Wood, 1976). Elman also demonstrated that the adaptation effect could be accounted for by changes in his subjects' labeling criteria. Furthermore, he found that when using a test series and adaptor taken from the vicinity immediately surrounding the phoneme boundary, an adaptation effect could still be obtained. If the feature detector account were correct, this result would have been impossible. An adaptor close to the phoneme boundary (and therefore within the response range of both detectors) would be unable to differentially affect one detector. Thus, the response bias account of adaptation seemed a plausible alternative to the feature detector model. If the perceptual mechanism suggested by this explanation is the interpreter and integrator proposed, it is reasonable that other manipulations of auditory stimuli also might produce effects similar to those found in the adaptation paradigm.

In the anchoring paradigm, one item in the test series is presented more often than the rest of the stimuli. This procedure is similar to adaptation because the more frequent presentation of the anchoring stimulus also can be assumed to cause subjects to rebalance the distributions of the phonemic categories and in this way create a shift in the phoneme boundary. Consistent anchoring effects have been observed for vowels (Sawusch & Nusbaum, 1979; Simon & Studdert-Kennedy, 1978) and more recently, for consonants (Simon & Studdert-Kennedy, 1978). There seemed to be ample evidence favoring a response bias explanation of the Simon and Studdert-Kennedy data, but the authors felt impelled to conclude that auditory contrast, not response bias, was responsible for the adaptation and anchoring results. They neglected, however, to specify how the auditory contrast account differs from response bias.

If it is assumed that auditory contrast operates at a level closer to consciousness and utilizes more immediate sensory experience (i.e., is less subject to the influence of linguistic experience) than response bias, there is good reason to propose that both feature detectors and response bias operate in the identification of phonemes. Neither mechanism alone can account for both the anchoring and adaptation data. The auditory contrast explanation has merit because it accounts for changes in phonemic decisions resulting in differences in the range occupied by a test series and adaptor (Brady & Darwin, 1978; Miller, 1975), a result which cannot be explained by the response bias account because the width of the categories should not alter the placement of the phoneme boundary as long as the probability of each linguistic category's occurrence remains the same. The results of Diehl et al. (1978), showing that a reliable adaptation effect could be obtained even with a single presentation of the adaptor, also present difficulties for the response bias account which predicts that one presentation of an adaptor should be insufficient and thus unable to alter the already established probabilities. On the other hand, the auditory contrast hypothesis suffers shortcomings as well, for it cannot offer an explanation for the results of Ainsworth (1977) and Miller (1975) who revealed that adaptation affected the identification of the adaptor, as well as other items in the test series. The auditory contrast hypothesis would suggest that an adaptor cannot contrast with itself. Furthermore, auditory contrast assigns a minor role to linguistic experience, and therefore differences in the successfulness of adaptation as a function of the subject's native language (Foreit, 1977) are unexplained. A response bias account is able to offer explanations for both these studies, because shifting probabilities also should affect identification of the adaptor, and prior linguistic experience is hypothesized to be a major determinant of these distributions.

Other data also suggest that both auditory contrast and response bias are at work. Sawusch, Nusbaum, and Schwab (1980), using a combination of the anchoring paradigm and an analysis of signal detectability, examined changes in between- and within-category discriminability for vowels. They found that changes in sensitivity coincided with changes in the perception of /i/, while changes in the perception of /I/ seemed mediated primarily by a shift in their subjects' labeling criterion. These authors also reported that within-category discriminability was found to change for the vowel /i/, but not for /I/. On the basis of these results, Sawusch et al. concluded that auditory contrast operates to shift the points of reference, while response bias operates to redistribute categories between these reference points. Thus, both auditory contrast and response bias play a role in the identification of vowels.

CONCLUSIONS

Having rejected the feature detector model's explanation of adaptation and having suggested a combination of response bias and auditory contrast in its stead, the task at hand becomes one of aligning this account with other speech perception research in an attempt to discover what mechanism (perceptually or physiologically) might operate in the manner proposed—using the immediate context and predetermined probabilities to our ultimate advantage in the perception of speech. Although the suggestion of alternative physiological mechanisms awaits a more complete understanding of sensory physiology, some necessarily tentative mechanisms underlying the phenomenon of adaptation include (a) mechanisms of efferent control, (b) neurochemically regulated mechanisms operating with a "selective attention" purpose, and (c) the neural changes mediating memory and learning.

In the perceptual realm, it should be noted that the distinctions between auditory contrast and response bias are paralleled by distinctions proposed for different stages of the memory process (Crowder & Morton, 1969; Studdert-Kennedy, 1973). Another interesting parallel in the perceptual domain can be found in the illusionary alterations discussed by Warren (1976). As the extent of context surrounding phonemic decisions increases, so do the predetermined probabilities for a linguistic segment's occurrence. This corresponds inversely to the degree of the segment's susceptibility to illusionary alterations, as well as to anchoring and adaptation. Because each of these techniques produces effects as a function of the manipulation of the surrounding context, it might be hypothesized that the mechanism tapped by these procedures is one normally responsible for the normalization of rate, interspeaker variation, speaker identity, and perceptual restorations such as those observed by Warren (1970) and Warren and Obusk (1971). As Warren (1976) suggested, this mechanism seems to operate at a level below consciousness, and in a top-down manner, exerting influence on our interpretation of the acoustic cues processed by the eighth nerve.

To summarize, adaptation has not conclusively determined the neuronal organization of the speech processor, but has helped to identify the pattern of speech processing employed by the auditory system. Studies employing this paradigm have revealed several distinct levels of analysis. The acoustic signal is first examined for the identity of the speaker and distinguished as either speech or nonspeech (Ades, 1977; Elman, 1980; Remez, 1979, 1980). Next, the extreme vowels (or an interpolation of their position relative to the fundamental frequency) are established as points of reference; the acoustic pattern of other vowels is interpreted on the basis of this established background (Sawusch & Nusbaum, 1979; Sawusch, Nusbaum, & Schwab, 1980; Simon & Studdert-Kennedy, 1978). Finally, in view of the fact that the amplitude- and frequency-modulated consonantal signal is laid over the vocalic signal, consonants are labeled as a function of the most outstanding variances produced in the vocalic pattern (Cooper, 1974b; Howell, 1980; Miller & Eimas, 1976; Sawusch & Pisoni, 1978). At each of these levels the acoustic signal encounters an interpretative mechanism which biases linguistic judgment according to the probabilities of occurrence established by prior linguistic experience and the contrasts created by the surrounding situational and sentential context.

REFERENCES

Abbs, J. H., & Sussman, H. M. Neurophysiological feature detectors and speech perception: A discussion of theoretical implications. *Journal of Speech and Hearing Research,* 1971, *14,* 23–36.

Ades, A. E. Some effects of adaptation on speech perception. *Quarterly Progress Report, Research Laboratory of Electronics,* MIT, 1973, *111,* 121–129.

Ades, A. E. How phonetic is selective adaptation? Experiments on syllable position and vowel environment. *Perception & Psychophysics,* 1974, *16,* 61–66. (a)

Ades, A. E. A bilateral component in speech perception. *Journal of the Acoustical Society of America,* 1974, *56,* 610–616. (b)

Ades, A. E. Adapting the property detectors for speech perception. In R. Wales & E. Walker (Eds.), *New approaches to language mechanisms.* Amsterdam: North-Holland, 1976.

Ades, A. E. Source assignment and feature extraction in speech. *Journal of Experimental Psychology: Human Perception and Performance,* 1977, *3,* 673–688.

Ainsworth, W. A. The influence of precursive sequences on the perception of synthesized vowels. *Language and Speech,* 1974, *17,* 103–109.

Ainsworth, W. A. Mechanisms of selective feature adaptation. *Perception and Psychophysics,* 1977, *21,* 365–370.

Bailey, P. J. *Perceptual adaptation to speech: Some properties of detectors for acoustic cues to phonetic distinctions.* Unpublished doctoral dissertation, University of Cambridge (1975, as cited in Cooper), 1979.

Barlow, H. B., & Hill, R. M. Selective sensitivity to direction of movement in ganglion cells of the rabbit retina. *Science,* 1963, *139,* 412–414.

Blumstein, S. E., & Stevens, K. N. Acoustic invariance in speech production: Evidence from measurements of the spectral characteristics of stop consonants. *Journal of the Acoustical Society of America,* 1979, *66,* 1001–1017.

Blumstein, S. E., & Stevens, K. N. Perceptual invariance and onset spectra for stop consonants in different vowel environments. *Journal of the Acoustical Society of America,* 1980, *67,* 648–662.

Blumstein, S. E., Stevens, K. N., & Nigro, G. N. Property detectors for bursts and transitions in speech perception. *Journal of the Acoustical Society of America,* 1977, *61,* 1301–1313.

Bondarko, L. V., Zagorujko, N. G., Kozevnikov, A. P., Molcanov, A. P., & Čistovič, L. A. A model of speech perception by humans [trans. I. Lehiste]. In *Working papers in linguistics, No. 6* (pp. 88–132). Ohio State University, 1970.

Brady, S. A., & Darwin, C. Range effect in the perception of voicing. *Journal of the Acoustical Society of America,* 1978, *63,* 1556–1558.

Campbell, F. W., & Maffei, L. The Tilt after-effect: A fresh look. *Vision Research,* 1971, *11,* 833–840.

Campbell, F. W., & Kulikowsky, J. J. Orientation of selectivity of the human visual system. *Journal of Physiology,* 1966, *197,* 437–445.

Capranica, R. R., Frishkopf, L. S., & Nevo, E. Encoding of geographical dialects in the auditory system of the cricket frog. *Science,* 1973, *182,* 1272–1274.

Cole, R. A., & Cooper, W. E. Perception of voicing in English affricates and fricatives. *Journal of the Acoustical Society of America,* 1975, *58,* 1280–1287.

Cole, R. A., & Cooper, W. E. Properties of friction analyzers for /j/. *Journal of the Acoustical Society of America,* 1977, *62,* 177–182.

Cooper, W. E. Adaptation of phonetic feature analyzers for place of articulation. *Journal of the Acoustical Society of America,* 1974, *56,* 617–627. (a)

Cooper, W. E. Selective adaptation for acoustic cues of voicing in initial stops. *Journal of Phonetics,* 1974, *2,* 255–266. (b)

Cooper, W. E. Selective adaptation to speech. In F. Restle, R. M. Shiffrin, N. J. Castellan, H. Lindman, & D. B. Pisoni (Eds.), *Cognitive theory* (Vol. 1). Hillsdale, NJ: Erlbaum, 1975.

Cooper, W. E. *Speech perception and production: Studies in selective adaption.* Norwood, NJ: Ablex, 1979.

Cooper, W. E., & Blumstein, S. E. A 'labial' feature analyzer in speech perception. *Perception & Psychophysics,* 1974, *15,* 591–600.

Cooper, W. E., Ebert, R. R., & Cole, R. A. Perceptual analysis of stop consonants and glides. *Journal of Experimental Psychology,* 1976, *2,* 92–104.

Crowder, R. G. Precategorical acoustic storage for vowels of short and long duration. *Perception & Psychophysics,* 1973, *13,* 502–506.

Crowder, R. G., & Morton, J. Precategorical acoustic storage (PAS). *Perception & Psychophysics,* 1969, *5,* 365–373.

Cutting, J. E., & Eimas, P. D. Phonetic feature analyzers in the processing of speech by infants. In J. F. Kavanagh & J. E. Cutting (Eds.), *The role of speech in language.* Cambridge, MA: MIT Press, 1975.

Cutting, J. E., Rosner, B. S., & Foard, C. F. Perceptual categories for musiclike sounds: Implications for theories of speech perception. *Quarterly Journal of Experimental Psychology,* 1976, *28,* 361–378.

Diehl, R. L. The effect of selective adaptation on the identification of speech sounds. *Perception & Psychophysics,* 1975, *17,* 48–52.

Diehl, R. L. Feature analyzers for the phonetic dimension stop vs. continuant. *Perception & Psychophysics,* 1976, *19,* 267-272.

Diehl, R. L. Feature detectors for speech: A critical reappraisal. *Psychological Bulletin,* 1981, *89,* 1-18.

Diehl, R. L., Elman, J. L., & McCusker, S. B. Contrast effects on stop consonant identification. *Journal of Experimental Psychology: Human Perception and Performance,* 1978, *4,* 599-609.

Diehl, R. L., & Rosenberg, D. M. Acoustic feature analysis in the perception of voicing contrasts. *Perception & Psychophysics,* 1977, *21,* 418-422.

Egan, J. P. *Signal detection theory and ROC analysis.* New York: Academic Press, 1975.

Eimas, P. D. Auditory and linguistic processing of cues for place of articulation by infants. *Perception & Psychophysics,* 1974, *16,* 513-521.

Eimas, P. D. Speech perception in early infancy. In L. B. Cohen & P. Salapatek (Eds.), *Infant perception.* New York: Academic Press, 1975.

Eimas, P. D., Cooper, W. E., & Corbit, J. D. Some properties of linguistic feature detectors. *Perception & Psychophysics,* 1973, *13,* 247-252.

Eimas, P. D., & Corbit, J. D. Selective adaptation of linguistic feature detectors. *Cognitive Psychology,* 1973, *4,* 99-109.

Eimas, P. D., & Miller, J. L. Effects of selective adaptation on the perception of speech and visual patterns: Evidence for feature detectors. In R. D. Walk & H. L. Pick, Jr. (Eds.), *Perception and experience.* New York: Plenum Press, 1978.

Eimas, P. D., Siqueland, E. R., Jusczyk, P., & Vigorito, J. Speech perception in infants. *Science,* 1971, *171,* 303-306.

Elam, J. L. Perceptual origins of the phoneme boundary effect and selective adaptation to speech: A signal detection theory analysis. *Journal of the Acoustical Society of America,* 1979, *65,* 190-207.

Elman, J. L. Intonation-contingent adaptation to speech. *Perception & Psychophysics,* 1980, *27,* 258-262.

Elman, J. L., Diehl, R. L., & Buchwald, S. E. Perceptual switching in bilinguals. *Journal of the Acoustical Society of America,* 1977, *62,* 971-974.

Evans, E. F. Central mechanisms relevant to the neural analysis of simple and complex sounds. In *Pattern recognition in biological and technical systems.* Heidelberg: Springer, 1971, 327–343.

Foreit, K. G. Linguistic relativism and selective adaptation for speech: A comparative study of English and Thai. *Perception & Psychophysics*, 1977, *21*, 347–351.

Ganong, W. F. III. The elective adaptation of burst cued stops. *Perception & Psychophysics*, 1978, *24*, 71–83.

Helson, H. *Adaptation-level theory: An experimental and systematic approach to behavior.* New York: Harper, 1964.

Helson, H. Adaptation-level theory: 1970 and after. In M. H. Appley (Ed.), *Adaptation level theory.* New York: Academic Press, 1971.

Hirsh, I. J. Auditory perception of temporal order. *Journal of the Acoustical Society of America*, 1959, *31*, 759–767.

Hirsh, I. J., & Sherrick, C. E. Perceived order in different sense modalities. *Journal of Experimental Psychology*, 1961, *62*, 423–432.

Howell, P. Vowel contingent feature detection. *Perception & Psychophysics*, 1980, *27*, 37–42.

Hubel, D. H., & Wiesel, T. N. Receptive fields, binocular interaction and functional architecture in the cat's visual cortex, *Journal of Physiology*, 1962, *160*, 106–154.

Kay, R. H., & Matthews, D. R. On the existence in human auditory pathways of channels selectively tuned to the modulation present in frequency-modulated tones. *Journal of Physiology*, 1972, *225*, 657–677.

Kuhl, P. K., & Miller, J. D. Speech perception by the chinchilla: The voiced–voiceless distinction in alveolar plosive consonants. *Science*, 1975, *190*, 69–72.

Kuhl, P. K., & Miller, J. D. Speech perception by the chinchilla: Identification functions for synthetic VOT stimuli. *Journal of the Acoustical Society of America*, 1978, *63*, 905–917.

Ladefoged, P., & Broadbent, D. E. Information conveyed by vowels. *Journal of the Acoustical Society of America*, 1957, *29*, 98–104.

Lettvin, J. Y., Maturana, H. R., McColloch, W. S., & Pitts, W. H. What the frog's eye tells the frog's brain. *Proceedings of the Institute of Radio Engineers*, 1959, *47*, 1940–1951.

Liberman, A. M., Cooper, F. S., Shankweiler, D. P., & Studdert-Kennedy, M. Perception of the speech code. *Psychological Review*, 1967, *74*, 431–461.

Liberman, A. M., Mattingly, I. G., & Turvey, M. T. Language codes and memory codes. In A. W. Melton & E. Martin (Eds.), *Coding processes in human memory*. Washington, DC: Winston, 1972.

Lisker, L. Is it VOT or a first formant detector? *Journal of the Acoustical Society of America*, 1975, *57*, 1547–1551.

Miller, C. L., & Morse, P. A. Selective adaptation effects in infant speech perception paradigms. *Journal of the Acoustical Society of America*, 1979, *65*, 789–798.

Miller, J. L. Properties of feature detectors for speech: Evidence from the effects of selective adaptation on dichotic listening. *Perception & Psychophysics*, 1975, *18*, 389–397.

Miller, J. L., & Eimas, P. D. Studies on the selective tuning of feature detectors for speech. *Journal of Phonetics*, 1976, *4*, 119–127.

Pisoni, D. B. Auditory short-term memory and vowel perception. *Memory & Cognition*, 1975, *3*, 7–18.

Pisoni, D. B. Adaptation of the relative onset time of two-component tones. *Perception & Psychophysics*, 1980, *28*, 337–346.

Pisoni, D. B., & Tash, J. Auditory property detectors and processing place features in stop consonants. *Perception & Psychophysics*, 1975, *18*, 401–408.

Remez, R. E. Adaptation of the category boundary between speech and nonspeech: A consonantal case against feature detectors. *Cognitive Psychology*, 1979, *11*, 38–57.

Remez, R. E. Susceptibility of a stop consonant to adaptation on a speech-nonspeech continuum: Further evidence against feature detectors in speech perception. *Perception & Psychophysics*, 1980, *27*, 17–23.

Remez, R. E., Cutting, J. E., & Studdert-Kennedy, M. Cross-series adaptation using song and string. *Perception & Psychophysics*, 1980, *27*, 524–530.

Samuel, A., & Newport, E. Adaptation of speech by nonspeech: Evidence for complex acoustic cue detectors. *Journal of Experimental Psychology: Human Perception and Performance*, 1979, *5*, 563–578.

Sawusch, J. R. Selective adaptation effects on end-point stimuli in a speech series. *Perception & Psychophysics*, 1976, *20*, 61–65.

Sawusch, J. R. Processing of place information in stop consonants. *Perception & Psychophysics,* 1977, *22,* 417–426. (a)

Sawusch, J. R. Peripheral and central processes in selective adaptation of place of articulation in stop consonants. *Journal of the Acoustical Society of America,* 1977, *62,* 738–750. (b)

Sawusch, J. R., & Pisoni, D. B. Simple and contingent adaptation effects for place of articulation stop consonants. *Perception & Psychophysics,* 1978, *23,* 125–131.

Sawusch, J. R., & Nusbaum, H. C. Contextual effects in vowel perception. I: Anchor-induced contrast effects. *Perception & Psychophysics,* 1979, *24,* 292–302.

Sawusch, J. R., Nusbaum, H. C. Auditory and phonetic processes in place perception for stops. *Perception & Psychophysics,* 1983, *34,* 560-568.

Sawusch, J. R., Nusbaum, H. C., & Schwab, E. C. Contextual effects in vowel perception II: Evidence for two processing mechanisms. *Perception & Psychophysics,* 1980, *27,* 421–434.

Scharf, B. Critical bands. In J. V. Tobias (Ed.), *Foundations of modern auditory theory* (Vol. I). New York: Academic Press, 1970.

Simon, H. J., & Studdert-Kennedy, M. Selective anchoring and adaptation of phonetic and nonphonetic continua. *Journal of the Acoustical Society of America,* 1978, *64,* 1338–1357.

Slis, J. H., & Cohen, A. On the complex regulating the voiced–voiceless distinction I, II. *Language and Speech,* 1969, *12,* 137–153.

Stevens, K. N. The potential role of property detectors in the perception of consonants. In G. Fant & M. Tatham (Eds.), *Auditory analysis and perception of speech.* New York: Academic Press, 1975.

Stevens, K. N., & Klatt, D. H. Role of formant transitions on the voiced–voiceless distinction for stops. *Journal of the Acoustical Society of America,* 1974, *55,* 653–659.

Studdert-Kennedy, M. Speech perception. *Language and Speech,* 1980, *23,* 45–66.

Swets, J. A. Detection theory and psychophysics: A review. *Psychometrika,* 1961, *26,* 49–63.

Tartter, V. C., & Eimas, P. D. The role of auditory feature detectors in the perception of speech. *Perception & Psychophysics,* 1975, *18,* 293–298.

Uttal, W. R. The psychobiological silly season—or—what happens when neurophysiological data becomes psychological theories. *The Journal of General Psychology,* 1971, *84,* 151–166.

Warren, R. M. Perceptual restoration of missing speech sounds. *Science,* 1970, *167,* 392–393.

Warren, R. Auditory illusions and perceptual processes. In N. J. Lass (Ed.), *Contemporary issues in experimental phonetics* (pp. 389–417). New York: Academic Press, 1976.

Warren, R., & Obusek, C. J. Speech perception and phonemic restorations. *Perception & Psychophysics,* 1971, *9,* 358–362.

Weisstein, N. Beyond the yellow-Volkswagen detector and the grandmother cell: A general strategy for the exploration of operations in human pattern recognition. In R. L. Solso (Ed.), *Contemporary issues in cognitive psychology: The Loyola symposium.* Washington, DC: Winston, 1973.

Whitfield, I. C., & Evans, E. F. Responses of auditory cortical neurons to stimuli of changing frequency. *Journal of Neurophysiology,* 1965, *28,* 655–672.

Winitz, H., LaRiviere, C., & Herriman, E. Variations in VOT in English initial stops. *Journal of Phonetics,* 1975, *3,* 41–52.

Wollberg, Z., & Newman, J. D. Auditory cortex of squirrel monkey: Response patterns of single cells to species-specific vocalizations. *Science,* 1972, *175,* 212–214.

Wood, C. C. Discriminability, response bias, and phoneme categories in discrimination of voice onset time. *Journal of the Acoustical Society of America,* 1976, *60,* 1381–1389.

6
SPEECH AND LANGUAGE ASSESSMENT FOR THE HEARING IMPAIRED

Daun C. Dickie
Ingham Intermediate School District, Mason, Michigan

Karen M. Krygier
Memphis State University

A s a result of current and federal legislation, educators and clinicians are presently faced with the task of assessing the language performance of severely and profoundly hearing-impaired students. Section 121a.532 of the Rules and Regulations for the Implementation of Part B of the Education of the Handicapped Act mandates state and local education agencies shall ensure, at a minimum, that tests and other evaluation materials are provided and administered in the child's native language or other mode of communication, unless it is clearly not feasible to do so, and have been validated for the specific purpose for which they are used. Evaluation materials used should be tailored to assess specific areas of educational need. Those selected and administered should ensure that the test results accurately reflect the child's aptitude or achievement level or whatever other factors the test purports to measure, rather than reflecting the child's impaired sensory, manual, or speaking skills (except where those skills are the factors which the test purports to measure). No single procedure is used as the sole criterion in the evaluation process, and the child's performance should be assessed in all areas related to the suspected disability (Federal Register, 1977, pp. 42496–42497).

While the vast majority of professionals would view such a charge as highly desirable, a paucity of standardized, appropriately normed tests exists which may be reliably used with severely and profoundly hearing-impaired students. In addition, professionals are typically unable to identify research efforts which clearly illustrate that existing standardized tests, which measure language skills, may be reliably used with hearing-impaired populations (Davis, 1974, 1977; Michigan State Department of Education, 1977; Presnell, 1973).

Efforts to comply with such legal mandates frequently result in the indiscriminate use of tests, which have been normed on nonimpaired populations, with hearing-impaired persons. Such tests may or may not be modified in an attempt to assess more accurately the performance of hearing-impaired individuals. For example, the written form may be added to oral presentations of test items in an attempt to minimize the disadvantages encountered as a result of limited auditory input. Modifications made may vary with the individual examiner, thus further confounding the accuracy or reliability of the results of such tests.

An additional alternative employed may be the use of clinician- or teacher-made forms of language assessment. An example of such a technique is suggested by the Michigan Department of Education Assessment Manual, whereby pictures are selected and presented to the child to elicit spontaneous written and expressive (spoken and/or signed) language samples. In such instances, no standardization of stimulus items exists, and results are largely based upon individual observations and judgments.

The above forms of assessment are generally recognized as being acceptable practices when used as a portion of a comprehensive testing battery. However, when used exclusively, they fall short of meeting the charge of providing a comprehensive and nondiscriminatory assessment of language performance for hearing-impaired children. The difficulty of adequately assessing language performance of such a population is compounded by the type of communication method utilized by the child being tested.

Presently, two major education and communication systems are used with hearing-impaired children in the United States. The first of these, the *aural–oral* approach, stresses the development of communication skills by emphasizing oral speech, speech reading, and auditory training. The use of any manual system is excluded in expressive or receptive strategies. The second approach, *total communication*, is defined by Denton (1970) as including "the full spectrum of language modes—child-devised gestures, formal sign language, speech, speech reading, fingerspelling, reading and writing."

Much controversy exists in the literature as to the benefits or appropriateness of either method (Bates, 1975; Drumm, 1972; Lane, 1976; Miller, 1970; Vernon, 1972). However, much of the available information is emotional in nature as opposed to data based. The reader is frequently confronted with position statements, rather than content-oriented sources addressing communication method and related testing implications.

The need exists to objectively examine appropriate standardized procedures for hearing-impaired populations as related to both education and communication methodologies. The following review examines research to date relative to communication methodology. In addition, speech–language testing strategies with hearing-impaired children are discussed.

AURAL–ORAL COMMUNICATION

The publications advocating the use of a strictly aural–oral approach for hearing-impaired children are characterized by a profound degree of enthusiasm, but minimal documentation. Such statements as "Oralism is not an academic exercise...It is a way of life" are typical of the highly zealous attitudes of its proponents (Miller, 1970). As has been stated, an aural–oral approach would stress the teaching of communication skills utilizing speech, speech reading, and auditory training. The use of sign language or finger spelling is forbidden, as it is felt that its inclusion would impede the development of speech (Olson, 1972; Van Uden, 1970). Much emphasis is placed upon early amplification and auditory training to maximize the use of any residual hearing which may be present.

The philosophical premise motivating such a commitment stresses the right of every deaf individual to function in society as a whole (Connor, 1972). To do so successfully, it is felt that the child must be adequately prepared to communicate in a normal environment (Position Paper, 1975; Stone, 1968). This end would negate the use of any "restricting" manual communication modes. The premise is that a child given the choice of speech only, versus a combination of speech and manual strategies, would most certainly choose the "easier" communication method at the expense of successful auditory-oral development (Owrid, 1972). Documentation for such a predicting attitude is not available in the literature to date. The difficulty of providing a truly aural-oral education is readily acknowledged by its proponents (Stone, 1968). However, enthusiastic position papers, plentiful in the literature, serve as motivating sources for continued application.

No data-based articles using large numbers of students have been identified which objectively legitimize an aural-oral approach. Further, in no report has the benefit of such an approach for speech, speech reading, or auditory training development been shown to be superior to that of total communication. The majority of articles typically describe specific successful case studies, or deal with broad generalizations relative to the needs of the hearing-impaired population as a whole (Blevins, 1976; Connor, 1972; Lane, 1976; Miller, 1970). Proponents frequently point out the need for quantifiable, supportive research to illustrate the superiority of an aural-oral approach. Such a charge was made to the profession as early as 1917 by Goldstein and continues to be reiterated by current authors. However, to date, no such quantifiable results are available.

TOTAL COMMUNICATION

Total communication is typically understood to include all aspects of the aural-oral approach, as well as the addition of finger spelling and the use of signs (Furfey, 1974). Proponents of this approach stress the utilization of all available forms of input and claim that the hearing-impaired child is better able to assimilate language. This belief is predicated upon such factors as the following:

1. The "invisibility" of numerous speech sounds (Hardy, 1970);

2. The dual or multiple meanings of words in the English language which require contextual and/or visible cues to determine the meaning;

3. This importance of receptive language skills being established during the critical early years of life (Alterman, 1970) as a prerequisite skill to that of speech acquisition (Olson, 1972).

Although a broad definition of total communication is generally recognized and accepted by educators, several forms of the necessary manual aspects of communication presently exist (Bornstein, 1973). Examples of these are Seeing Essential English, Signed English, Signing Exact English, Amaslan, and Visual

English. The fact that multiple sign systems may be operating within the inclusive category of total communication has been criticized by professionals favoring an aural–oral approach (Blevins, 1976). Educators of both of these philosophical predispositions stress the need for quantifiable research documenting the benefits of each sign system, if such exist.

As is true for the aural–oral method, numerous subjective articles may be found which advocate the use of total communication. Vernon (1972) stresses the need for such an approach from a "common sense" point of view. He states that the National Association of the Deaf has officially endorsed the use of total communication. This endorsement by deaf persons themselves, who "know better than anyone else the terrible educational and psychological deprivation resulting from a restriction to just oralism" (p. 530), is felt by the author to be justification for the use of such a combined approach.

Many of the studies which do use any form of measurement techniques to document claims made often are based upon the performance of a single subject. Olson (1972) described the linguistic development of a preschool hearing-impaired child over a 3-year period during which "Sign Language therapy" was stressed. He concluded that "the child has a big jump on those acoustically handicapped children who are still not attending to lip movement at age three" (p. 399). Articles of this type, based upon isolated samples, lend minimal support for any approach.

During recent years, research has been undertaken to document, on a broad scale, the benefits of a total communication approach. Vernon, Westminster, and Koh (1971) studied the speech and language skills of 123 graduates of 3-year oral preschool programs. Their performance was compared to that of (1) deaf children of deaf parents (manual communication between parents and child assumed), and (2) deaf children who had received no preschool training. Their results showed that deaf students who had received early manual training and no preschool experience were superior in academic and language performance to those students who had experienced an oral preschool program. It should be noted, however, that the subjects studied were in their adolescent years at the time of the comparative investigation. Numerous variables were not controlled, including the fact that the majority of all subjects investigated did not remain in or attend aural–oral programs.

Several large-scale descriptive studies which are frequently used to support the use of total communication are described by Nix (1975). Babbidge (1965) reports educational and achievement data on 269 schools and classes for the deaf, involving a total of 23,330 children. The resulting implication of this study is that low achievement levels of hearing-impaired students are positively related to aural–oral program instruction.

In a survey of 26 public residential schools, Denton (1966) reported on the scores of deaf students on the Stanford Achievement Test. Those students obtaining the highest scores on grade equivalent averages and language performance areas were those who had deaf parents. The author concluded that the higher average scores may be attributed to the early learning of a manual communication system.

Furfey (1974) studied the social abilities of 137 deaf adults. A case study format, based upon rating scales completed following home visits, was used. The author concluded that proficiency in manual communication was highly important for the socialization skills of deaf persons. He further stated that persons who had attended oral schools often failed to learn effectively either aural–oral or a manual communication form. Letournea and Young (1975) described the implementation of a total communication program at a school for the deaf in New York, as well as the research procedures planned to study its effectiveness. The results at the time of publication, however, relied upon teacher impressions of related language gains and social–emotional benefits.

Although articles and research efforts such as those previously described may serve to promulgate much discussion and/or dissension among professionals, they do little to provide conclusive, objective findings for the issue under investigation. The designs of such studies are most frequently descriptive in nature and are not appropriately conducted to determine the advisability or superiority of either method. Efforts to control for such variables as degree of hearing loss, type of instruction, use of standardized assessment tools, and age at onset of loss have not been evidenced in the majority of these studies.

In an attempt to address needs such as those previously mentioned, White and Stevenson (1975) examined the effectiveness of the manual form of communication using an experimental research design. They studied the performance of 45 students between the ages of 11.0 and 18.7 years, who were enrolled in one of two public residential schools for the deaf. Variables such as intelligence quotient and degree of hearing loss were controlled in a stratified random sample selection of students. A language assessment task was presented to each student through oral, manual, total communication, and reading modes, in an attempt to determine the most effective method for assimilation of information. Their results showed that the highest degree of information was transmitted through the written form, followed by manual communication and total communication, respectively. The amount of information assimilated through the oral presentation was less than that of any of the other above-mentioned approaches.

A replication of this study was conducted at a residential school for the deaf, at which the staff espoused an aural–oral philosophy for the training of students. The results of this second study supported those of the previous investigation in terms of the effectiveness of language reception using the various communication methods.

A study by Moores (1978) involved a longitudinal evaluation of seven early education programs. These programs differed as to educational methodology (total communication, auditory, oral–aural, Rochester method), settings (day, residential), orientation (nursery, cognitive, academic), emphasis (parent or child centered), and placement (integrated, self-contained). Evaluation continued over a 4-year period. Relative to receptive communication, the results determined that the mode that provided the greatest understanding was the combined use of sound, speech reading and signs when compared to printed messages, sound alone, and sound and speech reading, and sound, speech reading, and finger spelling. In addition, results of receptive and expressive communication performance suggested that manual communication did not have a negative effect on the use of residual hearing or speech reading.

Moulton and Beasley (1975) studied the verbal coding strategies of 26 severely hearing-impaired students using a total communication approach. The stimulus items selected consisted of four lists of word pairs which were described as sharing either (1) similar sign–similar meaning, (2) dissimilar sign–similar meaning, (3) similar sign–dissimilar meaning, or (4) dissimilar sign–dissimilar meaning. The study was designed to obtain information relative to the verbal coding strategies used by hearing-impaired subjects as related to proficiency in processing verbal information on a sign or semantic basis. Their results showed that while coding was possible using either basis, the semantic coding strategy appeared to be the more efficient method. That is, hearing-impaired subjects performed best when words shared either a similar meaning ("clean–wash") or a similar meaning and similar sign ("pretty–beautiful").

When contrasting studies dealing with auditory–oral and total communication modes, the variability inherent in hearing impaired children's communication skills should be considered. Therefore, several scales have been developed in an attempt to assist in the evaluation of young hearing-impaired children's communication performance. One such scale is the Deafness Management Quotient (DMQ) developed by Downs (1974). The DMQ assesses five major areas including (1) residual hearing, (2) central intactness, (3) intellectual factors, (4) family constellation, and (5) socioeconomic situation. The respective scores in these five areas are weighted and the resultant overall score assists in making a recommendation for either a total communication or auditory–oral mode of communication to be used with the child.

Another scale that was designed to determine the most appropriate route for language stimulation is "Feasibility Scale for Language Acquisition Routing" (FSLAR) developed by Rupp, Smith, Briggs, Litvin, Banachoueski, and Williams (1977). The scale addresses seven major areas identified as prognostic factors for language acquisition. These include (1) amount and configuration of residual hearing, (2) age of the child, (3) parental interaction, (4) other possible handicaps, (5) the child's general behavior in the testing situation, (6) the present form of communication used by the child, and (7) possible subjective responses to amplification. These factors have been analyzed as they apply to preprimary hearing-impaired students in an attempt to ascertain the appropriateness of an aural–oral or total communication form of communication training. The actual documentation for the predictive capabilities of the scale have been assessed through case study follow-up procedures.

These latter studies are among the first to provide experimental data relative to methodologies (aural–oral and total communication) being examined and serve as a point of departure for continued scientific investigation in this area. They do not, however, utilize or provide standardized assessment techniques for measuring the language performance of public school elementary age hearing-impaired students. In addition, no similar articles have been identified which experimentally demonstrate the benefits of an aural–oral approach for such a population.

INVESTIGATIONS RELATED TO TESTING PROCEDURES FOR HEARING–IMPAIRED CHILDREN

Vernon and Brown (1964) describe general considerations for psychological testing of hearing-impaired students and offer subjective evaluations as to the appropriateness of tests normed on hearing populations for use with the deaf and hard of hearing. Sachs, Trybus, Koch, and Falberg (1974), in addressing the issue of psychological evaluations of deaf individuals, point out that attention is increasingly being directed to better measurement instruments for use with the hearing impaired. The lack of normative data on hearing-impaired students for the majority of test instruments presently in use is identified as being a severe limitation to adequate evaluation. Schildroth (1976) has identified factors which may influence the legitimate application of existing tests to hearing-impaired populations. Among these is the need by the examiner to possess a knowledge of deafness, as well as familiarity in communicating with deaf individuals.

Large-scale standardized testing efforts of the performance of hearing-impaired students have focused primarily on the areas related to academic achievement. A Special Edition for Hearing Impaired of the 1973 Stanford Achievement Test was standardized nationally using a stratified random sample of 6,871 hearing-impaired subjects. Data are now available for students' performance from all 50 states and several foreign countries. Using this instrument, Trybus and Karchmer (1977) reported on the national school achievement scores of hearing-impaired children over a 3-year period. As a result of the existing norms for this evaluation tool, it is possible to compare an individual child's performance with those of both hearing and hearing-impaired populations. Further, the establishment of such an instrument enables the use of test scores to assist in the monitoring of pupil and program progress. In addition, accommodations for special requirements of testing hearing-impaired students using the Stanford Achievement Test have been reported by Allen, White, and Karchmer (1983). Modifications of the previous edition of the Stanford Achievement Test were made in order to make this test a more reliable and valid instrument to be used with hearing-impaired children.

While gains have been demonstrated in the area of assessment procedures for hearing-impaired students in the academic and psychological domains, minimal attempts have been undertaken to address this need in the measurement of receptive language skills. Rather, Siegel and Broen (1976) state that formal tests in general are inadequate in dealing with the wide range of children encountered. They are of the opinion that an excessive amount of time is spent in trying to "fit the child to the model." They describe the best form of language assessment as being an informed clinician who is not overly attached to a single method of assessment. While such an opinion may have subjective appeal, the fact remains that very few formal tests or documented models of assessment have been proven to be appropriate for hearing-impaired populations.

One such test designed for hearing-impaired children includes the Test of Syntactic Abilities (Quigley, Wilber, Power, Montanelli, & Steinkamp, 1976). This test was designed to assess hearing-impaired children's knowledge of a wide variety of syntactic structures of English. It was developed specifically for deaf children who range in age from 10 to 18 years. This test is presented in written form and must therefore be used with children who are able to read. It can be a useful tool when used as part of a battery of tests in evaluating a hearing-impaired child's language skills. The test has several important design factors which support its use, including normative data on deaf individuals in addition to the age range of 10 to 18 years.

Since so few tests have proven to be appropriate for use with the hearing-impaired population, some major studies have recently been conducted in an attempt to address this need. Davis (1977) examined the reliability of the Test of Auditory Comprehension of Language (Carrow, 1973) when used with 18 elementary age hearing-impaired children. Ten of the subjects demonstrated mild to moderate levels of hearing loss and used an aural–oral communication approach. The remaining eight subjects demonstrated severe to profound losses and utilized a total communication approach. The test was administered to each child on two occasions using the communication presentation method with which each child was familiar. Results indicated high reliability of responses for both groups of children. Error patterns for each group were examined and proved to be similar in type. No description of individual or group scores on the test was presented.

Davis concluded that the Test of Auditory Comprehension of Language appeared to be an appropriate and reliable test for use in assessment of receptive language skills of hearing-impaired children. While numerous variables were not controlled in subject selection, and comparisons of individual and group performance is not possible, this study does serve as an indicator of a possible measure of receptive language performance for use with hearing-impaired children.

In an earlier investigation, Davis (1974) addressed the need for language assessment tools. She studied the performance of 24 hard-of-hearing children (ages 6 years to 8 years, 11 months) on the Boehm Test of Basic Concepts (1971). Their performance on this task was compared to that of 24 normal-hearing children of a similar age range. Responses were analyzed according to age level and degree of hearing loss. Percentile rankings revealed that 75% of the hearing-impaired children scored at or below the 10th percentile when compared to the norms of normal-hearing children of the same age or younger. This finding was particularly significant in view of the fact that none of the hearing-impaired subjects of the study were more than 2 years behind the normal-hearing subjects in academic placement, and seven were enrolled in grade levels appropriate to their chronological ages. Therefore, the fact that 75% of the hearing-impaired subjects scored below the 10th percentile in terms of knowledge of basic language concepts raises crucial questions as to the probability of academic success for this population.

Results indicated that significant differences in test performance were associated with the degree of hearing loss. That is, the greater the loss of hearing, the poorer were the language skills as measured by the test. However, the author did not specify levels of hearing loss other than by the use of the labels "mild" and "moderate." No significant differences in test performance were found between the older and younger hearing-impaired children.

The Davis studies are limited in the number and type of subjects selected, and do not report attempts to control for numerous possible confounding variables. However, they do serve to illustrate test procedures which may be utilized in the assessment of language performance in hearing-impaired populations.

A study was conducted which demonstrated that an existing standardized test of receptive language performance may be reliably used with severely and profoundly hearing-impaired children. Dickie (1979) investigated the receptive language performance of elementary age severely and profoundly hearing-impaired children using the Boehm Test of Basic Concepts. Fifteen of the subjects had been taught using an aural–oral approach, and another fifteen were educated in a total communication environment, resulting in a total of thirty subjects. Each of the 50 test items of the Boehm Test of Basic Concepts was presented to each child twice, using the communication method with which each subject was familiar. The subjects' task was to mark a pictorial representation of the stimulus item. The results revealed that the children of the total communication group performed significantly better than did their aural–oral counterparts. Age of subjects was not found to be related to test performance for either group. The reliability of results obtained during test–retest administration was found to be high for both groups of subjects. However, the internal reliability of this test was higher for subjects of the aural–oral group. This was due to a ceiling effect for scores correct which was evidenced for subjects using a total communication approach.

Very few tests have been designed for multiply handicapped children. A scale which was specifically designed to assess deaf–blind and other multiply handicapped children is the Callier-Azuza Scale (Stillman, 1976). This scale assesses the areas of (1) motor development, (2) perceptual development, (3) daily living skills, (4) language development, and (5) socialization. It was developed for children from 0 to 108 months of age and can be useful in identifying a child's level of language development. The accuracy of the scale is somewhat questionable without a large number of observations of the child's behavior.

DISCUSSION

Public Law 94-142 mandates that handicapped children must be educated in the least restrictive environment which is deemed appropriate to meet individual needs. As a result, numerous hearing-impaired children are being considered for placement in general education classrooms for varying portions of the school day. Trybus and Karchmer (1977) report that, at the time of investigation, 19% of hearing-impaired students were being served in integrated programs consisting of part-time classes, resource rooms, or itinerant services. Such forms of integration may stress social, academic, or a combination of these areas of need for each child.

Decisions as to the appropriateness of such placements continue to be predicated primarily upon staff and parental input, as well as academic performance in selected subjects. The need exists, both as a result of legal mandates as well as concern for successful experiences for children, to identify instruments which may be reliably used to measure the language performance of these children. The documentation obtained could then be used, in combination with staff input and academic performance, to make more appropriate recommendations for programming.

The results of studies reviewed to date would suggest that elementary level hearing-impaired children of both aural–oral and total communication groups, regardless of chronological age, demonstrate severe limitations in their receptive language abilities. The tests discussed measure a very limited sampling of the multitude of concepts which the hearing-impaired child may be expected to encounter in the very early elementary grades. If, however, these tests are indeed indicative of the broader range of language concepts necessary for academic and social success, then all of the hearing-impaired students tested demonstrate severe limitations and are highly disadvantaged.

It would appear that the Boehm Test of Basic Concepts and the Test of Auditory Comprehension of Language are instruments which could be used with hearing-impaired children in an attempt to more objectively assess the appropriateness of placement in a regular education classroom. In addition, the Test of Syntactic Abilities can be a useful tool in the assessment of a hearing-impaired child's knowledge of syntactic structures. Examiners, of course, should realize that test performance represents behavior which may be expected to occur under more ideal conditions than are encountered in an ongoing classroom experience. Nevertheless, when used as an additive source of input to existing procedures, these instruments could serve to enhance the validity of judgments made relative to appropriate child placement and programming.

IMPLICATIONS FOR RESEARCH

The studies discussed above have demonstrated that the overall performance of the subjects investigated was found to be low when compared to normal-hearing children of younger ages. Further research is needed to determine the percentile or criteria of performance on assessment instruments necessary for successful academic performance in regular educational placements. Research designed to correlate test scores with an "integration adequacy index" could result in a predictive instrument which would strengthen present subjective judgments of recommendations for student placement and programming.

An obvious area requiring further research is that with regard to the nature of the test used in these studies. A single test, designed to assess receptive language performance through a representative sampling of basic concepts, was employed in the studies reviewed. While data-based information has recently been obtained, the need exists to expand such investigations to other standardized instruments for use with hearing-impaired children. Further, the need continues to exist for the identification of instruments which assess additional areas of language performance which have been demonstrated as reliable for use with children who use total communication.

Additional research is needed to determine whether the findings of the studies to date, with regard to subject performance, would be similar for students using a variety of sign systems. Also, future research efforts should include a variety of subject ages and degrees of hearing loss in order to permit broad-based applications of results.

Research also is needed to address the question of how hearing-impaired students of aural–oral and total communication programs perform on measures of receptive language, controlling for the amount of prior exposure to the concept presented in the testing situation. In the studies reviewed, it is impossible to determine conclusively why the total communication subjects perform better than their aural–oral counterparts. The question must be raised as to the degree of exposure to the various concepts presented that the children of each program had experienced. A study designed to match the number of exposures for children of both groups could better ascertain the effectivenss of conceptual learning by children as related to presentation method.

Finally, numerous hearing-impaired students exhibit multiple handicaps, thereby increasing the difficulty of appropriate performance assessment. However, the need most definitely exists to identify additional instruments which may be reliably used with this population.

Jensema and Trybus (1978) state that too often educators favor a "quick jump to the bottom line" approach to obtain information related to highly complex issues. They stress that the factors related to the communication patterns and achievement levels of hearing-impaired students cannot be properly understood or evaluated, except in their complexity. The critical need for continued experimental examination, to determine appropriate assessment procedures, is an absolute necessity for meeting the goal of providing more effective programming for hearing-impaired children.

REFERENCES

Allen, T., White, C. & Karchmer, M. Issues in the development of a special edition for hearing-impaired students of the seventh edition of the Stanford Achievement Test. *American Annals of the Deaf*, 1983, *128*, 34–39.

Alterman, A. Language and the education of children with early profound deafness. *American Annals of the Deaf*, 1970, *115*, 514–521.

Babbidge, H. *Education of the deaf. A report to the secretary of health, education and welfare by his advisory committee on the education of the deaf.* Washington, DC: U.S. Government Printing Office, 1965.

Bates, A. Controversy in the education of the deaf. *The Teacher of the Deaf*, 1975, *73*, 272–281.

Blevins, B. The myth of total communication. *AOEHI Bulletin*, 1976, 2–6.

Boehm, A. *Boehm Test of Basic Concepts manual.* New York: Psychological Corporation, 1971.

Bornstein, H. A description of some current sign systems designed to represent English. *American Annals of the Deaf*, 1973, *118*, 454–463.

Carrow, E., *The test for auditory comprehension of language.* Austin, TX: Learning Concepts, 1973.

Connor, L. That the deaf may hear and speak. *The Volta Review*, 1972, *74*, 518–527.

Davis, J. Performance of young hearing impaired children on a test of basic concepts. *Journal of Speech and Hearing Research*, 1974, *17*, 342–351.

Davis, J. Reliability of hearing impaired children's responses to oral and total presentations of the test of auditory comprehension of language. *Journal of Speech and Hearing Disorders*, 1977, *42*, 520–527.

Davis, H. & Silverman, S. *Hearing and deafness*. New York: Holt, Rinehart, & Winston, 1970.

Denton, D. *A study in the educational achievement of deaf children*. Report of the proceedings of the 42nd meeting of the convention of American Instructors of the Deaf (pp. 428–433). Washington, DC: U. S. Government Printing Office, 1966.

Denton, D. *Total communication*. Maryland School for the Deaf, October, 1970.

Dickie, D. Performance of severely and profoundly hearing impaired children on auditory/oral and total communication presentations of the Boehm Test of Basic Concepts. Unpublished doctoral dissertation, Michigan State University, 1979.

Downs, M. The deafness management quotient. *Hearing and Speech News*, 1974, *42*, 8–9; 26–28.

Drumm, P. Total communication—fraud or reality? *The Volta Review,* 1972, *74*, 564–569.

Federal Register. *Education of handicapped children* (Implementation of Part B of the Education of the Handicapped Act). Department of Health, Education and Welfare, Office of Education, August, 1977.

Furfey, P. Total communication and the Baltimore deaf survey. *American Annals of the Deaf*, 1974, *119*, 377–381.

Goldstein, M. The society of progressive oral advocates: Its origin and purpose. *The Volta Review*, 1917, *19*, 443–447.

Hardy, M. Speechreading. In H. Davis & S. Silverman (Eds.), *Hearing and deafness*. New York: Holt, Rinehart, & Winston, 1970.

Jensema, C., & Trybus, R. *Communication patterns and educational achievement of hearing impaired students*. Washington, DC: Office of Demographic Studies, Galludet College, 1978.

Lane, H. Thoughts on oral advocacy today...with memories of the society of oral advocates. *The Volta Review*, 1976, *78*, 136–143.

Letournea, N., & Young, V. Total communication shuffles off to Buffalo. *American Annals of the Deaf*, 1975, *120*, 493–498.

Michigan State Department of Education. *Information necessary for the placement of students*. Lansing: Department of Education, 1977.

Miller, J. Oralism is not an academic exercise—it is a way of life. *The Volta Review*, 1970, *72*, 211–217.

Moores, D. *Educating the deaf: Psychology, principles, and practices*. Boston: Houghton Mifflin, 1978.

Moulton, R., & Beasley, D. Verbal coding strategies used by hearing impaired individuals. *Journal of Speech and Hearing Research*, 1975, *18*, 559–570.

Nix, G. Total communication: A review of studies offered in its support. *The Volta Review*, 1975, *77*, 470–494.

Olson, J. A case for the use of sign language in critical years. *American Annals of the Deaf*, 1972, *117*, 397–400.

Owrid, H. Education and communication. *The Volta Review*, 1972, *74*, 225–234.

A position paper of the American organization for the education of hearing impaired. *The Volta Review*, 1975, *77*, 16–19.

Presnell, L. Hearing impaired children's comprehension and production of syntax in oral language. *Journal of Speech and Hearing Research*, 1973, *16*, 12–21.

Quigley, S., Wilbur, R., Power, D., Montanelli, D., & Steinkamp, H. *Syntactic structures in the language of deaf children*. Champaign—Urbana: University of Illinois Press, 1976.

Rupp, R., Smith, M., Briggs, P., Litvin, K., Banachoueski, S., & Williams, R. A feasibility scale for language acquisition routing for young hearing-impaired children. *Language, Speech and Hearing Services in Schools*, 1977, *8*, 222–232.

Sachs, B., Trybus, R., Koch, H. & Falberg, R. Current developments in the psychological evaluation of deaf individuals. *Journal of Rehabilitation of the Deaf*, 1974, *8*, 132–141.

Schildroth, A. The relationship of nonverbal intelligence test scores to selected characteristics of hearing impaired students. In C. Williams (Ed.), *Proceedings of the third Gallaudet symposium on research in deafness: Educational development research problems*. Washington DC: Gallaudet College Press, 1976.

Siegel, G., & Broen, P. Language assessment. In L. Lloyd (Ed.), *Communication assessment and intervention strategies.* Baltimore: University Park Press, 1976.

Stillman, E. (Ed.). *The Callier-Azuza Scale.* Dallas: Callier Center for Communication Disorders, University of Texas at Dallas, 1976.

Stone, A. Oral education—a challenge and a necessity. *The Volta Review,* 1968, *70,* 289–292.

Trybus, R., & Karchmer, M. School achievement scores of hearing impaired children: National data on achievement status and growth patterns. *American Annals of the Deaf Directory of Programs and Services,* 1977, *122,* 62–69.

Van Uden, A. New realizations in the light of the pure oral method. *American Annals of the Deaf,* 1970, *72,* 524–536.

Vernon, M. Mind over mouth—A rationale for total communication. *The Volta Review, 1972, 74,* 529–539.

Vernon, M., & Brown, D. A guide to psychological tests and testing procedures in the evaluation of deaf and hard-of-hearing children. *Journal of Speech and Hearing Disorders,* 1964, *29,* 414–423.

Vernon, M., Westminster, M., & Koh, S. Effects of oral preschool compared to early manual communication on education and communication in deaf children. *American Annals of the Deaf,* 1971, *116,* 569–573.

White, A., & Stevenson, V. The effects of total communication, oral communication and reading on the learning of factual information in residential school for deaf children. *American Annals of the Deaf,* 1975, *120,* 48–57.

7
THE ROLE OF VESTIBULAR FUNCTION IN THE DEVELOPMENT OF COMMUNICATION

David G. Cyr

Kathryn A. Beauchaine
Boys Town National Institute for Communication Disorders in Children

*T*he vestibular system interacts with the proprioceptive and visual centers to provide information for the maintenance of head and body posture, eye position and movement, muscle tonus, and equilibrium (de Quiros, 1978; Eviatar & Eviatar, 1979; Eviatar, Eviatar, & Naray, 1974; Molina-Negro, Betrand, Martin, & Gioani, 1980; White, Post, & Leibowitz, 1980). The acquisition of these abilities is a prerequisite to the development of motor skills and eventual academic abilities such as reading and writing.

The systematic physical and cognitive development of a child's ability to interact successfully with his environment has been documented extensively (Ginsberg & Opper, 1969; Knobloch & Pasamanick, 1974). Deficits in sensorimotor and/or cognitive systems impose obstacles to environmental adaptation and to the subsequent acquisition of skills needed for communication and learning. Normal acquisition of these skills is impaired when there are deficits in major sensory systems such as hearing or vision. Investigators in the fields of communication and learning disabilities have begun to document relationships between learning disorders and subtle signs of dysfunction within these sensory systems (de Quiros, 1976a, 1976b, 1978; Lloyd & Pavlidis, 1978; Pavlidis, 1981; Pavlidis, 1979; Steinberg & Randle-Short, 1977). For example, de Quiros (1979) has described vestibular dysfunction that results in postural disorders, as a potential factor in learning and/or language disabilities, a contention which has been supported by several investigators. Ayers (1975) has proposed that disordered muscle tonus, secondary to vestibular pathology, may be a factor in visual perception in learning-disabled children. Further, the occurrence of vestibular disorders has been investigated in children with unilateral and bilateral hearing loss (Brookhouser, Cyr, & Beauchaine, 1982; Eviatar & Eviatar, 1978; Hyden, Odkvist, & Kylen, 1979; Stool, Black, Craig, & Laird, 1981). Eviatar and Eviatar (1978) have suggested that delayed acquisition of postural control in children with congenital deafness may be related to vestibular dysfunction. Seldom, however, are vestibular disorders suspected as contributing to postural delays or disorders that relate to the inability to effectively control head position and/or eye movement in children with normal peripheral hearing, an idea that has significant intuitive appeal. Recently, attention has been directed to this area, specifically as it relates to dyslexia (de Quiros, 1976b; Levinson, 1980, 1981).

In this chapter, a discussion of the vestibular and ocular motor systems and how these systems interact in the development of learning and communication is presented.

THE MAINTENANCE OF BALANCE, POSTURE, AND EQUILIBRIUM

The vestibular apparatus of the inner ear and the ascending ocular pathways are connected intimately with both proprioceptive and visual motor systems in the maintenance of equilibrium. The interaction between these systems and the regulation and control exercised by brainstem and cerebellar structures is critical to the acquisition of developmental reflexes and postural control.

The vestibular end organs provide information to the brain for detection of both linear and angular acceleration and head position relative to gravity. The inner ear vestibular apparati do not respond to loss of balance until head movement of approximately 2 to 3° occurs, whereas visual and ocular motor systems detect velocity and acceleration at frequency levels lower than the threshold level of the vestibular system. This lends credence to the assumption that the vestibular end organs may function primarily to control eye and head movement and position, rather than to solely respond to loss of equilibrium (Barnes, 1975). Indeed, the immediate reaction to loss of balance while in the standing position is a proprioceptive response rather than a vestibular response. Since most proprioceptive input is mediated at the spinal level, while equilibrium and visual inputs are mediated at the brainstem/midbrain and cortical levels, it could be argued that the reaction to loss of balance follows the hierarchy of central nervous system development (Fiorentino, 1978).

The integration of vestibular and visual inputs occurs centrally and coordinates head and eye movements during visual search. This is true whether the individual is in motion relative to the environment, or the environment is in motion relative to the individual. The vestibular portion of the reflex can enhance visual pursuit when the head is turning rapidly by generating compensatory eye movements that stabilize an image on the retina (Bohmer & Pfaltz, 1980). Conversely, the vestibular system can inhibit visual pursuit and fixation by creating an inappropriate nystagmus such as in unilateral labyrinthitis, Meniere's Disease, or benign paroxysmal vertigo. In other words, the vestibular end organs can affect ocular motor movements in an inhibitory or facilitory manner. Since vestibular response is measured through the ocular motor system, dysfunction in the vestibulo-ocular pathways can affect measures of vestibular integrity.

METHODS OF VESTIBULAR EVALUATION

In order to delineate the interaction between vestibular function and ocular motor movements as they relate to skills such as writing or reading, a sensitive measure of vestibular function is necessary. Some of the methods which have been used to assess vestibular function include: observation of postural reflexes, as is a common practice in the field of physical and occupational therapy (Fiorentino, 1978), post-rotary testing (Ayers, 1975), consistency board and postural platform testing (Black, O'Leary, Wall, & Furman, 1977; Black, Wall, & O'Leary, 1978; de Quiros, 1978), modifications of the standard electronystagmographic (ENG) procedure including caloric and per-rotational testing (Cyr, 1980), and attempts to record evoked potentials from the vestibular system (McCabe & Ryu, 1979).

There are shortcomings with each of these methods. Examination of vestibular function via postural reflexes relies on intact muscular and central nervous systems. This type of testing also includes proprioceptive and visual inputs (White et al., 1980), and it may be difficult to separate these from the vestibular response. Similar problems exist when using consistency boards and posture platforms, which are designed to evaluate the vestibulospinal tracts.

Vestibular evoked response testing has been attempted with limited success (McCabe & Ryu, 1979). The vestibular system is a complex series of pathways and has numerous afferent and efferent inputs between the vestibular, visual, and proprioceptive systems. These occur within the peripheral end organs, spinal cord, brainstem, midbrain, and cortex. Consequently, it is difficult to isolate a common vestibular pathway which would allow investigation of vestibular function using evoked potential techniques.

The caloric test is a nonphysiologic method of determining vestibular contributions to the maintenance of body posture and head and eye control. The caloric stimulus temperature produces a response much greater than the organism typically encounters. In addition, the caloric test evaluates only a small portion of the vestibular end organs' operating range. As a result, its clinical utility is limited.

The majority of rotational testing has focused on either post-rotary stimulation, which is a highly variable procedure, or per-rotary stimulation, which may yield an invalid measure of peripheral vestibular symmetry (Cyr, 1980). The frequency of nystagmic beats during per-rotary stimulation is influenced by factors such as spontaneous nystagmus. Therefore, results may suggest a unilateral peripheral vestibular weakness where none exists. Recently, a computerized rotary chair system (Wolfe, Engelken, Olson, & Kos, 1978a) has been developed which is sensitive to subtle peripheral vertibular pathologies, and has the capability of eliminating some of the extraneous effects, such as spontaneous nystagmus. Wall, Black, and O'Leary (1978) have stated: "Although rotational stimulation has been used for some time in attempts to infer vestibular function through the vestibular ocular reflex, recent advances in signal process and parameter estimation coupled with the inexorable decrease in cost of laboratory computers have brought the use of rotational testing near the realm of clinical reality."

Currently, the ENG evaluation (Coats, 1975) is considered one of the most sensitive and clinically practical measures of peripheral vestibular and vestibulo-ocular function. One of the major shortcomings of this procedure is that it measures only a fraction of the peripheral vestibular apparatus. Subtests are designed to evalute the horizontal semicircular canal, the utricle, and the superior branch of the vestibular nerve, as the neural response ascends the medial longitudinal fasciculus to the extraocular muscles. This makes up the vestibulo-ocular reflex. The remainder of the peripheral vestibular system, including the posterior and inferior branches of the vestibular nerve, the saccule, and the posterior and superior semicircular canals are not assessed. The vestibulospinal tracts are also not evaluated.

Although the ENG modifications have been detailed for use with children (Cyr, 1980, 1981; Eviatar & Eviatar, 1977a, 1978b), sufficient normative data for this population is lacking.

Binocular and monocular counterrolling of the eyes has been used to evaluate peripheral vestibular output (Diamond & Markham, 1981; Howard & Evans, 1963). This has been evaluated during dynamic rotation and with static studies using photographic methods (Diamond et al., 1979). This latter procedure only evaluates otolith (utricular) function and, consequently, yields limited information.

In summary, the most frequently used methods for evaluation of peripheral vestibular function are incomplete. Only when the above-mentioned limitations are overcome will we be able to make assumptions about the specific effect of the vestibular apparatus on ocular movements.

COMPUTERIZED HARMONIC ACCELERATION

The most sensitive measure of peripheral vestibular function appears to be a computerized rotary chair (low-frequency harmonic acceleration). For this procedure, the patient is rotated in a computer-controlled chair in an upright position at several rotational speeds. This procedure measures per-rotary nystagmus, which appears to be a more sensitive measure of peripheral vestibular output than postrotary nystagmus. Eye velocity versus head velocity, as estimated by chair velocity, is the primary response parameter. Wolfe et al. (1978a) have reported that: "Low frequency harmonic acceleration (rotary chair test) can be used to detect unilateral peripheral deficits that agree with caloric findings. However, the responses to sinusoidal acceleration are less variable than the caloric responses and allow one to more clearly evaluate changes in pathology with time." In addition, the computerized rotary chair does not create the vertigo and occasional vagal response (nausea, vomiting, etc.) that is common to the caloric test and, as a result, should be the method of choice in cases of minor peripheral vestibular end organ dysfunction. This method can be contrasted to caloric tests which are so nonphysiologic that the sensitivity level is suspect and repeatability is poor even over short periods of time.

OCULAR MOTOR SYSTEMS

Vestibulovisual integration can be described by a series of eye movements that were initially classified by Dodge (1903). These are saccadic, slow continuous, coordinate compensatory, reactive compensatory, and convergence or divergence.

Daroff and Del-Osso (1976) have described the ocular motor system as a dual mode system consisting of a vergence mode and a version mode. Version mode stimuli include fixation, motion, volition, optokinetic, audition, afterimage, and vestibular, and result in slow or fast eye movements, called pursuits or saccades. Vergence stimuli include retinal blur or diplopia from refixation or motion. These result in output called vergence eye movements and are disconjugate or opposing eye movements.

The types of version stimuli important in the ocular motor abilities needed for the acquisition of reading and writing are fixation, refixation, and optokinetic. These will be discussed as visual pursuit (Robinson, 1965), saccades (Robinson, 1964), and optokinetic (Smith & Cogan, 1959).

Visual pursuit, resulting in a slow eye movement, functions in the stabilization of retinal images. This is accomplished by matching the angular velocity of the eye with that of a moving target (Young, 1971). The result is the smooth pursuit of an image moving in space. Smooth ocular pursuit movements are affected by lesions in the central vestibular system, primarily in the brainstem, and may be affected by peripheral vestibular pathology.

A type of fast eye movement, called a saccade, is the most rapid eye movement of which the ocular motor system is capable. Saccades redirect the eyes from one target in the visual field to another in the shortest possible time. During most saccadic movements, visual acuity is suppressed markedly. When the eyes reach the intended target, visual acuity is reestablished. Saccadic eye movements facilitate the maintenance of an image on the fovea of the eye by a series of separate, high-velocity jumps. The fovea is the region of the retina where the best visual acuity exists. Eye velocity, symmetry, gain, and latency abnormalities may be seen with brainstem/vestibular pathology and are common in early demyelinating disease such as multiple sclerosis (Mastaglia, Black, & Collins, 1979). It has been shown that saccades can be induced by electrical stimulation in the frontal and occipital cortex, superior colliculus, cerebellum, and the paramedial pontine reticular formation (PPRF) (Baloh, Kumley, & Honrubia, 1976). Typically, saccades are not affected by peripheral vestibular lesions.

Optokinetic (compensatory) movements are those which act to maintain visual fixation on a target when the head is in motion. These compensatory movements consist of a slow pursuit phase in one direction and a fast saccade in the opposite direction. Asymmetrical responses often are identified in central vestibular pathologies that unilaterally affect the optokinetic system, such as in cortical space-occupying lesions or infarctions. In some instances, the optokinetic response cannot be suppressed. An "involuntary" optokinetic nystagmic response can be elicited by filling the visual field with a stimulus such as alternated black and white stripes. The morphology of the resultant nystagmic waveform and the symmetry of the response between the eyes are the parameters used to judge normalcy (Coates, 1975).

Optokinetic responses are altered when the peripheral vestibular system is impaired (Jenkins, Honrubia, & Baloh, 1977; Karlan, Todd, Stein, Adams, & Goldstein, 1979; Zee, Yee, & Robinson, 1976). This has been identified during opto-kinetic stimulation and for optokinetic afternystagmus (OKAN) (Cohen, Uemura, & Takemori, 1973). A right-beating peripheral spontaneous nystagmus can cause a right-beating dominant optokinetic response that is secondary to a peripheral lesion rather than an abnormality within the optokinetic system. Regardless of the type of eye movement (a saccade, optokinetic nystagmus, or caloric/rotational-induced nystagmus), it is the same neural network in the paramedial pontine reticular formation that appears to be employed (Henriksson, Pyykko, Schalen, & Wennmo, 1980).

RECENT ASSUMPTIONS

Over the past decade, claims have been made that performance on vestibular function tests, as well as on a variety of ocular motor tests, differs between normal-reading children and learning-disabled children (Levinson, 1980). Levinson has reported that children with dyslexia produce eye tracking patterns that are different from those noted in normal-reading children. The sensitivity level of the tests used to evaluate the vestibular response and the ocular movement patterns of these children does not appear to be sufficient to definitively demonstrate vestibulovisual differences. Most of these claims are based on the assumption that a primary function of the inner ear vestibular mechanism is to control eye movement and position. As a result of this thinking, generalizations are being made in the literature and in the media relative to the reading-impaired population. If the ocular motor tracking system or the vestibulo-ocular system are contributory to reading problems, then the computerized tracking and rotary chair systems should be the most sensitive methods to assess this hypothesis.

In order to pursue these suggestions, a variety of research investigations need to be undertaken. These include studies that address the following questions:

• Do differences exist between normal-reading children and dyslexic children for saccadic eye velocity, latency, and gain? Do the eyes move disconjugately during saccades for the two groups, and if so, can we infer lateral ocular muscle differences between the two groups?

• Since the optokinetic response is an involuntary ocular action, can this response be used to separate the two groups? Do differences exist between the two groups relative to the slow phase versus the fast phase of optokinetic nystagmus?

• Are there differences in the smooth ocular pursuit systems between and/or within these two groups?

• Do nystagmic differences exist between the two groups during rotary chair tests and can we consistently identify reading-disabled children on the basis of these tests? If so, can that information be used in the diagnosis and remediation of reading disorders?

Only after these questions have been addressed effectively and the functional interrelationships of these systems established, can we discuss their role in specific communication and learning skills, such as writing and reading.

SUMMARY AND FUTURE DIRECTION

The observation that dyslexia is related to abnormal ocular motor function is by no means recent. For almost 100 years, there has been speculation about how eye movements are made during reading. A significant amount of research has centered around a variety of eye movements during reading, specifically saccadic movements (Lloyd & Pavlidis, 1978; Pavlidis, 1978, 1979; Tinker, 1958; Zangwell & Blakemore, 1972).

One of the primary considerations in determining saccadic function during reading is the number of saccades made by normal-reading versus dyslexic subjects while reading a specific phrase or sentence. Proponents of the visual motor perception theories (Getman, 1965) have long addressed the role of ocular movements in dyslexia, especially for remediation purposes. Several investigators (Leisman & Schwartz, 1975; Levinson, 1980; Lloyd & Pavlidis, 1978; Pavlidis, 1979, 1981; Rayner & McConkie, 1976; Tinker, 1958; Zangwell & Blakemore, 1972) have studied eye movement patterns in dyslexic subjects and found them to differ from normal-reading subjects, at least for saccades and certain pursuit movements. The primary difference between normal and dyslexic subjects was found to be in the size and duration of the eye movements that occurred during reading tasks. The eye movements of dyslexic subjects appeared to be of shorter size and longer duration (Pavlidis, 1981); however, the overall ocular wave morphology between the two groups was similar.

Some investigators (Pavlidis, 1981; Pirozzolo & Rayner, 1978; Zangwell & Blakemore, 1972) have demonstrated eye movement patterns that were qualitatively and quantitatively different between normal and dyslexic subjects. Leisman and Schwartz (1975) have attempted to evaluate saccadic eye velocities during reading; however, the latency and gain of saccades in the dyslexic population have not been investigated systematically. In addition, the optokinetic (involuntary) and smooth pursuit movements have not been evaluated critically in the dyslexic population.

Ocular motor performance in children with dyslexia may be evaluated only after contributions from the vestibular apparatus are ruled out. If that is possible, then ocular motor performance can be measured with sensitive and specific procedures.

In order to sensitively evaluate peripheral vestibular output at a physiologic level, a computerized rotary accelerating chair, mounted on a rate table, with controlled acceleration and deceleration can be used. The chair rotates horizontally at acceleration rates ranging from .01 to .16 Hz. Eye velocity, gain, and phase is matched against head velocity and used to measure the vestibular response and to assess symmetry.

Recent research at the Boys Town National Institute suggests that performance on ENG and computerized rotational tests does not differ between normal readers and dyslexics, although there are marked sex differences (Cyr, 1983 unpublished). These findings either refute the assumptions of Levinson and de Quiros, or support the fact that current methodology for measuring vestibular response is inadequate.

A second research project (Cyr, unpublished data) suggests that differences do exist between dyslexics and normal readers for ocular saccades. The differences primarily relate to higher velocity eye movements in normal readers compared to their dyslexic counterparts. Interestingly, the above data was obtained on nonreading tasks. In other words, fast eye movement differences appear to exist within the saccade system between normal readers and dyslexics which are not based upon a reading task.

In summary, we feel that the vestibular and ocular motor performance differences between dyslexic and normal readers has not yet been evaluated adequately. Before statements can be made about this relationship, sensitive measurement of the ocular motor systems (saccade, pursuit, and optokinetic) must be made to include monocular and binocular measures of velocity, gain, phase, and latency. This can be accomplished only after the effects of vestibular output are isolated and accounted for systematically.

REFERENCES

Ayers, A. J. *Sensory integration and learning disorders.* Los Angeles: Western Psychological Services, 1975.

Bahill, A. T., & Stark, L. The trajectories of saccadic eye movements. *Scientific American,* 1979, *240,* 108–117.

Baloh, R. W., Kumley, W. E., & Honrubia, V. Algorithm for analyses of saccadic eye movements using a digital computer. *Aviation, Space, and Environmental Medicine,* 1976, *47,* 523–527.

Barnes, G. R. The role of the vestibular system in head–eye coordination. *Journal of Physiology,* 1975, *246,* 99.

Black, F. O., O'Leary, D. P., Wall, C., & Furman, J. The vestibulospinal stability test: Normal limits. *Journal for Oto-Rhino-Laryngology and its Borderlands,* 1977, *84,* 549–560.

Black, F. O., Wall, C., & O'Leary, D. P. Computerized screening of the human vestibulospinal system. *Annals of Otology, Rhinology, and Laryngology,* 1978, *87,* 853–860.

Bohmer, A., & Pfaltz, C. R. Interaction of vestibular and optokinetic nystagmus in patients with peripheral vestibular and central nervous disorders. *Journal for Oto-Rhino-Laryngology and its Related Specialties,* 1980, *42,* 125–141.

Brookhouser, P. E., Cyr, D. G., & Beauchaine, K. A. Vestibular findings in the deaf and hard of hearing. *Otolaryngology—Head and Neck Surgery,* 1982, *90,* 773–778.

Coats, A. C. Electronystagmography. In L. Bradford (Ed.), *Physiological measures of the audio-vestibular system* (pp. 37–85). New York: Academic Press, 1975.

Cohen, B., Uemura, T., & Takemori, S. Effects of labyrinthectomy on optokinetic nystagmus (OKN) and optokinetic after nystagmus (OKAN). *Equilibrium Research,* 1973, *3,* 88–93.

Cyr, D. G. Vestibular testing in children. *Annals of Oto-Rhino-Laryngology* (Supplement 74), 1980, *89,* 63–69.

Cyr, D. G. Vestibular testing in children: Rationale, technique, and application. *Audiology: An audio journal for continuing studies.* New York: Grune & Stratton, 1981.

Daroff, R. B., & Del-Osso, L. F. The control of eye movements. *Neurological Reviews,* 1976, 143–170.

de Quiros, J. B. Significance of some therapies on posture and learning. *Academic Therapy,* 1976a, *11,* 261–270.

de Quiros, J. B. Diagnosis of vestibular disorders in the learning disabled. *Journal of Learning Disabilities,* 1976b, *9,* 39–44.

de Quiros, J. B. *Neurophysiological fundamentals in learning disabilities.* California: Academic Therapy, 1979.

Diamond, S. G., Markham, C. H., Simpson, N. E., & Curthoys, I. S. Binocular counterrolling in humans during dynamic rotation. *Acta Oto-laryngologica* (Stockholm), 1979, *87,* 490–498.

Diamond, S. G., & Markham, C. H. Binocular counterrolling in humans with unilateral labyrinthectomy and in normal controls. In B. Cohen (Ed.), *Vestibular and oculo-motor physiology: International meeting of the Barany Society,* 1981, 69–79.

Dodge, R. Five types of eye movements in the horizontal meridian plane of the field of regard. *American Journal of Physiology,* 1903, *8,* 307–329.

Eviatar, L., & Eviatar, A. Electronystagmography and neuro-otologic examination of infants and children. *American Academy of Ophthalmology and Otolaryngology,* Course 44, 1977.

Eviatar, L., & Eviatar, A. Vertigo in children: Differential diagnosis and treatment. *Pediatrics,* 1977, *59,* 833–838.

Eviatar, L., & Eviatar, A. Aminoglycoside ototoxicity in the neonatal period: Possible etiologic factor in delayed postural control. *Otolaryngology—Head and Neck Surgery,* 1978, *80,* 818–821.

Eviatar, L., & Eviatar, A. Neurovestibular examination of infants and children. *Advances in Otol-Rhino-Laryngology,* 1978, *23,* 169–191.

Eviatar, L., & Eviatar, A. The normal nystagmic response of infants to caloric and perrotatory stimulation. *Laryngoscope,* 1979, *89,* 1036–1044.

Eviatar, L., Miranda, S., Eviatar, A., Freeman, K., & Borkowski, M. Development of nystagmus in response to vestibular stimulation in infants. *Annals of Neurology,* 1979, *5,* 508–514.

Eviatar, L., Eviatar, A., & Naray, I. Maturation of neurovestibular responses in infants. *Developmental Medicine and Child Neurology,* 1974, *16,* 435–446.

Fiorentino, M. *Reflex testing methods for evaluating c.n.s. development* (2nd ed.). Springfield, IL: Thomas, 1978.

Getman, G. H. The visuo-motor complex in the acquisition of learning skills. In B. Straub & J. Hellmath (Eds.), *Learning disorders* (Vol. 1). Seattle: Special Child Publications, 1965.

Ginsberg, H., & Opper, S. *Piaget's theory of intellectual development, an introduction.* NJ: Prentice–Hall, 1969.

Henriksson, N. G., Pyykko, I., Schalen, L., & Wennmo, C. Velocity patterns of rapid eye movements. *Acta Oto-laryngologica* (Stockholm), 1980, *89,* 504–512.

Howard, I. P., & Evans, J. A. The measurement of eye torsion. *Vision Research,* 1963, *3,* 447.

Hyden, D., Odkvist, L. M., & Kylen, P. Vestibular symptoms in mumps deafness. *Acta Oto-laryngology* (Supplement), 1979, *360,* 182–183.

Jenkins, H. A., Honrubia, V., & Baloh, R. W. Modification of optokinetic nystagmus by horizontal semicircular canal stimulation in normal humans and patients with cerebellar degeneration. *ORL Transactions,* 1977, *85,* 400–406.

Kanter, R. M., Clark, D. L., Allen, L. C., & Chase, M. F. Effects of vestibular stimulation on nystagmus response and motor performance in the developmentally delayed infant. *Journal of the American Physical Therapy Association,* 1976, *56,* 414–421.

Karlan, M. S., Todd, J., Stein, G. H., Adams, C. K., & Goldstein, M. K. Optokinetic suppression of aberrant vestibular reaction: An observation. *Annals of Otology,* 1979, *88,* 109–111.

Knobloch, H., & Pasamanick, B. (Eds.). *Gesell and Amatruda's developmental diagnosis: The evaluation and management of normal and abnormal neurophysiologic development in infancy and childhood* (3rd ed.). New York: Harper & Row, 1974.

Leisman, G., & Schwartz, A. Oculo-motor function and information processing: Implications for the reading process. In M. Kling (Ed.), *Promising new methodological approaches in understanding the reading/language process.* Newark: International Reading Association, 1975.

Levinson, H. N. *A solution to the riddle dyslexia.* New York: Springer-Verlag, 1980.

Levinson, H. N. Dyslexia: Transcript 08171 from The Donahue Show, September 7, 1981.

Lloyd, P., & Pavlidis, G. The child language and eye movements: The relative effects of sentence and situation on comprehension in young children. *Bulletin of British Psychological Society,* 1978, *31,* 70–71.

Mastaglia, F. L., Black, J. L., & Collins, D. W. K. Quantitative studies of saccadic and pursuit eye movements in multiple sclerosis. *Brain,* 1979, *102,* 817–834.

McCabe, B. F., & Ryu, J. H. *Vestibular physiology in understanding the dizzy patient.* Rochester, MN: American Academy of Otolaryngology, 1979.

Molina-Negro, P., Betrand, R. A., Martin, E., & Gioani, Y. The role of the vestibular system in relation to muscle tone and postural reflexes in man. *Acta Otolaryngologica* (Stockholm), 1980, *89,* 524–533.

Pavlidis, G. The dyslexics' erratic eye movements: Case studies. *Dyslexia Review,* 1978, *1,* 22–28.

Pavlidis, G. How can dyslexia be objectively diagnosed? *Reading,* 1979, *13,* 3–15.

Pavlidis, G. Do eye movements hold the key to dyslexia? *Neuropsychologia,* 1981, *19,* 57–64.

Pirozzolo, F. J., & Rayner, K. In H. A. Whittaker (Ed.), *Advances in neurolinguistics and psycholinguistics.* New York: Academic Press, 1978.

Rayner, K., & McConkie, G. W. What guides a reader's eye movements? *Vision Research,* 1976, *16,* 837–839.

Robinson, D. A. The mechanics of human saccadic eye movement. *Journal of Physiology,* 1964, *174,* 245–264.

Robinson, D. A. The mechanics of human smooth pursuit eye movement. *Journal of Physiology,* 1965, *180,* 569–591.

Smith, J. L., & Cogan, D. G. Optokinetic nystagmus: A test for parietal lobe lesions. *American Journal of Ophthalmology,* 1959, *48,* 187.

138   *Cyr/Beauchaine*

Steinberg, M., & Randle-Short, J. Vestibular dysfunction in young children with minor neurological impairment. *Developmental Medicine and Child Neurology,* 1977, *19,* 639-651.

Stool, S. E., Black, F. O., Craig, H., & Laird, M. Otologic care in a school for the deaf. *Otolaryngology—Head and Neck Surgery,* 1981, *89,* 651-657.

Takahashi, M., Uemura, T., & Fujishiro, T. Studies of the vestibulo-ocular reflex and visual-vestibular interactions during active head movements. *Acta Otolaryngologica* (Stockholm), 1980, *90,* 115-124.

Tinker, M. A. Recent studies of eye movements in reading. *Psychological Bulletin,* 1958, *55,* 215-231.

Wall, C., Black, F. O., & O'Leary, D. P. Clinical use of pseudorandom binary sequence white noise in assessment of the human vestibulo-ocular system. *Annals of Otology, Rhinology and Laryngology,* 1978, *87,* 845-853.

White K. D., Post, R. B., & Leibowitz, H. W. Saccadic eye movements and body sway. *Science,* 1980, *208,* 621-623.

Wolfe, J. W. Monocular nystagmic responses to caloric stimulation. *Annals of Otology,* 1979, *88,* 79-85.

Wolfe, J. W., Engelken, E. J., & Kos, C. M. Low-frequency harmonic acceleration as a test of labyrinthine function: Basic methods and illustrative cases. *ORL Transactions,* 1978, *86,* 130-142.

Wolfe, J. W., Engelken, E. J., Olson, J. W., & Kos, C. M. Vestibular responses to bithermal caloric and harmonic acceleration. *Annals of Otology, Rhinology and Laryngology,* 1978a, *87.*

Wolf, J. W., Engelken, E. J., Olson, J. W., & Allen, J. P. Cross-power spectral density analysis of pursuit tracing: Evaluation of central and peripheral pathology. *Annals of Otology, Rhinology and Laryngology,* 1978b, *87.*

Young, L. R. Pursuit eye tracking movements. In P. Bach-y-Rita, C. C. Collins, & J. E. Hyde (Eds.), *The control of eye movements,* (pp. 429-443). New York: Academic Press, 1971.

Zangwell, O. L., & Blakemore, C. Dyslexia: Reversal of eye movements during reading. *Neuropsychologica,* 1972, *10,* 371-373.

Zee, D. S., Yee, R. D., & Robinson, D. A. Optokinetic responses in labyrinthine-defective human beings. *Brain Research,* 1976, *113,* 423-428.

8
AUDITORY REASSEMBLY OF SEGMENTED CONSONANT–VOWEL–CONSONANT (CVC) SYLLABLES BY GOOD AND POOR THIRD- AND FIFTH-GRADE READERS

Judith B. Amster
Helen K. Smith
Thomas H. Shriner
University of Miami

It is believed that this manuscript, based upon the doctoral dissertation of Dr. Judith Amster, represents the last student-related research effort with which Tom Shriner was involved prior to his untimely death. It is, therefore, published in the form and style used in scientific publications—a form and style reminiscent of Tom's writing, as will be readily apparent to those who knew Tom and his work.

A n intact and adequately developed system of processing auditory stimuli has been postulated as essential to the acquisition of reading skills. The early results of Monroe (1932), Bond (1935), and Orton (1937) observed the presence of auditory processing difficulties among poor readers.

One aspect of auditory processing is auditory reassembly, which requires the listener to synthesize or blend auditorily presented phonemes of a syllable or word and to reproduce verbally the integrated whole. Placed within a model of speech perception (Halle & Stevens, 1964), the reassembly process is viewed as a task of perception, synthesis, and matching of stimuli in a rule-governed paradigm.

If, as Conrad (1974) suggests, a phonetic code is employed to store visually presented letters or words, the relationship between the ability to blend sounds and reading becomes more understandable. This relationship would impact particularly during the earliest stages of learning to read, in which phonologic and visual relationships are being established and manipulated. Conrad's (1974) findings in addition to those of Hintzman (1967) and Mark, Shankweiler, Liberman, and Fowler

(1977) reveal that phonetic representations may be employed to facilitate access to the reader's mental lexicon or listening vocabulary and to reconstruct the prosodic information necessary to understand speech. Mark et al. (1977) further suggest that the readers of a language may continue to use a phonetic representation, just as listeners do, in processing the written code. The child who cannot effectively access the phonological cues of spoken language may be the child who evidences difficulties in the primary activity of speech production and the secondary activity of reading.

In a comprehensive review of the literature on sound blending, Richardson, DiBenedetto, and Bradley (1977) conclude that auditory reassembly is linked to the decoding process and that this task may be fundamentally related to reading achievement. It would, therefore, correlate most significantly with those reading methods which stress decoding of words through a phonics approach.

Sound blending has been shown experimentally to be correlated concurrently and predictively with reading achievement by Gates (1939), Reynolds (1953), Mulder and Curtin (1955), Chall, Roswell, and Blumenthal (1963), Alshan (1965), Kass (1966), Dykstra (1966), Bruininks (1969), Balmuth (1971), and McNinch (1971). Its ability to discriminate good from poor readers was identified by Monroe (1932), Bond (1935), McLeod (1966), Golden and Steiner (1969), and Flynn and Byrne (1970).

Investigations in the area of articulation have demonstrated that differences in auditory reassembly exist between children with normal speech productions and those with deviant patterns (Goldman & Dixon, 1974; Gray, 1963; Lerea, 1963; Monsees, 1968; Pratt & Butler, 1968; Van Riper, 1954).

The findings from such investigations, although provocative, may be of restricted value in view of the methodological diversity of the auditory reassembly measures used. Such tasks have been characterized by variety as well as subjectivity of the intervals between phonemic stimuli, the frequent presence of visual cues created by the examiner's articulatory movements, the use of meaningful or nonmeaningful stimuli and the presentational and response modes employed.

More recent investigations which provided experimental control of the foregoing variables (Beasley & Beasley, 1973; Beasley, Shriner, Manning, & Beasley, 1974; Shriner & Daniloff, 1970; Stovall, Manning, & Shaw, 1977) show that differences in performance on auditory reassembly measures are affected by the subject's age, the time intervals between phonemes (interphonemic intervals), and use of meaningful versus nonmeaningful stimuli.

A review of the literature reveals no reported studies which explicitly controlled for presentational, temporal, and semantic variables in examining possible differences in the reassembly performance of good and poor readers. Such an approach is essential if assumptions regarding auditory reassembly are to become more than merely conventional wisdom based upon widely diverse experimental procedures. If differences in auditory reassembly by good and poor readers do exist and if auditory reassembly tasks are to be used to assess these abilities, then the variables of meaningfulness and nonmeaningfulness, interphonemic interval, mode of presentation, and response requirements must be taken into consideration. These factors appear to have been neglected in previous investigations of auditory reassembly within the context of reading. This investigation was designed to study the following question: Is there a difference in the performance of good and poor readers with respect to the auditory reassembly of both meaningful and nonmeaningful consonant–vowel–consonant (CVC) monosyllables under varied interphonemic intervals (IPI)? The following subsidiary questions were generated:

1. Is there an age-related difference in the ability of good and poor readers to blend auditorily presented segmented consonant–vowel–consonant monosyllables?

2. Is performance on an auditory reassembly task related to reading ability?

3. What is the effect of varying the length of the interval between phonemes on the blending of segmented CVC stimuli?

METHOD

Subjects

A sample of 160 subjects was drawn from the total third- ($N = 337$) and fifth-grade ($N = 452$) populations of three public elementary schools located in a suburban community. All third- and fifth-grade students who had scored at or above the 80th percentile (good readers) and at or below the 30th percentile (poor readers) on the Paragraph Meaning subtest of the Stanford Achievement Test were identified. A total of 401 students met the initial stratification criteria of grade level and reading level. Additional stratification criteria for inclusion in the study were average or above average intellectual functioning, middle-class or above socioeconomic status, the absence of visual, auditory, speech, gross neurological and/or psychological dysfunction, membership in a regular class, and use of English as the native language of the child. Information relative to the visual, auditory, speech, gross neurological and psychological status of each child ($N = 401$), and the absence of dysfunction in these areas was obtained from cumulative records.

The speech adequacy of each child was further evaluated individually by a speech pathologist using the Templin–Darley Tests of Articulation (1960). Any child who evidenced articulatory deficiencies or foreign dialectal patterns was excluded from the study.

An estimate of at least average verbal intelligence was obtained through the use of the Peabody Picture Vocabulary Test. Children who did not meet average or above average intellectual criteria were not included in the sample.

Of the students initially identified as good readers or poor readers through use of the Stanford Achievement Test ($N = 401$), a total of 208 (54 third-grade good readers, 47 third-grade poor readers, 58 fifth-grade good readers, 49 fifth-grade poor readers) met all stratification criteria for inclusion in the study. Of these 208 students a sample of 160 subjects (40 good third-grade readers, 40 poor third-grade readers, 40 good fifth-grade readers, 40 poor fifth-grade readers) was drawn by stratified random sampling procedures.

Stimulus Materials

One of the major purposes of this research was to clarify the possible effect of time intervals between segmented phonemes in an auditory reassembly task.

In order to avoid possible confounding of issues through the presence of uncontrolled interphonemic intervals, use of a taped auditory reassembly measure, which would not only control for but also examine the factor of interphonemic interval, was essential. In addition, the use of a taped measure allowed for experimental control of the signal-to-noise ratio, as well as the removal of any visual cues which might be provided by the examiner.

The experimental tapes used to assess auditory reassembly performance in the present study were developed at the University of Illinois Speech Research Laboratory by Shriner and Daniloff (1970) and modified by Beasley and Beasley (1973). Specific procedures for their preparation are outlined by Shriner and Daniloff (1970). The stimuli tapes consisted of 10 meaningful and 10 nonmeaningful CVC monosyllables which had been made into like pairs (Table 8-1) with only the central vowel differing and controlling the semantic factor.

Specified segments of blank tape containing intervals of 100, 200, 300, and 400 msec had been inserted between each of the phonemes comprising a complete CVC monosyllable. Each segmented CVC item was placed in the carrier phrase "Repeat——Please" with 10 sec between phrases. Each tape contained a randomized version of all 20 (10 meaningful and 10 nonmeaningful) CVC items at only one of the four interphonemic conditions.

Presentation Procedures

Subjects were randomly assigned on the basis of reading level (good vs. poor) and grade level (third vs. fifth) to one of four interphonemic interval conditions (100, 200, 300, and 400 msec). There were 40 subjects (10 good and 10 poor third-grade readers, 10 good and 10 poor fifth-grade readers) under each of the four interphonemic interval conditions.

The auditory reassembly measure was presented via an Ampex tapedeck (Model 601) and Ampex amplifier–speaker combination (Model 620) to all subjects individually in a testing room in each of three schools. Sound level meter measurements revealed highly satisfactory and relatively equivalent signal-to-noise (S/N) ratios for the three testing rooms.

Directions were administered orally by the experimenter, with several meaning-ful and nonmeaningful CVC examples being provided. If the subject correctly reassembled the segmented phonemes into the correct meaningful or nonmean-ingful monosyllables, he was then asked to listen to and assemble the two practice items included on each tape. If he did so, the entire tape was run nonstop. No subjects were unable to perform the practice auditory reassembly task. Each subject in the final sample received the randomized 10 meaningful and 10 nonmeaningful CVC stimuli under only one interphonemic interval condition (100, 200, 300, or 400 msec).

Analysis of the Data

Responses on the reassembly task were taped and hand recorded and scored as to correct or incorrect. Responses of each subject were tape-recorded by means of a Sony Cassette Recorder (TC-110A) with a microphone placed directly in front

TABLE 8-1
List of meaningful and nonmeaningful CVC monosyllable stimulus items

Meaningful		*Nonmeaningful*	
/noz/	nose	/nez/	nāz
/mæn/	man	/mɑn/	män
/bɛd/	bed	/bɑd/	bäd
/dɔg/	dog	/dɛg/	dĕg
/dʒʌg/	jug	/dʒig/	jēg
/tʃɪn/	chin	/tʃʌn/	chŭn
/ʃuz/	shoes	/ʃez/	shāz
/sʌn/	sun	/sɛn/	sĕn
/lɛg/	leg	/lʊg/	lōōg
/rɛd/	red	/rʌd/	rŭd

of the seated subject, who was seated 12 in. from the amplifier–speaker unit. In order to establish the reliability of the examiner's judgment in recording and scoring responses, a panel of three speech pathologists listened to the taped responses of eight subjects chosen at random (two from each grade by reading level) and scored each response as correct or incorrect. Interjudge percentage of agreement was 97%, while the percentage of agreement between the examiner and judges was 98%. The number of items correctly reassembled for each subject was converted into a percentage correct score. Three such scores were obtained for each subject: (1) the percent correct responses on the total reassembly task; (2) the percent correct for the 10 meaningful stimuli; and (3) the percent correct for the 10 nonmeaningful stimuli. The mean percentage correct scores for these data are shown in Table 8-2.

Data were placed into a $4 \times 2 \times 2$ completely crossed fixed effect factorial design. Two 3-way ($4 \times 2 \times 2$) analysis of variance designs (Clyde, 1969) which examined the effect of grade level, reading ability, and temporal conditions and six 2-way (4×2) analysis of variance designs which examined the effect of reading level and temporal condition were performed.

A one-way analysis of variance BMD08V (Dixon, 1973) was performed to examine the difference between percent correct on meaningful versus nonmeaningful stimuli. Computerized trend analysis using orthogonal polynomials was performed to determine the nature of the response curve for the total reassembly task collapsed across grade level, reading level, and temporal condition.

RESULTS

Effect of Grade Level

A summary of the results of the analysis of variance comparing the performance of all fifth-grade versus all third-grade subjects for all monosyllables is presented

TABLE 8-2

Mean percent correct response scores for the auditory reassembly task

Grade		Interphonemic interval (msec)				Total Percent Correct
		100	200	306	400	
All 3rd-Grade Subjects % correct	Meaningful	87.5	66.5	62.5	83.5	75.0
	Nonmeaningful	49.0	37.0	46.0	48.0	45.1
	Combined	68.2	51.8	54.3	66.0	60.1
3rd-Grade Good Readers % correct	Meaningful	87.0	71.0	66.0	85.0	77.3
	Nonmeaningful	59.0	39.0	50.0	61.0	55.2
	Combined	73.0	55.0	58.0	73.0	64.8
3rd-Grade Poor Readers % correct	Meaningful	88.0	62.0	59.0	82.0	72.8
	Nonmeaningful	39.0	35.0	42.0	36.0	38.0
	Combined	63.5	48.5	50.5	59.0	55.4
All 5th-Grade Subjects % correct	Meaningful	87.5	73.0	71.0	84.0	78.9
	Nonmeaningful	56.0	46.0	57.0	51.0	52.5
	Combined	71.8	59.5	64.5	67.8	65.9
5th-Grade Good Readers % correct	Meaningful	89.0	76.0	80.0	93.0	84.5
	Nonmeaningful	56.0	48.0	68.0	54.0	56.5
	Combined	72.5	62.0	74.0	74.0	70.6
5th-Grade Poor Readers % correct	Meaningful	86.0	70.0	63.0	75.0	73.5
	Nonmeaningful	56.0	44.0	47.0	48.0	48.8
	Combined	71.0	57.0	55.0	61.0	61.1
All 3rd- and 5th-Grade Readers % correct	Meaningful	87.5	69.8	67.0	83.8	77.0
	Nonmeaningful	52.5	41.5	51.7	49.8	48.9
	Combined	70.0	55.6	59.4	66.8	62.9
All 3rd- and 5th-Grade Good Readers % correct	Meaningful	88.0	73.5	73.0	89.0	80.6
	Nonmeaningful	57.5	43.5	59.0	57.5	54.4
	Combined	72.8	58.5	66.0	73.3	67.7
All 3rd- and 5th-Grade Poor Readers % correct	Meaningful	87.0	66.0	61.0	78.5	73.1
	Nonmeaningful	47.5	39.5	44.5	42.0	43.4
	Combined	67.3	52.8	52.8	60.3	58.5

TABLE 8-3
Summary of an analysis of variance performed on total correct CVC reassembly scores for all third- and fifth-grade subjects

Source	df	MS	F
Grade (G)	1	1351.407	9.071*
Reading Level (R)	1	3562.655	23.914**
Temporal Level (T)	3	1753.906	11.773**
GR	1	.156	.001
GT	3	150.990	1.014
RT	3	193.906	1.302
GRT	3	167.239	1.123
Within	144	148.976	

$*p < .01.$
$**p < .001.$

in Table 8-3. Performance for meaningful and nonmeaningful monosyllables are displayed graphically in Figure 8-1.

These findings show the marked advantage held by fifth-grade subjects as compared to third-grade subjects on the total reassembly task (F (1,144) = 9.071, $p < .003$) when scores were collapsed across reading levels and temporal conditions. Results further revealed that although a trend in the predicted direction for older subjects to perform better than younger subjects can be seen (Figure 8-1), the main effect of grade level on the blending of meaningful stimuli did not reach significance. However, a significant grade level effect (Figure 8-1) is present for assembly of nonmeaningful stimuli, indicating the increased ability of older (fifth-grade) subjects to perform the reassembly task when semantic cues were not available.

Effect of Reading Level

Further analysis of variance results shown in Table 8-3 reveal that good readers performed significantly better (F (1,144) = 23.91, $p < .001$) than poor readers on the total reassembly of all CVC stimuli when scores were collapsed across grade level. Significance beyond the .01 level was also obtained for a comparison of all good versus all poor readers on meaningful and nonmeaningful stimuli. These results are displayed graphically in Figure 8-2.

FIGURE 8-1
Percent correct for meaningful (filled symbols) and nonmeaningful (open symbols) reassembly responses for third- and fifth-grade subjects as a function of interphonemic interval. Each datum point represents a mean score for 20 subjects and 200 responses.

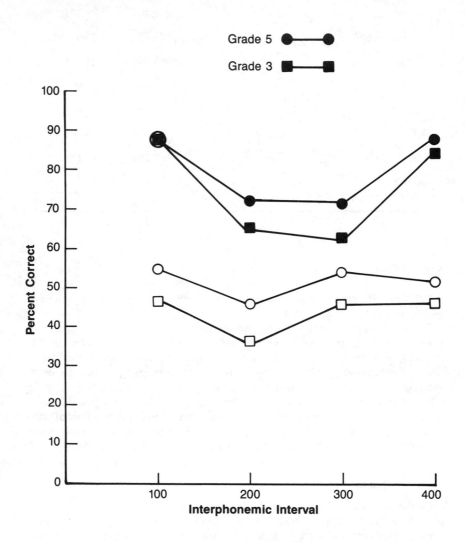

FIGURE 8-2
Percent correct for meaningful (filled symbols) and nonmeaningful (open symbols) reassembly responses produced by good readers versus poor readers as a function of interphonemic interval with scores collapsed across grade level. Each datum point represents a mean score for 20 subjects and 200 responses.

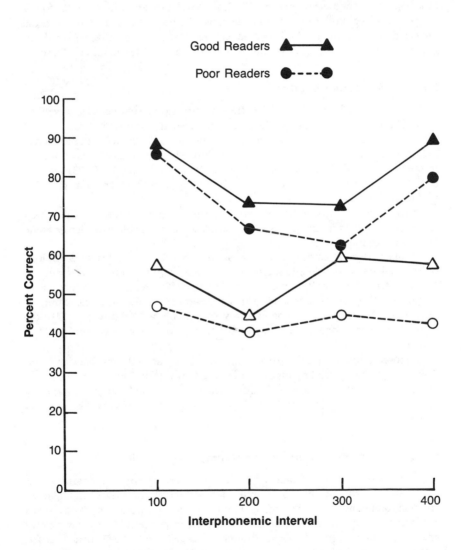

Analysis of the data revealed that good fifth-grade readers performed significantly better than poor fifth-grade subjects on the total reassembly task (Figure 8-3) and the meaningful reassembly task. Differences between good and poor fifth-grade subjects in the predicted direction were evidenced on the reassembly of nonmeaningful stimuli which approached but did not reach significance (F (1,72) = 5.52, $p < .021$).

With respect to third-grade subjects, results showed that good third-grade readers performed significantly better than poor third-grade readers on the total reassembly task (Figure 8-3) and the nonmeaningful task. No significant difference was found for performance on the blending of meaningful stimuli although a trend in the predicted direction for good third-grade readers to perform better than poor third-grade readers on meaningful stimuli was observed at all temporal conditions.

Effect of Temporal Condition

It can be seen (Table 8-3) that the effect of varying interphonemic intervals on the total reassembly process by all subjects produced an F ratio significant beyond the .001 level. The point at which interval size most markedly affected percentage of correct responses was at 200 msec, a finding which is consistent with related investigations by Shriner and Daniloff (1970), Beasley and Beasley (1973), Beasley et al. (1974), and Stovall et al. (1977). These findings can be observed in Table 8-2 and Figures 8-1, 8-2, and 8-3.

Temporal condition significantly affected the blending of meaningful as well as nonmeaningful stimuli by all subjects when scores were collapsed across grade levels and reading levels.

The main effect of temporal condition on performance by all third-grade subjects on the total assembly task and the assembly of meaningful stimuli was significant. However, temporal condition did not significantly affect reassembly of nonmeaningful stimuli by third-grade readers. For third-grade subjects, the reassembly of nonmeaningful stimuli was apparently a very difficult task, and variations in the interval between phonemes did not appear to help or hinder reassembly performance appreciably.

Temporal condition affected performance for fifth-grade subjects to a significant degree for the total blending task and the meaningful task. The blending of nonmeaningful stimuli was not significantly affected by temporal condition, a finding similar to that produced for third-grade subjects. A graphic display of these findings is presented in Figure 8-1.

Reassembly of Meaningful Versus Nonmeaningful Stimuli

Results revealed a significant difference in reassembly of meaningful versus nonmeaningful stimuli when socres were collapsed across grade level, reading level, and temporal condition. The large F ratio (F (1,159) = 189.45, $p < .001$) reflects the extent of the difference in percent of correct responses between meaningful and nonmeaningful stimuli. These differences range from a 15.3% advantage for meaningful stimuli at the 300-msec interval to a 35.0% advantage at the 100-msec level. A comparison of the combined means produced at all temporal conditions

FIGURE 8-3

Percent correct for total CVC reassembly responses for good versus poor fifth-grade subjects and good versus poor third-grade subjects as a function of interphonemic interval. Each datum point represents a mean score for 20 subjects and 400 responses.

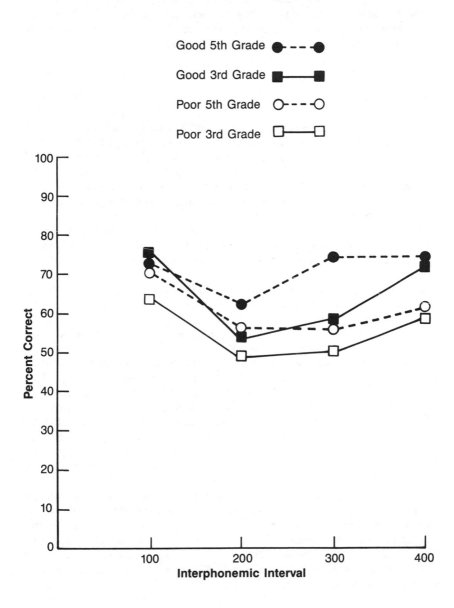

for meaningful stimuli revealed a mean of 77.0% correct while for nonmeaningful stimuli the mean was 48.8% correct. The results show that meaningful stimuli elicit significantly more frequent correct reassembly than nonmeaningful stimuli.

A significant quadratic curvature of the treatment means (F (1,156) = 28.6, p <.001) revealed that for total reassembly by all subjects performance was most depressed by temporal condition at the 200-msec (55.6% correct) and 300-msec (59.4% correct) IPI conditions while performance at the 100-msec (70.3% correct) and 400-msec (67.3% correct) condition was less affected. Figure 8-1 shows that when examined separately this trend is pronounced for meaningful stimuli while reassembly accuracy for nonmeaningful stimuli does not follow the same pattern.

DISCUSSION

The results of this investigation permit the following conclusions:

1. Older subjects, in general, are able to reassemble segmented auditory stimuli with greater proficiency than younger subjects. The marked superiority in total auditory reassembly of older (fifth-grade) subjects when compared to the performance of younger (third-grade) subjects appears to be related to the age-correlated increase in auditory skills in general which has been reported consistently in the literature (Lerea, 1963; Maccoby & Konrad, 1960; Sabatino & Hayden, 1970). Older children, who have presumably overlearned the phonemic cues of language, apparently were able to use this knowledge in restricting incorrect responses to the distorted CVC stimuli, while for younger subjects their less constrained field of response was detrimental.

2. Good readers, as a whole, are superior to poor readers in auditory reassembly. This superiority exists for performance on meaningful and nonmeaningful stimuli and functions across grade level and temporal conditions. Notwithstanding the minimal lexical clues provided by nonmeaningful stimuli, good readers were able to perform this task more efficiently than poor readers. These findings are in essential agreement with earlier research indicating the presence of auditory reassembly (sound blending) problems in groups of poor readers.

3. Performance on a reassembly task is affected by manipulation of the length of the interphonemic interval. These findings are in essential agreement with related investigations by Shriner and Daniloff, 1970, Beasley and Beasley, 1973, Beasley et al., 1974, and Stovall et al., 1977. The insertion of specific acoustic pauses between stimuli appears to be a crucial factor in subject performance and should be taken into consideration in the development or administration of auditory reassembly measures. Differences observed in response to manipulation of the IPI may be explained on the basis of differences in the nature of the stimulus material and the perceptual strategies used by the subject. For meaningful stimuli it appears that the additional time provided by longer IPI contributed to more effective strategies of auditory reassembly. In contrast, the added time available under longer IPI conditions for nonmeaningful stimuli may have been detrimental to the reassembly process in view of the increased difficulty in retaining and manipulating these low associational stimuli.

4. The semantic nature of the stimuli is an important variable in the auditory reassembly task. Meaningful CVC stimuli are significantly easier to reassemble than nonmeaningful stimuli, a finding in agreement with the results of previous related investigations (Beasley & Beasley, 1973; Beasley et al., 1974; Shriner & Daniloff, 1970; Stovall et al., 1977).

As Denes (1963) suggests, the acoustic characteristics of an auditory stimulus do not identify the phonemes precisely. The listener must use his knowledge of linguistic, conceptual, and phonemic constraints to resolve the ambiguities of the signal. The use of meaningful stimuli appeared to allow for more systems (lexical, morphological, syntactical) to be brought into play, contributing to ease of reassembly. The ability to exploit the redundancy of spoken language (McLeod, 1966) is enhanced when the stimulus material is meaningful. Distortion of the auditory stimulus via insertion of interphonemic intervals produces a smaller loss in the intelligibility of meaningful stimuli. For nonmeaningful stimuli where linguistic cues are minimal, such distortion has a debilitating effect on the reassembly process.

Samuels (1973) cautions that the results of research which focuses on the testing of auditory skills may be invalidated by task variables which are not controlled as well as other procedural shortcomings. The current discussion concerning the presence or absence of auditory perceptual skills in poor readers (Hammill & Larsen, 1974) may be clarified if future investigations address these shortcomings, thereby reducing the vulnerability of the results.

Children who are identified as being deficient in auditory reassembly abilities might begin to learn to read using a more holistic approach while auditory reassembly deficits are being ameliorated. Although this suggestion has been made much earlier (Hildreth, 1954; Chall et al., 1963), the concept of systematically adapting programs of beginning reading to meet the needs of the child who is weak in reassembly and other related auditory processing skills is not universally accepted.

Training programs in auditory analysis and synthesis have been developed and used effectively with speech- and language-impaired children (Katz & Burge, 1971; Katz & Medol, 1972; Rosner, 1973) and reading-disordered subjects (Richardson & Collier, 1971). Such programs should be evaluated experimentally with regard to their use in establishing readiness for beginning reading as well as remediating children who exhibit poor word decoding skills.

With increasing evidence that reading problems generate from inadequate language function (Vellutino, 1977) further research designed to examine the performance of good and poor readers on the auditory processing of longer language units would be a logical extension of the present findings. Questions which might be raised would concern the effect of phonologic, syntactic, and semantic constraints in addition to the factors of stimulus duration and the age of the listener.

This investigation attempted to minimize the presence of such possibly confounding variables as the semantic nature of the stimuli, interphonemic interval, method of presentation, and response requirements. The results obtained from this investigation reflect a more stringent examination of the auditory reassembly process from which generalizations concerning good and poor readers may be drawn. The findings of this study support earlier research with respect to auditory reassembly difficulties in groups of poor readers and further substantiate the findings of closely related investigations (Beasley et al., 1974; Shriner & Daniloff, 1970; Stovall et al., 1977) regarding the significant effects on reassembly performance of interphonemic interval and use of meaningful versus nonmeaningful stimuli. In addition, findings obtained in this study added the dimensions of an older population and the performance of good and poor readers to present theoretical knowledge.

Implications regarding the more proficient auditory reassembly performance of good readers as a whole when compared to poor readers can be viewed within the context of language ability. Within this framework, the better performance of good readers may reflect a more efficient use of phonemic, morphemic, and morpho-phonemic rules to assist in perception and reassembly. The ability to use this knowledge to reduce the uncertainty of the phonemes, even when nonmeaningful stimuli are used, appears to be characteristic of good readers. Further examination of the underlying language competence of good and poor readers would seem a logical extension. The conclusion reached by Vellutino (1977) "that many children have not become aware of the phonetic structure of both spoken and printed language and are, therefore, unable to make the important connections between these representations" is relevant.

It would appear that teachers and clinicians should become increasingly aware of the nature of auditory reassembly and its potential impact on the reading process. There is substantial evidence (Richardson et al., 1977) that auditory reassembly is fundamental to the decoding of words and that direct instruction in auditory blending can improve the decoding skills of retarded readers in a laboratory setting. Although not yet empirically substantiated, the relationship of auditory reassembly to reading, particularly when a phonics approach is used, seems logical. This relationship may be particularly critical during beginning reading when auditory and visual equivalence must be established. The results of the present investigation further imply that diagnostic measures for the assessment of auditory reassembly difficulties should control for the variables of interphonemic interval and the semantic level of the stimuli. Such refined measurement techniques would allow for defensible generalizations to be drawn.

With increasingly compelling evidence concerning the language-based status of reading, further well-defined and controlled evaluation of those linguistic factors which may impact on reading should be a major research goal. In this respect, auditory reassembly may be only one of a number of nonmutually exclusive language-based problems which delimit reading success or failure.

REFERENCES

Alshan, L. Reading readiness and reading achievement. In A. Figurel (Ed.), *Reading and inquiry.* Newark, DE: IRA, 1965.

Balmuth, M. *Phoneme blending and silent reading achievement.* Paper presented at the meeting of the International Reading Association, Atlantic City, NJ, 1971. (ERIC Document Reproduction Service ED052912).

Beasley, D. S., & Beasley, D. C. Auditory reassembly abilities of black and white first and third grade children. *Journal of Speech and Hearing Research,* 1973, *16,* 213–221.

Beasley, D. S., Shriner, T. H., Manning, W. H., & Beasley, D. C. Auditory assembly of CVCs by children with normal and defective articulation. *Journal of Communication Disorders,* 1974, *7,* 127–133.

Bond, G. L. Auditory and speech characteristics of good and poor readers. *Teachers college contributions to education,* New York: Columbia University, 1935.

Bruininks, R. H. Auditory and visual perceptual skills related to the reading performance of disadvantaged boys. *Perceptual and Motor Skills,* 1969, *29,* 179–186.

Chall, J., Roswell, J., & Blumenthal, S. H. Auditory blending ability: A factor in success in beginning reading. *The Reading Teacher,* 1963, *29,* 113–118.

Clyde, D. J. *Multivariate analysis of variance on large computers.* Miami, FL: Clyde Computing Service, 1969.

Conrad, R. Acoustic confusions in immediate memory. *British Journal of Psychology,* 1974, *55,* 75–83.

Denes, P. B. On the statistics of spoken English. *The Journal of the Acoustical Society of America,* 1963, *35,* 892–904.

Dixon, W. J. *Biomedical computer programs* (BMD). Berkeley, CA: University of California Press, 1973.

Dykstra, R. Auditory discrimination abilities and beginning reading ability. *Reading Research Quarterly,* 1966, *1,* 5–34.

Flynn, P. L., & Byrne, M. C. Relationships between reading and selected auditory abilities of third grade children. *Journal of Speech and Hearing Research,* 1970, *13,* 731–740.

Gates, A. I. An experimental evaluation of reading readiness tests. *Elementary School Journal,* 1939, *39,* 497–508.

Golden, N. E., & Steiner, S. R. Auditory and visual functions in good and poor readers. *Journal of Learning Disabilities,* 1969, *2,* 476–481.

Goldman, R., & Dixon, S. D. The relationship of vocalphonic and articulatory abilities. *Journal of Learning Disabilities,* 1974, *4,* 21–26.

Gray, E.   *A study of the vocal phonic ability of children six to eight and one-half years.* Unpublished doctoral dissertation, University of Oklahoma, 1963.

Halle, M., & Stevens, K. N.   Speech recognition: A model and a program for research. In J. A. Fodor & J. J. Katz (Eds.), *The structure of language: Readings in the philosophy of language.* Englewood Cliffs, NJ: Prentice-Hall, 1964.

Hammill, D. D., & Larsen, S. C.   The relationship of selected auditory skills and reading ability. *Journal of Learning Disabilities,* 1974, *7,* 429-435.

Hildreth, G. H.   The role of pronouncing and sounding in learning to read. *Elementary School Journal,* 1954, *55,* 141-147.

Hintzman, D. L.   Articulatory coding in short-term memory. *Journal of Verbal Learning and Verbal Behavior,* 1967, *6,* 312-316.

Kass, C. E.   Psycholinguistic disabilities of children with reading problems. *Exceptional Children,* 1966, *32,* 533-539.

Katz, J., & Burge, C.   Auditory perception training for children with learning disabilities. *Menorah Medical Journal,* 1971, *2,* 18-29.

Katz, J., & Medol, E.   The use of phonemic synthesis in speech therapy. *Menorah Medical Journal,* 1972, *3,* 10-18.

Lerea, L.   Phonemic analysis: Synthesis skills of normal and speech defective children. *Psychological Record,* 1963, *14,* 327-333.

Maccoby, E., & Konrad, K. W.   Age trends in selective listening. *Journal of Experimental Child Psychology,* 1960, *3,* 113-122.

Mark, L. S., Shankweiler, D., Liberman, I. Y., & Fowler, C. A.   Phonetic recoding and reading difficulty in beginning readers. *Memory & Cognition,* 1977, *5,* 623-629.

McLeod, J.   Some psycholinguistic correlates of reading disability in young children. *Reading Research Quarterly,* 1966, *1,* 5-30.

McNinch, C.   Auditory perceptual factors. *Reading Research Quarterly,* 1971, *1,* 482-492.

Monroe, M.   *Children who cannot read.* Chicago: University of Chicago Press, 1932.

Monsees, E. K.   Temporal sequence and expressive language disorder. *Exceptional Children,* 1968, *35,* 141-147.

Mulder, R. V., & Curtin, J. T. Vocal phonic ability and silent reading achievement: A first report. *Elementary School Journal*, 1955, *56*, 121–123.

Orton, S. T. *Reading, writing and speech disorders in children: A presentation of certain types of disorders in the development of the language faculty.* New York: Norton, 1937.

Pratt, J. E., & Butler, K. *Normative study of auditory closure skills in school age children.* Paper presented to Annual American Speech and Hearing Association Convention, Denver, CO, 1968.

Reynolds, M. D. A study of the relationships between auditory characteristics and specific silent reading abilities. *Journal of Educational Research*, 1953, *46*, 439–449.

Richardson, E., & Collier, L. Programmed tutoring of decoding skills with third and fifth grade non-readers. *The Journal of Experimental Education*, 1971, *39*, 57–64.

Richardson, E., DiBenedetto, R., & Bradley, C. M. The relationship of sound blending to reading achievement. *Review of Educational Research*, 1977, *47*, 319–334.

Rosner, J. Phonic analysis training and beginning reading skills. Learning Research and Development Center, University of Pittsburgh, 1971. Cited in S. J. Samuels, Success and failure in learning to read. *Reading Research Quarterly*, 1973, *8*, 200–239.

Sabatino, D. A., & Hayden, D. L. Variation in information processing behavior. *Journal of Learning Disabilities*, 1970, *3*, 404–412.

Samuels, S. J. Success and failure in learning to read: A critique of the research. *Reading Research Quarterly*, 1973, *8*, 200–239.

Shriner, T. H., & Daniloff, R. G. Reassembly of segmented CVC syllables in children. *Journal of Speech and Hearing Research*, 1970, *13*, 537–547.

Stovall, J. V., Manning, W. H., & Shaw, C. K. Auditory assembly ability of children with mild and severe misarticulation. *Folia Phoniatric*, 1977, *29*, 163–172.

Templin, M., & Darley, F. *The Templin-Darley Test of Articulation.* University of Iowa: Bureau of Educational Research and Service, Division of Extension and University Services, 1960.

Van Riper, C.   *Speech correction principles and methods* (3rd ed.). Englewood Cliffs, NJ: Prentice-Hall, 1954.

Vellutino, F. R.   Alternative conceptualizations of dyslexia: Evidence in support of a verbal deficit hypothesis. *Harvard Educational Review,* 1977, *47,* 334-354.

9
A PRELIMINARY INVESTIGATION OF THE AUDITORY ASSEMBLY ABILITIES OF BRAIN-DAMAGED AND NON-BRAIN-DAMAGED ADULTS

Walter W. Amster
Thomas H. Shriner
G. Robert Hopper

Veterans Administration Medical Center, Miami, Florida

Judith B. Amster

University of Miami

> It is believed that this was the final formal research investigation in which Tom Shriner participated in a major role as a scientist and thus it is printed in the traditional research format and style characteristic of Tom's writing.

*P*resent models of communication postulate an encoding–decoding paradigm which forms the basis of language function. The communication process, involving both receptive and expressive components, has been disrupted for the aphasic individual due to neurological insult. Schuell (1964) indicated that there is almost always demonstrable impairment of auditory processes in aphasia.

Brookshire (1978) in an incisive review of the literature concerning auditory comprehension in aphasia states: "Because comprehension of spoken language requires that the individual decode a temporal sequence of acoustic stimuli, a number of investigators have evaluated aphasic individuals' ability to recognize and report the temporal order of sequences of various kinds of stimuli" (p. 105).

Efron (1963) stated a major problem in aphasic patients is the assignment of time labels to incoming stimuli. He found that aphasics required longer interstimulus intervals between paired tones (high and low) than normals, to correctly indicate sequential order.

Investigations following Efron's seminal research by Edwards and Auger (1965), Ebbin and Edwards (1967), and Brookshire (1972) with adult aphasics and Lowe and Campbell (1965) with aphasoid children using nonlanguage stimuli or discrimination of syllable pairs are in essential agreement with Efron's major premise that aphasics as a group do suffer from a profound deficit in auditory sequencing. Brookshire (1978) concurs in this respect stating that " at this point the temporal sequencing disabilities in aphasic subjects is an interesting phenomenon but it does not help the aphasiologist to understand the aphasic patient's difficulties in understanding speech" (p. 110).

Available research in its use of primarily nonlanguage or at best simple phonemic stimuli for the measurement of processing abilities, has produced findings which do not reflect on and cannot be generalized to basic aspects of linguistic competence and performance. The use of a language task in the measurement of auditory processing deficits would reflect upon a communication model to a far greater degree than those tasks which have been previously utilized. Futher insight into the role of semantic clues involved in the auditory processing of aphasics could be gained through the use of a task which presents both meaningful and nonmeaningful language stimuli. If differences do exist, an auditory reassembly task in which the listener must synthesize the phonemes of a word and verbally reproduce the integrated whole would appear to be sensitive to the measurement of this basic auditory ability in the aphasic. In this respect the following questions were generated: (1) Do non-brain-damaged and brain-damaged subjects differ in their ability to assemble CVC monosyllabic stimuli? (2) Do non-brain-damaged and brain-damaged subjects differ in their ability to assemble CVC stimuli as a function of four different silent interphonemic intervals when information is held constant? (3) Do non-brain-damaged and brain-damaged subjects differ in their ability to assemble meaningful and nonmeaningful CVC stimuli?

METHOD

Subjects

The subjects consisted of 40 non-brain-damaged and 26 brain-damaged adults of whom 20 were classified aphasic. All subjects (in-patients, out-patients, employees, and volunteers) were affiliated with the Veterans Administration Medical Center, Miami, Florida. The brain-damaged group was composed of in-patients and out-patients. The age range of the non-brain-damaged group was 18–81 years with a mean of 47 years while the brain-damaged group was 30–97 years with a mean of 59 years. The 26 brain-damaged subjects met the stratification criteria of adequate auditory acuity, auditory comprehension, and speech performance with respect to correct articulatory production of those consonants found in the experimental task, and absence of gross psychiatric dysfunction. For this group, the neurological symptomatology must have existed at least 3–6 months prior to inclusion in the study. Information pertaining to the neurological and psychiatric status of the brain-damaged group was obtained through review of individual medical protocols. The non-brain-damaged subjects met all stratification criteria.

TABLE 9-1
List of meaningful and nonmeaningful CVC monosyllable stimulus items

Meaningful		Nonmeaningful	
/noz/	nose	/nez/	nāz
/mæn/	man	/mɑn/	män
/bɛd/	bed	/bɑd/	bäd
/dɔg/	dog	/dɛg/	dĕg
/dʒʌg/	jug	/dʒig/	jēg
/tʃɪn/	chin	/tʃʌn/	chŭn
/ʃuz/	shoes	/ʃez/	shāz
/sʌn/	sun	/sɛn/	sĕn
/lɛg/	leg	/lʊg/	lōōg
/rɛd/	red	/rʌd/	rŭd

Experimental Tapes

The experimental tapes used to assess auditory reassembly performance in the present study were developed at the University of Illinois Speech Research Laboratory by Shriner and Daniloff (1970) and modified by Beasley and Beasley (1973). Their method of preparation is described in Shriner and Daniloff (1970). These tapes consist of 10 meaningful and 10 nonmeaningful CVC monosyllables which met vocabulary and phonic requirements and had been made into like pairs with only the central vowel differing and controlling the semantic factor (e.g., /noz/ vs /nez/) (see Table 9-1). Specified segments of blank tape containing intervals of 100, 200, 300, and 400 msec have been inserted between each of the phonemes comprising a complete CVC monosyllable. Each segmented CVC item was placed in the carrier phrase, "Repeat——please," with 10 sec between phrases. Each tape contained a randomized version of 20 (10 meaningful and 10 nonmeaningful) CVC items at only one of the four interphonemic conditions.

Empirical evidence has substantiated the essential validity of auditory assembly measures in delineating children who are adequate or deficient in assembling segmented phonemes (Beasley & Beasley, 1973; Beasley, Shriner, Manning, & Beasley, 1974; Shriner & Daniloff, 1970).

Experimental Session

The experimental tapes were played by a loudspeaker through a high-quality tape deck and amplifier combination to each subject seated alone in a quiet room with a satisfactory signal-to-noise ratio. A training session was provided for each subject prior to the playing of each tape using procedures developed by Shriner and Daniloff (1970). These procedures are as follows:

In a given session, each subject heard a CVC sense-nonsense pair of practice items, /wɪtʃ/ and /witʃ/, at the delay appropriate to his experimental tape. The procedure was as follows: The experimenter said, "You are going to hear some words like this: d-o-g." (At this point, the experimenter spoke several meaningful and meaningless CVC constructions such as /dog, lig/ with a silent delay between each phoneme and without any delays.) After the experimenter spoke the word *dog* with and without delays, the subject was asked to repeat the syllable. If he did so successfully, then he was told to listen, and to repeat the two practice items on the tape. If he did so successfully, then the whole tape of 20 items was played nonstop and his responses recorded on a stereo tape recorder for replay scoring. If he did not, further examples were given until he was responding successfully.

Analysis

Three scores were obtained for each subject: Percent correct for (1) total, (2) meaningful, and (3) nonmeaningful reassembly. Recordings of each subject's responses were played to a group of three trained listeners. Responses were scored as correct or incorrect with a majority decision, two of three listeners agreeing, sufficient to score a response. An interjudge reliability of 95% was obtained. Each subject was scored for 10 meaningful and 10 nonmeaningful CVCs at only one of four values of the interphonemic interval. The data were treated statistically via computerized ANOVA procedures.

RESULTS

Mean CVC synthesis response scores are presented in Table 9-2. Figures 9-1, 9-2, 9-3, and 9-4 show these mean data in graphic form.

Effect of Brain Damage

With respect to the effect of brain damage, the results revealed that non-brain-damaged (normal subjects) performed significantly better than brain-damaged subjects on the overall task ($F(1, 58) = 14.33, p < .001$). The large difference between the performance contour of the normal (non-brain-damaged) and that of the brain-damaged except in the 100-msec interphonemic level can be observed in Figure 9-1. The non-brain-damaged also did significantly better than the brain-damaged on both the meaningful ($F(1, 58) = 9.57, p < .003$) and the nonmeaningful task ($F(1, 58) = 14.99, p < .001$) (Figure 9-2).

Effect of Temporal Level

The effect of interphonemic intervals (100 through 400 msec) did not significantly affect performance on the total ($F(3, 58) = .972, p < .41$), meaningful ($F(3, 58) = 1.1, p < .36$) or nonmeaningful tasks ($F(3, 58) = .985, p < .40$). Although the overall temporal effect was not statistically significant, the performance contours reveal a distinct decline for both meaningful and nonmeaningful stimuli for the brain-damaged subjects between 100 and 200 msec (Figure 9-1).

TABLE 9-2
Mean correct response scores for word reassembly task

Group		Interphoneme Interval (msec)				
		100	200	300	400	Combined
Non-Brain-Damaged						
% Correct	Meaningful	30.9	31.1	31.7	41.1	33.4
	Nonmeaningful	16.9	21.1	20.8	27.2	20.8
	Total	47.8	52.2	52.5	68.3	54.1
Brain-Damaged						
% Correct	Meaningful	36.4	15.7	15.8	17.5	21.7
	Nonmeaningful	13.6	3.6	7.5	10.8	8.8
	Total	50.0	18.6	23.3	28.3	30.6

FIGURE 9-1
Percent correct for total CVC assembly responses for non-brain-damaged
versus brain-damaged subjects as a function of interphonemic interval.

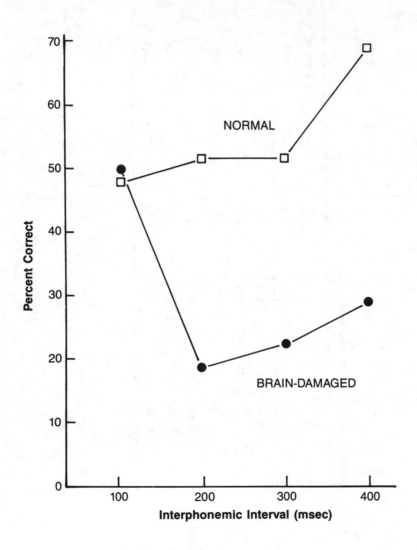

FIGURE 9-2

Percent correct for meaningful and nonmeaningful assembly responses produced by non-brain-damaged versus brain-damaged subjects as a function of interphonemic interval.

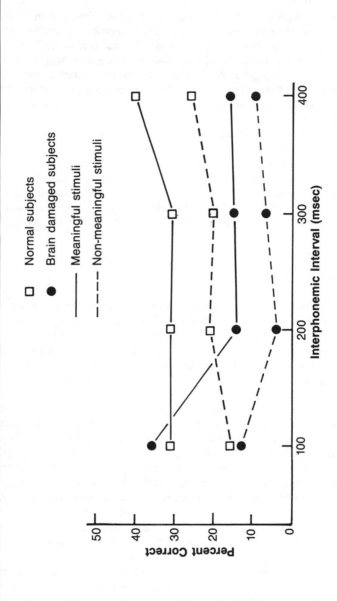

164   Amster/Shriner/Hopper/Amster

Meaningful versus Nonmeaningful Stimuli

With respect to the semantic level of the stimuli (meaningful versus nonmeaningful) meaningful stimuli elicited significantly greater correct responses than nonmeaningful stimuli when scores for the brain-damaged and non-brain-damaged were combined and collapsed across temporal levels (F (1, 130) = 24.20, $p < .001$) (see Figure 9-3). Within-group performance revealed significant differences between meaningful and nonmeaningful performance for non-brain-damaged subjects (F (1, 78) = 14.72, $p < .001$) and brain-damaged (F (1, 50) = 13.43, $p < .001$).

Information is available regarding performance on this task by children (Figure 9-4). The lower line illustrates the auditory assembly performance of the brain-damaged for the total task. It is most interesting to note the sharp decline between 100 and 200 msec produced by brain-damaged adults and its striking similarity to the performance of children in investigations of articulation and ethnic factors. It is to be noted that the normal (non-brain-damaged) adults did not evidence this type of decline (Figure 9-1).

DISCUSSION

The overall purpose of this study was to determine if an auditory assembly task could be used to differentiate non-brain-damaged from brain-damaged subjects. The task was to have each subject listen to separate phonemes and then to repeat whole syllabic units which consisted of 10 pairs of both meaningful and nonmeaningful stimuli under four different segmentation intervals. Non-brain-damaged subjects did significantly better than brain-damaged subjects on all aspects of the task.

It was assumed the assembly task would reflect upon encoding (or performance) and hence upon each subject's knowledge of grammar. Subjects in this study had to identify isolated, sustained phone productions, a type of speech signal not usually encountered in speech production or perception. Under the present assembly task, subjects were asked to connect their perceptions of the isolated sounds with their stored patterns as heard in running speech. The subject was then asked to assemble the phone perceptions into a meaningful or nonmeaningful response. The process would have been more natural and easier on each subject's speech processing recognition mechanism had real words been spliced into quasi-phonemic segments. This is decidedly an unnatural perceptual recognition task and may not reflect the subject's ability to function in an everyday language environment. Just what is stored or disrupted in memory, whether it is the phoneme, contextual allophone, distinctive feature, or, more importantly, coarticulatory feature is not known, nor do we know whether such stored sounds are placed in auditory (sensory) modality, articulatory (motor or kinesthetic), or an abstract verbal modality. To even extrapolate these findings at this time to the brain-damaged may be premature.

Certain interesting findings, however, do emerge as a function of the results of this study. The study does reflect construct validity because the non-brain-damaged performed significantly better than the brain-damaged subjects. One would have

FIGURE 9-3

Percent correct for meaningful and nonmeaningful assembly responses for all non-brain-damaged and brain-damaged subjects (N = 66) as a function of interphonemic interval.

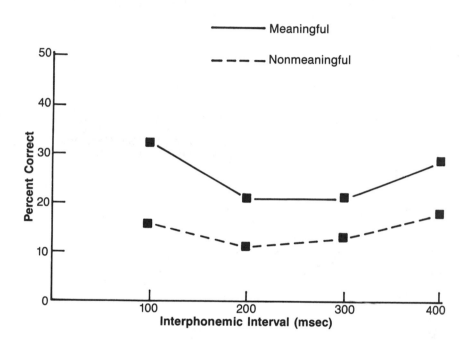

predicted, however, that non-brain-damaged subjects would have performed significantly better than the brain-damaged subjects only on the meaningful stimuli but not on the nonmeaningful stimuli. Since most researchers are in agreement with Schuell's contention that aphasia is a language disturbance that crosses all modes of stimulus and response, it seems reasonable to assume that non-brain-damaged would apply their superior knowledge (competence) of grammar to aid them with assembly of meaningful CVCs but not to nonmeaningful CVCs. Nonmeaningful CVCs should not place that great a burden on an adult's linguistic competence, non-brain-damaged or brain-damaged. Both groups would have performed in a similar fashion on the nonmeaningful stimuli if rules of phonological–perceptual processing were not required. Obviously, this is not the case. The non-brain-damaged subjects performed significantly better than the brain-damaged subjects.

With respect to the effects of temporal intervals, it has been assumed and reported, that if the brain-damaged individual is given more time (within sufficient limits of short-term memory recall) to process the stimuli, then his recall accuracy would increase. The results of this study found that these subjects perform equally well,

FIGURE 9-4
Percent correct for total CVC assembly responses for all non-brain-damaged and brain-damaged subjects (*N* = 66) as a function of interphonemic interval compared to assembly data for children.

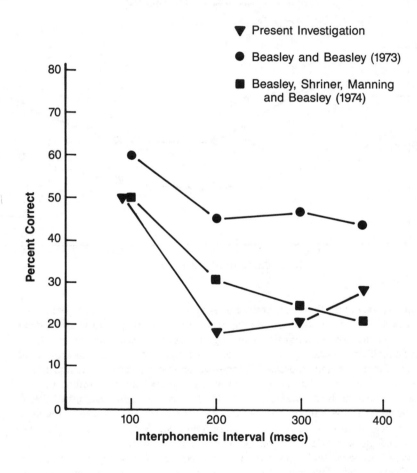

percentagewise, at the 100-msec interval as they do at the 400-msec interval. Moreover, the results revealed that the contour or the slope over segmentation interval is highly similar to the non-brain-damaged subjects and also highly similar to studies completed on children. The contours are highly similar but their percentage of correct responses is depressed. When the results of the non-brain-damaged adults are compared to results from other studies on young children, one also finds their scores lower, percentagewise, but not as depressed as the brain-damaged scores.

Since this was a highly unnatural task, even though the results were revealing, it may be more natural and germane to an individual's everyday language environment to use an auditory assembly segmented sentence task. In this instance one would be able to systematically study the semantic word error rate for both non-brain-damaged and brain-damaged subjects.

REFERENCES

Beasley, D. S., & Beasley, D. C. Auditory reassembly abilities of black and white first and third grade children. *Journal of Speech and Hearing Research*, 1973, *16*, 213–221.

Beasley, D. S., Shriner, T. H., Manning, W. H., & Beasley, D. C. Auditory assembly of CVC's by children with normal and defective articulation. *Journal of Communication Disorders*, 1974, *7*, 127–133.

Brookshire, R. H. Visual and auditory sequencing by aphasic subjects. *Journal of Communication Disorders*, 1972, *5*, 259–269.

Brookshire, R. H. Auditory comprehension and aphasia. In D. F. Johns (Ed.), *Clinical management of neurogenic communicative disorders*. Boston: Little, Brown, 1978.

Ebbin, J., & Edwards, A. E. Speech sound discrimination of aphasics when inter-sound interval is varied. *Journal of Speech and Hearing Research*, 1967, *10, 120–125*.

Edwards, A. E., & Auger, R. The effect of aphasia in the perception of precedence. *Proceedings of the 73rd Annual Convention of the American Psychological Association*, 1965.

Efron, R. Temporal perception, aphasia and deja vu. *Brain*, 1963, *86*, 403–424.

Lowe, A., & Campbell, R. Temporal discrimination in aphasoid and normal children. *Journal of Speech and Hearing Research*, 1965, *8*, 313–314.

Schuell, H., Jenkins, J., & Jimenez-Pabon, E. *Aphasia in adults: Diagnosis, prognosis and treatment*. New York: Harper & Row, 1964.

Shriner, T. H., & Daniloff, R. G. Reassembly of segmented CVC syllables by children. *Journal of Speech and Hearing Research*, 1970, *13*, 537–547.